User Experience M

Enhance UX with User Story Map, Journey Map
and Diagrams

Peter W. Szabo

BIRMINGHAM - MUMBAI

User Experience Mapping

Copyright © 2017 Packt Publishing

First published: May 2017

Production reference: 1240517

Published by Packt Publishing Ltd.
Livery Place
35 Livery Street
Birmingham
B3 2PB, UK.
ISBN 978-1-78712-350-2

www.packtpub.com

Credits

Author
Peter W. Szabo

Reviewer
Jay Heal

Commissioning Editor
Ashwin Nair

Acquisition Editor
Reshma Raman

Content Development Editor
Aditi Gour

Technical Editor
Murtaza Tinwala

Copy Editor
Dhanya Baburaj

Project Coordinator
Ritika Manoj

Proofreader
Safis Editing

Indexer
Francy Puthiry

Graphics
Jason Monteiro

Production Coordinator
Shantanu Zagade

About the Author

Peter W. Szabo is one of the world's leading user experience consultants, the principal of the farZenith.com agency. He is a frequent conference speaker, workshop host, and user centricity evangelist. His UX blog, Kaizen-UX.com, gained its popularity for UX management articles and novel user experience approach. He used to be a senior manager leading the UX team at the world's biggest online gambling corporation, Amaya Inc. (known for brands such as PokerStars, BetStars or FullTilt). As UX Director at WhatUsersDo (Europe's largest remote testing platform), he contributed to the widespread acceptance of remote research in the UX industry.

Outside of the UX world, he is the proud father of Maya and Magor. He enjoys reading, writing, and playing games (not just computer ones). He is a cat person. Ok, that's an understatement, he is simply crazy for cats.

About the Reviewer

Jay Heal is a Cambridge-based UX consultant with expertise in user-centered design, service design, interaction design and user research.

His principle belief is that design is both a collaborative and interactive process of problem solving. Great design solutions are achieved from a deeper understanding and empathy of the people they are intended for.

As a practitioner, Jay is a vocal advocate of the *test early, test often* approach to UX, where numerous ideas and concepts can be quickly validated until the right solution is found.

Having graduated from the University of East London in New Technology and Multimedia Design in the early 2000s, his passion for designing for people has led him to work with organizations that include the BBC, Ministry of Justice, Just Eat, Virgin Trains East Coast, and Transport for London.

Away from design and research, Jay is a devoted family man to his children (Dennis, Yasmin and Max), a music enthusiast, home barista and self proclaimed foodie.

www.PacktPub.com

For support files and downloads related to your book, please visit `www.PacktPub.com`.

Did you know that Packt offers eBook versions of every book published, with PDF and ePub files available? You can upgrade to the eBook version at `www.PacktPub.com` and as a print book customer, you are entitled to a discount on the eBook copy. Get in touch with us at `service@packtpub.com` for more details.

At `www.PacktPub.com`, you can also read a collection of free technical articles, sign up for a range of free newsletters and receive exclusive discounts and offers on Packt books and eBooks.

`https://www.packtpub.com/mapt`

Get the most in-demand software skills with Mapt. Mapt gives you full access to all Packt books and video courses, as well as industry-leading tools to help you plan your personal development and advance your career.

Why subscribe?

- Fully searchable across every book published by Packt
- Copy and paste, print, and bookmark content
- On demand and accessible via a web browser

Customer Feedback

Thanks for purchasing this Packt book. At Packt, quality is at the heart of our editorial process. To help us improve, please leave us an honest review on this book's Amazon page at `https://www.amazon.com/dp/1787123502`.

If you'd like to join our team of regular reviewers, you can e-mail us at `customerreviews@packtpub.com`. We award our regular reviewers with free eBooks and videos in exchange for their valuable feedback. Help us be relentless in improving our products!

To Maya and Magor!

Table of Contents

Preface

There is no map to writing introductions. Fortunately, there are maps to great user experience and outstanding products. This book is about those maps.

Do you want to create better products and innovative solutions? *User Experience Maps* will help you understand users and communicate this understanding with others. Maps can also champion user-centricity within your organization. They will fight for your users.

But no map can carry the sway of product design battles alone. That's why you need an army of maps. And that's why we need you to wield them like the shining sword of user-centricity.

This book reveals two advanced mapping techniques for the first time in print, the behavioral change map and the 4D UX map. You will also explore user story maps, task models, and journey maps. You will create wireflows, mental model maps, ecosystem maps, and solution maps. In this book, we will show you how to use insights from real users to create and improve your maps and your product.

Start mapping your products now to change your users' lives!

What this book covers

Chapter 1, *How Will UX Mapping Change Your (Users') Life?*, gets the reader started with User Experience Mapping in a fun and engaging way. In this chapter, we will create a simple map, not worried about map types and UX mapping theory. We will use pen and paper, to give the reader the first taste in mapping and demonstrate its strength.

Chapter 2, *User Story Map - Requirements by Collaboration and Sticky Notes*, is a simple technique to visually tell the users' story. The linear map helps you create a narrative flow. Because it's quick and easy, it can be used in the early ideation phase of a product.

Chapter 3, *Journey Map - Understand Your Users*, the journey maps is a tool, that helps us to understand and communicate users' behavior as they progress through a route using interactions, trying to accomplish their goals.

Chapter 4, *Wireflows - Plan Your Product,* wireflows are journey maps where key interactions are represented by wireframes of the relevant views. They allow you to create, explore, communicate, and improve the interactions in detail.

Chapter 5, *Remote and Lab Tests for Map Creation,* by watching users while they interact with a solution, we gain understanding. This understanding leads to better maps and better experiences.

Chapter 6, *Solution Mapping Based on User Insights,* a solution map is a tool that will help us find solutions and communicate them. They are visual representations of an actionable project plan. Ideally, solution maps should be based on user testing sessions with real users.

Chapter 7, *Mental Model Map - A Diagram of the Perceived Reality,* a mental model map is a visual representation of a user group's thought process and patterns. The mental model shifts the focus from designing a solution to understanding the user's state of mind, and how we can support those states.

Chapter 8, *Behavioral Change Map - The Action Plan of Persuasion,* a behavioral change map is a path to changing a user group's behavior. It should be simple and impactful, based on a real understanding of our user's mindset and thought processes.

Chapter 9, *The 4D UX Map - Putting It All Together,* the 4D UX map is a compact summary of a UX project, a high-impact deliverable to visualize how the users' needs are met.

Chapter 10, *Ecosystem Maps - A Holistic Overview,* the ecosystem map places our solution in the greater context of the holistic user experience. This map aids the identification and integration of complex, interdisciplinary information concerning the user experience ecosystem.

Chapter 11, *Kaizen Mapping - UX Maps in Agile Product Management,* you can use the Kaizen-UX framework to structure your product design and user experience efforts. The agile framework defines the three core roles within the UX team, it has a UX strategy at its core, and it leads to better products and better communication within the team and with stakeholders.

What you need for this book

To draw a map, you only need a pen and a slightly larger sheet of paper. But software can help tremendously. That's why this book contains detailed, beginner-level tutorials on creating maps using different software products, including Adobe Illustrator, Balsamiq Mockups, Axure RP, or even Microsoft Word. Remember, even if you don't have access to any of those, each map type can also be drawn using a broad range of software or even freehand.

Who this book is for

This book is for Product Managers, Service Managers, Designers, and anyone who is keen on learning User Experience Mapping techniques to improve how they communicate their ideas. It's for You!

Conventions

In this book, you will find a number of text styles that distinguish between different kinds of information. Here are some examples of these styles and an explanation of their meaning.

Code words in text, database table names, folder names, filenames, file extensions, pathnames, dummy URLs, user input, and Twitter handles are shown as follows: "If you do, you can share your results with me on my Twitter account: `@wszp`".

New terms and **important words** are shown in bold. Words that you see on the screen, for example, in menus or dialog boxes, appear in the text like this: "If you want, you can rotate the text from the **Format Shape** panel (**Text Options** | **Text direction** dropdown)".

Warnings or important notes appear in a box like this.

Tips and tricks appear like this.

Reader feedback

Feedback from our readers is always welcome. Let us know what you think about this book-what you liked or disliked. Reader feedback is important for us as it helps us develop titles that you will really get the most out of.

To send us general feedback, simply e-mail `feedback@packtpub.com`, and mention the book's title in the subject of your message.

If there is a topic that you have expertise in and you are interested in either writing or contributing to a book, see our author guide at `www.packtpub.com/authors`.

Customer support

Now that you are the proud owner of a Packt book, we have a number of things to help you to get the most from your purchase.

Downloading the color images of this book

We also provide you with a PDF file that has color images of the screenshots/diagrams used in this book. The color images will help you better understand the changes in the output. You can download this file from `https://www.packtpub.com/sites/default/files/down loads/UserExperienceMapping_ColorImages.pdf`.

Errata

Although we have taken every care to ensure the accuracy of our content, mistakes do happen. If you find a mistake in one of our books-maybe a mistake in the text or the code-we would be grateful if you could report this to us. By doing so, you can save other readers from frustration and help us improve subsequent versions of this book. If you find any errata, please report them by visiting `http://www.packtpub.com/submit-errata`, selecting your book, clicking on the **Errata Submission Form** link, and entering the details of your errata. Once your errata are verified, your submission will be accepted and the errata will be uploaded to our website or added to any list of existing errata under the Errata section of that title.

To view the previously submitted errata, go to `https://www.packtpub.com/books/conten t/support` and enter the name of the book in the search field. The required information will appear under the **Errata** section.

Piracy

Piracy of copyrighted material on the Internet is an ongoing problem across all media. At Packt, we take the protection of our copyright and licenses very seriously. If you come across any illegal copies of our works in any form on the Internet, please provide us with the location address or website name immediately so that we can pursue a remedy.

Please contact us at copyright@packtpub.com with a link to the suspected pirated material.

We appreciate your help in protecting our authors and our ability to bring you valuable content.

Questions

If you have a problem with any aspect of this book, you can contact us at questions@packtpub.com, and we will do our best to address the problem.

If you want to contact the author, use peter@kaizen-ux.com.

1

How Will UX Mapping Change Your (Users') Life?

In this book, I will change your life. I will show you techniques that will help you to understand your users, gain strategic insights, and improve communication within the team and with stakeholders.

In this introductory chapter, we will perform the following things:

- Create our first User Experience Map.
- Similar to the other chapters of this book, we will solve a real-world problem, but for this one, we will start with a rather fun and unusual one.
- After setting the scene, we will take a look into the shortcomings of the old requirements document from the waterfall product management model.
- This naturally leads to the solution that states that most problems can and will be solved with improved communication.
- We will see how mapping can be the ideal tool to facilitate communication.
- We will have to discuss some basic mapping terms, output, outcome, and opportunity.
- The next sections of this chapter are about visualizing and creating a backlog.
- All this should equip the reader to create their first UX map on paper.
- Then, they should be able to do it digitally. (You should use the software you are most comfortable with to map. In the following chapters, we will use a wide array of software tools, but for this chapter, I have chosen Microsoft Word.)

Getting started with User Experience Mapping

Now, let's talk about cats, and improving their lives. After all, cats always come first, when you need to improve someone's life. Later in this book, we will create maps for complex apps, websites and other digital projects, but in this introductory chapter, we will get started with a low-tech problem.

Imagine having a cat. You can imagine any other pet, but the example will be a bit different with longhorn or other cattle. You are planning an extended holiday with limited phone and no Internet access, and you need to leave your cat at home. (Not because of the lack of Internet access. Unlike UX designers, cats can survive prolonged periods of time without the Internet.) Fortunately, you have found a cat-sitter. Now, for the plot twist--although the cat-sitter has watched thousands of cat videos, she never had a cat.

You could tell her what to do. Chances are you would forget something obvious to you, but surprising for her. On top of that, you would have to rely on her memory and understanding.

Why did the requirements document fail?

Why shouldn't you give a 100 page document to your cat-sitter? Writing a documentation and sharing that with your cat-sitter might seem like a better idea. In the "information stone-age" of the early 90's, software delivery was based on a requirements document created as the first phase of the waterfall model. It seemed like a good idea back then. In this analysis phase, a long document was written. This document contained many details about what's being built, ahead of time, as well as an executive summary and product description and possibly many other sections. The requirements document was then approved and signed, and it represented a commitment. Requirements documents assumed that it's possible to know every eventuality up front and that priorities would not change. Obviously, they were not cast in stone. They were often revised, and sometimes even drastically changed.

Now, imagine our cat-sitter getting a 100-page requirements document with many sections. What are the chances that she misses or misunderstands something? Software developers cursed with a massive documentation feel the same.

In my experience, companies who still work based on burdensome requirements documents have more "firefighting jobs", as in very urgent jobs for consultants. On a Sunday afternoon, my mobile rang. The IT director of a well-known Hungarian eCommerce site was calling, seemingly in distress. The summary of the call was that they created a new responsive website with new design and information architecture. Now, it's been live for two weeks, and our sales plummeted, especially on mobile. That was odd because the site was not responsive before. Why the call on Sunday? It was because the solution he presented on Monday was to review the documentation, especially the user experience bits, to find out which parts were not followed. For this, he needed an unbiased third party.
I got the documentation and opened the site. There was a sitemap in it, a bit hard to read, as it continued across many pages, but suggested a fairly well thought out information architecture. Some subcategories appeared under multiple categories, and individual products could be found in one or more categories or subcategories. In the footer of the website, there was a link titled "Sitemap". Although the other link titles were in Hungarian, this one was in English. This link led me to the sitemap.xml *file. The file contained everything from the documentation's relevant chapter, nicely prepared for Googlebot, but far from ideal for humans, it just looked gibberish.*
The desktop navigation contained unique icons for the categories with the category name next to it. On the other hand, the mobile menu was just nine big icons, visible after tapping the burger icon (three parallel lines, often found in the top left or right corner of a mobile site or app), with small hard-to-read labels under them. Category names were long, and the designer made sure that they would not ruin his nice design. The documentation was followed to the letter, but the developers and whoever created the information architecture had a different idea on what to do with the sitemap chapter.

According to Paul Vii and most other experts, waterfall was the most popular product management model in software development. In the first phase of waterfall, usually named analysis, the business analyst and the product owner will put together a set of requirements. Why has this approach failed?

- *The waterfall model's requirements document can lead to dysfunctional communication, lack of collaboration, and understanding. The emphasis is often put on negotiation.* Cat-sitting and software development share the hate for contract negotiations, and walls of text are usually a source of a few misunderstandings. I hope that you appreciate the irony of arguing against writing long texts, while my arguments are part of a long text in a printed book.

- *The requirements documents are intimidating,* not just for cat-sitters, but anyone involved in a project. When you get a requirements document, the first thing that might cross your mind is whether you will ever be done with this, or what exactly you will deliver at the end.

- *Documents usually don't break down projects into tiny functionality bits, and some functionalities can be lost among thousands of lines of text.* Now, imagine if the location of the cat food was on page 74, paragraph 8. Remember, there is no easy way to contact you.

- *Such a document places our process above people.* In our case, it would seem as though we cared more about the paperwork than the cat-sitter and her interactions with our cat.

- *Even if you could create the best masterplan ever, unforeseeable things can and will happen. Rigid documentations and plan-following mindsets will make responding to change backbreakingly hard.* What if your cat explodes while you are away? You cat-sitter will flip through your lengthy documentation over and over, not finding anything about exploding cats. Although cats very rarely, if ever, explode (unless you are playing the *Exploding Kittens* card game), in software development even more unexpected things can be produced by the machine-spirit.

- *Even the best ideas will need continuous improvement, to stay competitive.* If you regularly go on holiday, sooner or later technology will make most of your cat-sitting requirements document quite obsolete. With the **Internet of things** connected to your cat bowl, you will not need a cat-sitter to feed your cat manually. They can simply download the app to their phone.

- *People want to work on making the world better, not spend time creating or understanding a long documentation.* The cat-sitter wants to concentrate on making your cat happy, not lawyering a comprehensive documentation.

As you can see, our problem will not be solved by telling the cat-sitter what to do or writing a comprehensive documentation.

Most problems can and will be solved with improved communication. The goal of the improvements in communication is to achieve a shared understanding. I think that the best communication method for shared understanding is drawing a map.

In Chapter 2, *User Story Map – Requirements by Collaboration and Sticky Notes*, we will see how maps and improved communication will address the problems of rigidity, lack of collaboration, and inflexibility of traditional requirements documents.

This book will teach you many User Experience Map types so that you can pick the right tool for the situation. The examples in the other chapters are product management, usually software development problems. I certainly don't expect you to build software for your cat-sitter (at least not in this chapter.)

There is a communication technique much older than the writing technique. You guessed it, some 40,000 years ago our ancestors started to draw. At first, they didn't draw maps, but that changed more than 15,000 years ago. A prehistoric map of the night sky on the walls of the caves at Lascaux, France, testifies this. Obviously, the creators of that map preferred hand drawing over sophisticated software products, so we will also start with hand-drawn maps.

To solve the cat-sitter's communication problem, let's draw a map using pen and paper. Often sticky notes or other small pieces of paper are used because it's easier to rearrange them. We will create sticky notes based user story maps in Chapter 2, *User Story Map – Requirements by Collaboration and Sticky Notes*, but here, we will just use a sheet of paper. Don't worry if your drawing skills stop at stick figures. Maps can be composed of some simple lines and a few written words. Some people do this instinctively during meetings. The most important thing to remember is that although mapping is a powerful tool, maps should never replace conversations.

A map is a tool you should use to facilitate the conversation. You need both the map and a conversation to solve a problem.

It's easy to overdo mapping, hoping to reduce the need for conversation. Remember that the map is not a substitute for a conversation. It will also not work if you overdo it, as it will be confusingly complicated for others. It's a tempting idea to draw a map so detailed that you can simply send it to the cat-sitter and get done with it. Don't do that, it's a terrible idea. I have seen agencies creating journey maps as a deliverable and e-mailing it to project stakeholders. Although they can look great, they rarely--if ever--meet the goals or solve problems alone, without a conversation.

We agreed that you will draw a map, and you will have a conversation where the map will help. You could also create the map during the conversation if you are an experienced mapper, but most of the time it's better if you have the first version ready for the conversation, and create a new iteration together with the stakeholders--in our case, the cat-sitter.

Before you start drawing, you need to decide what to draw. It's perfectly fine if your approach and strategy are not crystal clear at this stage.

Mapping is a useful tool, not just in getting understood, but it also helps you to find holes and contradictions in your strategy and approach.

How to jump-start mapping?

First, you need an idea obviously, but we already have that. The idea is to go on holiday without your cat. A terrible idea if you ask your cat, but the world is not a perfect place, not even for our feline companions.

Another thing you should decide is the opportunity. What do you expect to happen because of our process? It's easy to confuse opportunity, outcome, and output, not just because they all start with "o", but because some people use the terms interchangeably.

 The **outputs** are products of the map's usage. In other words, whatever happens because of the map is an output of the map.

In our example, opening a can of cat food is the output, but so is the cat biting our cat-sitter. We want to minimize outputs. Your resources are always limited. Even if you somehow got virtually countless people and money for this project, time will never be unlimited. Throwing more money at a project is probably the worst thing you can do, so it makes sense to do as few things as possible.

 The **outcomes** are the results of the map's usage; in other words, how running the whole process impacts the outside world.

For example, the cat will not be hungry after the feeding process. While opening a can of cat food or putting food in front of the cat are outputs, the outcome can be a well-fed cat or a starving cat. We will not know the outcome until the map is put in production. This means that we will only know how our map changed our cat's life when we come home from the holiday, but not before we board the plane.

 The **opportunity** is the desired outcome we plan to achieve with the aid of the map. This is how we want to change the world.

We want our cat to be well-fed and healthy and, most importantly, happy while we are away. This is our opportunity, the outcome we would love to happen. We will know the results of our map after it's put into practice. For now, let's aim for a happy cat. It goes without saying that we want to have the biggest possible opportunity. It's human nature to be greedy, but cats also share this character trait with us.

Mapping will help you to achieve the most, with as little as possible. In other words, maximize the opportunity, while minimizing the outputs.

> Most of the time you should *start mapping with the opportunity*. It's important to initiate the discussion and the map with something positive and impactful. It also helps you focus on the goal, and grabs the attention of your conversation partners from the first minute. This is also why the first sentence of this chapter is, "In this book, I will change your life".

If you have an idea and opportunity, grab a piece of paper and a pen, and you can start drawing the solution.

Visualizing - what the cat wants you to know

This is not a cat-food advertisement, but a twist on Ram Charan's book, *What the Customer Wants You to Know*. Without delving too deep into sales, the main takeaway from the book is beginning with the customers' needs. To ensure that we maximize the opportunity and minimize the output, we need to visualize what our users want.

In Chapter 5, *Remote and Lab Tests for Map Creation*, we will research what our users need and what they usually do when interacting with similar products. Cats, unlike humans, really hate being researched, tested, and analyzed. So, we just assume what a cat needs and wants during our time away.

You need to make sure you **visualize something implementable**, something which helps you to fulfill the opportunities within the constraints of time, budget, and human resources. For our demo project, getting nine cat-sitters 24/7 in three shifts would certainly be nice, but that's probably way too expensive and way too hard to organize. Later in this book, we will see how mapping can help us in understanding our limits, but for now, we assume to know our limitations.

Creating a backlog for a cat-sitter

If you know what you want and what are your limitations, you need a **prioritized list** within those constraints. In the SCRUM agile software development framework, we call this list a **product backlog,** and it is one of the most iconic SCRUM artifacts. My favorite definition for a product backlog is from Ken Schwaber: "*Product Backlog: A prioritized list of project requirements with estimated times to turn them into completed product functionality. [...] The list evolves, changing as business conditions or technology changes.*"

Arrange the possible things in the descending order of importance. This is the first and most crucial step of creating a successful product backlog.

For our cat-sitter, the backlog's most important element should be to make sure that the cat has access to fresh, clean water at all times. Dehydration is definitely not an outcome we would want. A close second is making sure that the cat is well fed, but not overfed. If the cat survives, we need to make sure that she does so in good health. So, the cat-sitter should check whether the cat is sick or injured, then take it to a vet, if needed. The above three elements are strictly necessary for the survival of the cat. Among those, probably the health of the cat is the top priority. There is no time or point to feed the cat if it is about to die from some illness. Cleaning the litter box is the fourth element here, and those four elements are why we have the cat-sitter. There are many other things a good cat-sitter can and will do, for example, checking and cleaning the cat's ears and teeth, and brushing its coat. Some cat-sitters may even give the cat a bath, or at least try and usually end up with some claw marks and bites, but that's another story. Keeping the cat clean and groomed is obviously important, not just for the looks, but for the health of the cat; but let's be honest, the cat will be just fine if a human doesn't groom her for a week. They spend lots of time cleaning themselves anyhow. Sleeping is also an important biological need, but I haven't seen any cat who needed help with that. However, there is another backlog item, which is a must, but is easy to forget. This is making sure that the cat is not lost and can't escape. (We assume it is an indoor cat in this mapping example.) If you think about it, this is the most important backlog item. If the cat-sitter loses the cat, all of our efforts will be pointless, as we will have no cat. Even a sick cat is a bit better than a non-existent one.

So, our backlog will have the following five items, starting with the highest priority:

- As a cat-sitter, I want to *make sure that the cat is not lost, and it can't escape,* so the cat will be safe
- As a cat-sitter, I want to ensure that *the cat is not sick or injured and if it is, I need to take it to the vet* so that it will be healthy
- As a cat-sitter, I want to *provide fresh and clean water for the cat at all times,* so it doesn't become dehydrated
- As a cat-sitter, I want to *give the cat enough food, without overfeeding it* so that it will be well fed
- As a cat-sitter, I want to *clean the litter box* so that the environment of the cat is clean and fresh

At the visualization phase, we don't assign time estimates to the backlog items, but later that will become important. What's important to note here is the backlog item template we have used. This is what Paul VII and other SCRUM gurus call the **Three R format**. In the next chapter, we will see a few other formats, but this one is the most popular.

 When creating backlogs, you can use the Three R format, so each item will include the Role, the Requirement and the Reason. This can be templatized as: As a _____ *[role -> persona]*, I want _____ *[requirement -> output]*, so _____ *[reason -> outcome]*.

The role is the user type. It's easy to understand why we want a map that works for any cat-sitter, not just one specific cat-sitter. We also don't want any miscellaneous passer-by to fit into it. We don't expect the janitor to take our cat to the vet, for example. In Chapter 3, *Journey Map – Understand Your Users*, we will create maps with multiple user groups, personas with different goals and abilities, but for now, we will focus only on the cat-sitter user group. The requirement explains what will happen. The requirements generate the outputs of the map, whereas the reasons are a subset of the positive outcomes. For example, the cat being sick would also be an outcome of the map, but certainly not a reason. As long as all reasons are aligned with our opportunity, we should be able to reach and end up with a well-fed, happy, and healthy cat when we come back. The preceding list was easy to create because we know what's more important for our opportunity. We could have written a list with 10 or 100 items, but probably we would have neither the resources nor the time for anything beyond the 5th.

Setting priorities right usually means the difference between success and failure for corporations. A famous example is from the summer of 2002. Sergey Brin and Larry Page, the founders of Google, were about to sell their company. Yahoo's then-chief executive Terry Semel refused to pay three billion dollars for it. At that time, search was clearly not important for Yahoo. Of course, it's easy to pass judgement on them in 2017, knowing that Verizon acquired Yahoo for less than five billion, while Google is worth about 500 billion dollars. The web was vastly different 15 years ago. Semel couldn't foresee how it would evolve. Continuing the story, in 2006, Yahoo had a different company in sight: Facebook. Mark Zuckerberg turned down a one billion offer, but some reports suggest that Facebook's board would have forced him to sell if the offer had been increased by only 10%. Yet again, Yahoo's CEO refused to increase the offer. Although Semel approached both Google and Facebook with an acquisition offer, both offers were too low. Money and other resources are allocated based on a priority list. For some corporations, investing in the future is not high on the priority list. History suggests that those companies, such as Yahoo, Kodak, or Blockbuster, perish within a decade. Even if you don't run a multi-billion dollar corporation, you should always think about the future, embrace change, and set your priorities accordingly.

Pen and paper are all you need – but adding color makes the maps great

A piece of paper and a pen is all you really need for mapping. For our purpose, the only "drawing" you need to do is drawing lines. Sounds simple enough, right? We have all created millions of lines. When we connect those, shapes emerged. Writing is simply a set of lines, no matter the language. Alyona Nickelson goes beyond that and emphasizes that lines and shapes carry an emotional message to the viewer; straight lines convey a sense of accuracy, directness, solidity, and stiffness. On the other hand, curves create a feeling of compromise and agreement, and flexibility and indecisiveness. To balance our communication, we can incorporate both types of lines. Don't worry if you can't draw a straight line. You can use rulers, or better to avoid communicating stiffness and be 100% agile, use only freehand-drawn lines.

Any pen and paper will do, but if you had more than one color, that would be really helpful. The often neglected aspect of experience mapping is color. We use brightly colored sticky notes for our user story maps (see `Chapter 2`, *User Story Map – Requirements by Collaboration and Sticky Notes*), but many UX experts just pick colors to represent a group of notes or even worse, just randomly. I hope that after reading this book, you will have a different approach. Color is an important aspect of communication. Judy Martin argues that our response to color is instinctive. We use it as a means of recognition and analysis. It not only defines space and form, but we also use color cues as invitations or warning signals. It has a subconscious emotional appeal. We associate green with the idea of life, growth, youth, spring, hope, and recently, environmental consciousness. For the artists out there, that might be a shock, because there are few natural sources of green pigment and the green coloring agents in artists' materials have been chemically developed so make sure that no green pastel dust falls on your cat, or any pastel dust for that matter.

This is a fraction (the cleaner, more presentable fraction) of my drawing equipment, but don't let yourself be intimidated by that. You don't need such a wide range of equipment for User Experience Mapping. Simply use what is available to you. *A piece of printer paper and a pen is a good start.* Colored mud on the wall of a cave was the choice of our ancestors, and it worked wonderfully for their purposes. Remember Barber Barrington's famous quote: *A keen artist will draw with anything and make it work to his advantage.* All user experience experts are artists. Communication is an art after all.

Now, we really need to get started with drawing a map. I'm sure that the inner artist in you is itching to take a pencil in hand and draw something.

Drawing the diagram

Now things will get exciting. We will add the opportunity to the map. You can write "Opportunity: Happy Cat", or have some fun creating a happy cat line art like I did:

The main map elements in User Experience Mapping are often called cards. This is because you can use a blank card, or more often a sticky note to represent them.

If you draw two boxes or place two cards, one above the other, then people assume that the one above is more important. Horizontal alignment usually represents progress, so placing a card to the right, usually means something happening after or as a cause. This is only true where left-to-right writing is more popular and not as obvious as a vertical placement. So, for horizontal layouts, use arrows to reinforce the meaning.

For each map, you need to create a structure that can be easily understood at a glance. For many maps, it makes sense to name the card by the outcome. Geographic and route map elements have their name, but those names can also be outcomes. For example, if I want to go to Budapest by car, the outcome is getting to Budapest. All I need to do is find the map element name Budapest to use the map.

In the next chapter, we will use sticky notes to represent cards, as they have many advantages. Movable, easy-to-rearrange cards are vital in the early, ideation phase of a product. Fortunately, our vision is clear, and we cast our priorities into stone in a totally non-agile way. Please don't try this at home, and always maintain flexibility in product management and in life. However, for this demo, it's okay to draw the cards on the paper.

For each card, we also want to add a short version of the requirements associated with the outcome. For multi-user, multi-platform, or multi-channel cards, we want to add those classifications. As our map is only aimed at cat-sitters, it's pointless to define the cat-sitter user group.

The last step is *adding a title*. Usually, you want to give your maps a meaningful title. I have seen digitally created maps with titles ranging from "Untitled" and "UXMap" to the URL of the site. Needless to say, all those are terrible choices. People who are not familiar with the process used to generate the map should know instantly what it is describing. Titles are also helpful when distributing the maps to the wider organization to get buy-in.

When creating a title for your map, try to find something that the stakeholders can relate to. Something that stops them in their tracks and starts user-centric thinking based on the subject.

In our example, "How to make a cat happy?" will do the trick. I add the "Opportunity" to the title, if that can be spelled out with simple and short words. If not, then you might need to think a bit more about your opportunity. Remember that now you need to discuss this with your main stakeholder, the cat-sitter. You need both the map and a conversation to solve a problem. In the following chapters, we will see business situations and get into facilitating the conversation using the map, but this chapter's examples stop at the finished map:

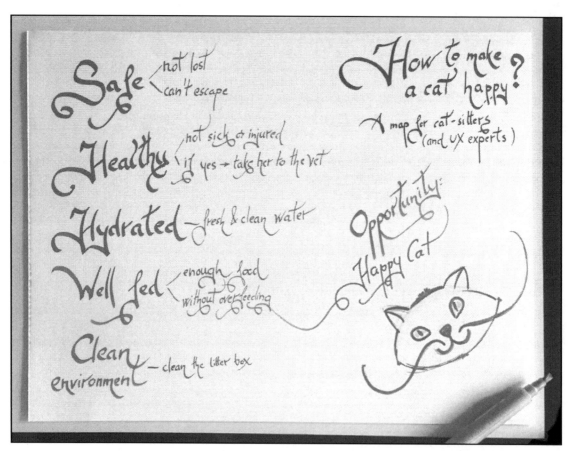

This map is also an example for cards not needing well-defined edges. It's customary to draw a rectangle or use a sticky note as a card, but sometimes it's not needed. I could have added a thin border around each card, but it would have added only visual clutter. As you can see, just a few words on a paper can form a map.

In the next section of this chapter, we will draw the same map with well-defined card boundaries, and more importantly using digital tools instead of free-hand.

Cats of the digital age use a computer

Drawing by hand is great fun, and all maps in the book can be done with pen and paper; each chapter will show you how to do the map with software. Digital tools will result in easier to edit and more readable maps while sacrificing the handmade charm. If you don't intend to sell your maps on Etsy or eBay, but use them as a communication tool, then digital might be the way to go.

I will use different software, my personal favorite for a map type. This, of course, doesn't mean that you need to use that software. This book is not intended to be a tutorial for any of those software products, so just use what's the easiest for you.

Always use the software you are the most familiar with for mapping. You want to focus on the users and the message, not on quirks of the software you are using to map.

In my eight years as a people manager, the most frequent software product I have seen in CVs is Microsoft's Office package, more specifically Word. Although Microsoft Word is rarely among job requirements for a UX job, most people will know the software at least to a basic level. Although people have Word installed on their machines and use it to write shorter or longer texts, most people would not think of it as a User Experience Mapping tool.

A few years ago I told a junior UX-er to do a simple journey map. She was new to UX, Adobe Illustrator, and most other software, but had a great attitude. I asked her what software she knew. She replied with "I have used Word to write my papers during Uni". She thought I was joking. When she realized that I wasn't, she jumped into the task. She did a good job, but it took her quite a bit, as she used a wild combination of special characters, tabs, and shapes. Then, I realized two things. First, that SmartArt is not something you can assume people will know about or use. Second, more importantly, you can do anything if you have the right attitude and approach to work. Skills come second. I could teach her User Experience Mapping in a few weeks, and I will try to share my knowledge with you through this book. What is much harder to teach is attitude and approach to work. (By the way, the heroine of our story is now the senior UX designer at a successful start-up, and she found real joy in researching users.)

On the screenshots, you will see Microsoft Word 2016, but you can use older versions to achieve similar effects. I will not use any feature new to Word 2016. I will use the Windows version, running on Windows 10. Again, you can use the Mac version to achieve the same look and feel.

To create our journey map, launch Word and **Insert a SmartArt Graphic** from the **Insert** tab's **Illustrations** group, selecting **SmartArt**:

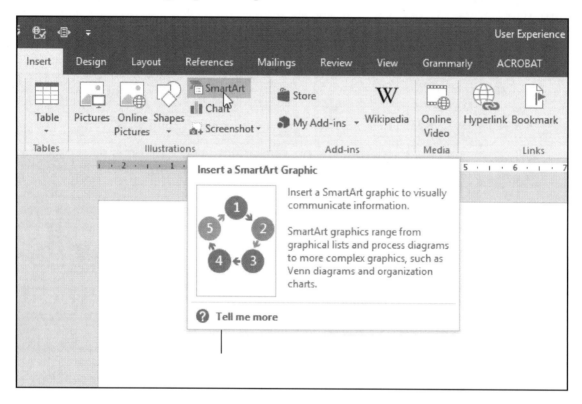

In the following choose a SmartArt graphic dialog box, click on the type and layout that you want. There are many types available, but for our mapping purposes, **Process** seems to be the best starting point. With that said, please experiment with other types too.

For now, let's just pick **Basic Process**:

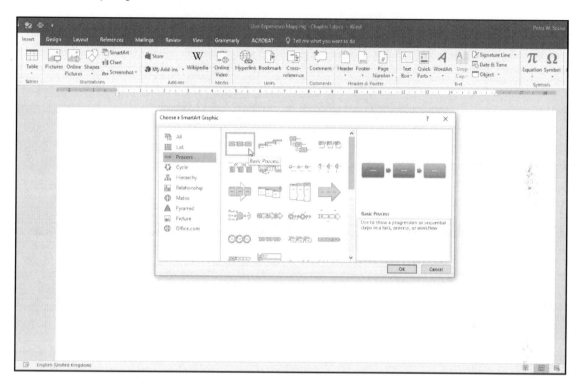

Choosing a SmartArt Graphic

Now, we can add our textual content. For this demo exercise, we will not specify user groups, just as we only intend to target cat-sitters. To add text to SmartArt, we can use the text pane. If it's not visible, you should click on the control button (that usually looks like a "<" character):

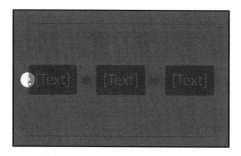

Once you are in the text pane, simply type in the text. Each top-level list item in the text pane will create a card as a map element. You can even copy and paste a list. If you press *Tab*, you can add sub-elements; those will be shown on the card as a list:

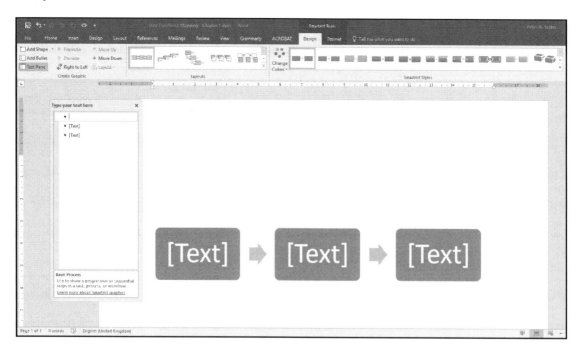

Text pane

Remember, for each map, you need to create a structure that can be easily and quickly understood by a miscellaneous passer-by. For our map, it makes sense to name the card by the outcome.

As the second level, we want to add a short version of the requirements associated with the outcome. Pressing the *Tab* key at the beginning of the line will enable you to make a first-level item a second-level item, pressing again will make it a third-level item, and so forth. Pressing the *Backspace* key at the beginning of the line will decrease the level, making the second-level item a first-level, for example:

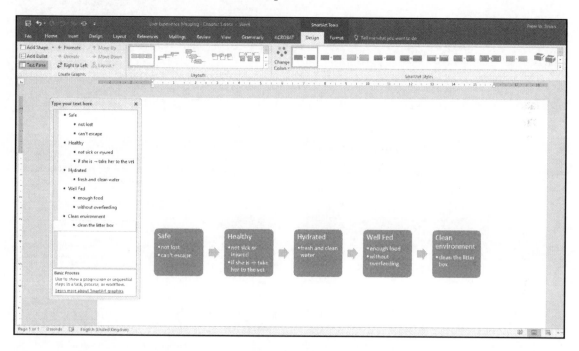

Adding text to different level items

At this point, you might realize that the **Basic Process** SmartArt type might not be the best for our map, as one card is not the result of the previous card, but they are all needed to make our cat happy. Fortunately, you don't need to recreate the SmartArt. You can change the type on-the-fly from the **Layouts** selection in the **Design** tab, as follows:

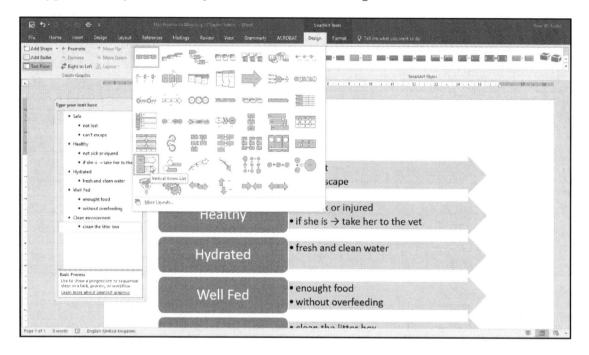

Deciding the design for our map

When you hover over different layout types, you can see their effect on our map, while clicking on one commits the change of type. For this map, arguably the best type would be **Vertical Arrow List**. All of our efforts should lead to fulfilling the opportunity, and they are not necessarily a result of the previous card's fulfillment. You can easily give food and water at the same time, no need to wait until the cat finishes drinking before you put down the food bowl.

Same as with the hand-drawn map, vertical placements of a color can be a good representation of importance here. Remember, if you draw two cards, one above the other, then people assume that the one above is more important. What's easier to do digitally is to gradually add tints of a color to highlight importance. A tint is the mixture of a color with white, which increases lightness. This means that the most important box will be the pure color, without white mixed in, and we add more and more white as we go down the importance scale.

To do this, Office has an easy solution. Just go to the **Design** tab and select **Change Colors**. There, you can find the gradient range of your chosen color. I have picked green because it is often associated with safety or the most important outcome. Moreover, it has a strong emotional correspondence with life, health, and clean environment. It is also the most restful color for the human eye. Another fun fact here is that cats don't see colors like we do. Reds and pinks appear greenish to them, whereas purple is just another shade of blue, but they can see shades of green similarly to how we see the color, according to Nickolay Lamm (`http://nickolaylamm.com/art-for-clients/what-do-cats-see/`):

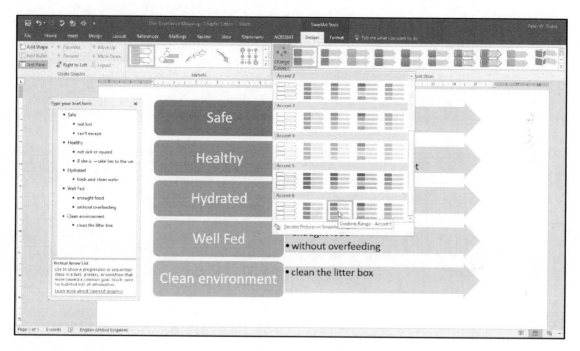

Changing the color scheme

You may find it odd that we started with the opportunity on the hand-drawn map, but not digitally. The main difference is that we are using the hand-drawn map as a guide for our digital map. Therefore, we know the opportunity and it's always in our focus, even if we haven't added it to the map yet, but now it's time.

Although you can add shapes inside the SmartArt, sometimes it's easier to add another SmartArt or Text Box next to it. To do so, we will start with resizing the SmartArt, so there is space to the left. In parts of the world where left-to-right writing is more common, it makes sense to add the opportunity to the right-hand side of the page. To resize the SmartArt, move the mouse cursor over the SmartArt's left edge. There should be a dot in the middle when the SmartArt is selected. Click on the SmartArt if it's not selected. Now, the cursor should turn into a double arrow, and you can start dragging it to the left to set the size. Most drawing elements in Word (and other software) can be resized the same way:

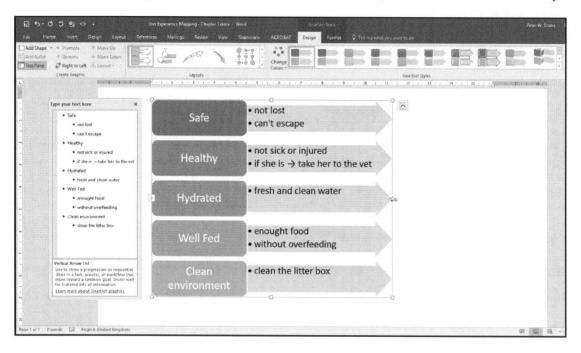

Resizing the SmartArt

Changing any element of the SmartArt is simple and intuitive. Just click on the element, and set the option in the **Format** panel. For example, I changed the text color for the second-level elements on the following screenshot to better match the rest of the map. This step is, of course, optional:

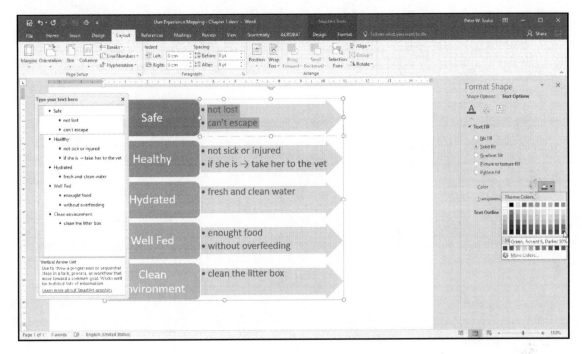

Customizing the elements

After you finish formatting your SmartArt, we will add the "Opportunity" as a **Text Box**; you can find that in the **Insert** tab's **Text** group. You can choose a **Simple Text Box** and format it later:

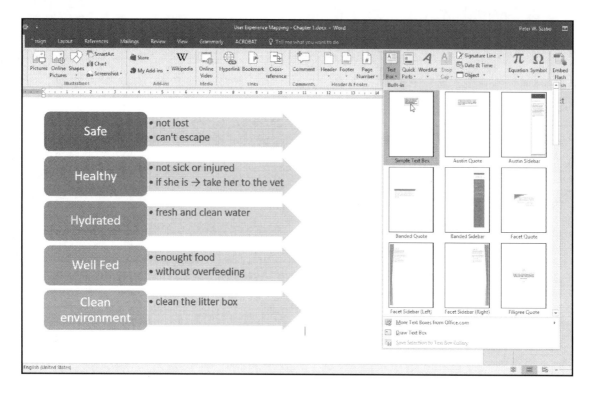

Now, you can move the Text Box to the right location by dragging and dropping with the mouse. Then, you can resize it by dragging the dots on the edges to make it the right size:

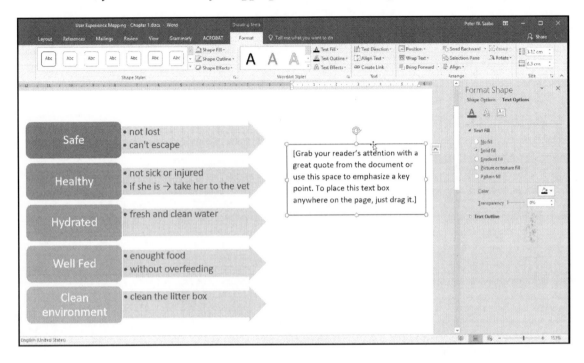

Optionally, you can change its appearance by selecting one of the **Theme Styles** or by manually setting your **Shape Fill** and **Shape Outline** colors:

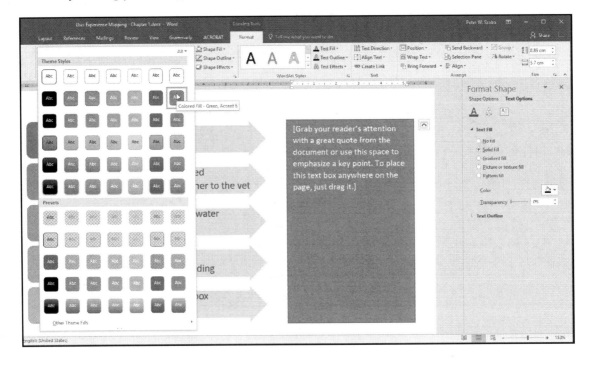

Now, you can rotate and add the text for our *Opportunity* box. If you want, you can rotate the text from the **Format Shape** panel (**Text Options** | **Text direction** dropdown):

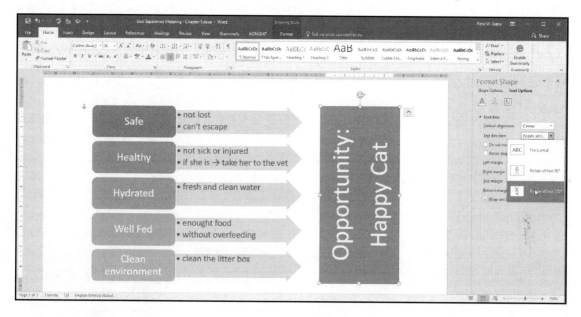

Rotating the text

The last step is adding a title. You can type in a title as your first line of text in the document. Remember, when creating a title for your map, try to find something that the stakeholders can relate to. Something that stops them in their tracks and starts user-centric thinking based on the subject.

How to make a cat happy? was my choice, because it introduces the "Opportunity" with simple and short words. Format the title to your liking and publish the final map by printing it. Don't forget that you need to discuss this with your cat-sitter. Both the map and a conversation are needed to solve the problem. In the following chapters, we will delve deeper into facilitating the conversation using the map, but this chapter stops at the finished map:

Summary

The finished map of the previous section summarizes the most important discovery of this chapter, *User Experience Mapping is a technique which will help you to understand the users, gain strategic insights, and improve communication.* Most problems can and will be solved with improved communication, which can be done by achieving shared understanding. The best communication method for shared understanding is drawing a map.

Before you start mapping, you need to visualize something implementable and create a backlog (list with the most important outcomes) to achieve the opportunity. When creating backlogs, each item should include the role, the requirement, and the reason. (To refresh the mapping lingo, the outputs are products of the map's usage, whereas the outcomes are the results. The opportunity is the desired outcome we plan to achieve with the aid of the map. This is how we want to change the world. We should start the map with the opportunity.)

This concludes our introduction to *User Experience Mapping*. In the next chapter, we will have some fun with sticky notes and learn to create User Story Maps.

2

User Story Map - Requirements by Collaboration and Sticky Notes

User story maps are the most common and popular map types by far. In this chapter, we will explore user story maps, and how they help you to create requirements through collaboration (and a few sticky notes). We will do the following in this chapter:

- We will create user stories and arrange them as a user story map
- We will discuss the reasons behind creating them
- We will cover how to tell a story
- The grocery surplus webshop's user story map will be the example I create in this chapter
- To do this, we will explore user story templates, characteristics of a good user story (INVEST) and epics
- With the three Cs (card, conversation, and confirmation) process, we will turn the stories into a reality
- We will create a user story map on a wall with sticky notes
- Then, create it digitally using StoriesOnBoard

 User stories are atomic functionality pieces, which provide value to the user. They are used to facilitate a conversation.

Jeff Patton wrote the first article about the subject in 2004, and a decade later in the book titled *User Story Mapping*, O'Reilly Media, 2014. Most people agree that he coined the term *user story map*, so it's only fair that we start this chapter with a quote from Jeff:

> *Story maps are for breaking down big stories as you tell them.*

- Jeff Patton

Systematically putting together atomic and valuable functionality pieces will produce a user story map.

Why should you create user story maps?

Contrary to the dreaded requirement document from the previous chapter, the discussion is an essential part of story maps, and we create them to help facilitate a healthy communication. My best answer to *why should you create user story maps?* is as follows:

User story maps solve the user's problems in the form of a discussion. Your job as a product manager or user experience consultant should be to make the world better through user-centric products, essentially by solving the user's problems.

Contrary to popular belief, user story maps are not just cash cows for agile experts. They will help a product to succeed, by increasing their understanding of the system. Not just what's inside it, but what will happen to the world as a result of such a system. By focusing on the opportunity and outcomes that will enable opportunity, the team can prioritize development. In reality, this often means stopping the proliferation of features and *underdoing* your competition.

Wait a minute, did you just read underdoing? As in, fewer features, not making bold promises, and significantly less customizability and options? Yes, indeed. The founders of Basecamp (formerly 37signals) are the champions of building less. In their book, *ReWork: Change the Way You Work Forever*, they tell Basecamp's success story while giving vital advice to anyone trying to run a build a product or a start-up:

When things aren't working, the natural inclination is to throw more at the problem. More people, time, and money. All that ends up doing is making the problem bigger. The right way to go is the opposite direction: cut back. So do less. Your project won't suffer nearly as much as you fear. In fact, there's a good chance it'll end up even better.

- Jason Fried

User story maps will help you to throw less at the problem, chopping down extras, until you reach an awesome product, which is actually done. One of the problems with long product backlogs or nightmarish requirement documents is that it never gets done, literally never.

Once I had to work on improving the user experience of a bank's backend. It was a gargantuan task, as this backend was a large collection of distributed microservices, which meant hundreds of different forms with hard-to-understand functions and a badly designed multi-level menu that connected them together. I knew almost nothing about banking, and they knew almost nothing about UX, so this was a match made in heaven. They gave me a twelve-page document. That was just the non-disclosure agreement. The project had many 100+ page documents, detailing various things and how they are done, complete with business processes and banking jargon. They wanted us to compile an expert review on what needs to be redesigned and create a detailed strategy for that. I found a better use of their money than wasting time on expert reviews and redesign strategies at that stage. Recording or even watching bank employees while they used the system during their work was out of the question. So we went for the quick win and did user story mapping in the first week of the project. Among the attendees of the user story mapping sessions, there were a few non-manager-level bank employees, who used the backend extensively. One of them was quite new to her job, but fortunately, quite talkative about it. It was immediately evident that most employees almost never used at least 95% of the functionality. Those were reserved for specially trained people, usually managers. After creating the user story map with the most essential and frequently used features, I suggested a backend interface, which only contained about 1% of the functionality of the old system at first, with the mention of other features to be added later. (As a UX consultant, you should avoid saying no, instead try saying later. It has the same effect for the project, but keeps everyone happy.) No one in the room believed that such a crazy idea would go through senior management, although they supported the proposal. Quite the contrary, it did go extremely well with their senior management. The senior managers understood that by creating a simple and fast backend user interface, they will be able to reduce the queues without hiring new employees. Moreover, if they need to hire people, training will be easier and faster. The new UI could also reduce the number of human errors. Almost all of the old backend was still online 2 years later, although used only by a few employees. This made both the product and the information security team happy, not to mention the HR. The functionality of the new application extended only slightly in 24 months. Nobody complained, and the bank's customers were happy with smaller queues. All this was achieved with a pack of colored sticky notes, some markers and, more importantly, a discussion and shared understanding.

This is just one example how a simple technique, such as user story mapping, could save millions of dollars for a company.

Just tell the story

Later in this chapter, we will discuss the basic conventions and formats of user story mapping, but first, let's discuss user story mapping without the burdens of using format constraints.

In Chapter 1, *How will UX Mapping Change Your (Users) Life?*, we saw that drawing a map, any map, will lead to solving the problem. In this one, we will focus on replacing document handovers by frequent discussions and collaboration.

 Enterprises tend to have some sort of formal approval process, usually with a sign-off. That's perfectly fine, and most of the time unavoidable. Just make sure that the sign-off happens after the mapping and story discussions. Ideally, right after the discussion, not days or weeks later.

There is a reason why product manager, UX experts, and all stakeholders love stories: they are humans. As such, we all have a natural tendency to love an emotionally satisfying tale. Most of our entertainment revolves around stories, and we want to hear good stories. A great story revolves around conflicts in a memorable and exciting way.

How to tell a story?

Telling a story is an easy task. We all did that as kids, yet we tend to forget about that skill we possess when we get into a serious product management discussion. How to tell a great story? There are a few rules to consider: the most important one is that you should talk about something that captivates the audience.

The audience

You should focus on the audience. What are their problems? What would make them listen actively, instead of texting or catching Pokémon, while at a user story discussion? Even if the project is about scratching your own itch, you should spin the story so it's their itch that is scratched. Engaging the audience can be indeed a challenge.

Once upon a time, I had written a sci-fi novel. Actually, it was published in 2000, with the title Tűzsugár, in Hungarian. The English title would be Ray of Fire, but fortunately for my future writing career, it was never translated into English. The book had everything my 15-16 years old self considered fun, for instance, a great space war or passionate love between members of different sapient spacefaring races. The characters were miscellaneous human and non-human lifeforms stuck in a spaceship for most of the story. Some of my characters had a keen resemblance to miscellaneous video game characters, from games such as Mortal Kombat 2 or Might & Magic VI. They certainly lacked emotional struggles over insignificant things such as mass-murder or the end of the universe. As I certainly hope that you will never read that book, I will spoil the fun for you by telling the end. A whole planet died, hinting that the entire galaxy might share the same fate, with a faint hope for salvation. This could have led to a sequel, but fortunately for all sci-fi lovers, I stopped writing the sequel after nine chapters.

The book seemed to be a success. A national TV channel did an interview with me, and I certainly got to all local newspapers, as a young author. Even more importantly, I had lots of fun writing it. However, the book itself was hard to understand and probably impossible to appreciate. My biggest mistake was writing only what I considered fun. To be honest, I still write for fun, but now I have an audience in mind. I tell the story of my passion for user experience mapping to a great audience: you. I try to find things that are fun to write and still interesting to my target audience. As a true UX geek, I create the main persona of my audience before writing anything and tell a story to them. We will get to personas in the next chapter. For this book, I call the main persona Maya, and she shares many traits with my daughter. Could I say, I'm writing this book for my daughter? Of course, I do, but I also keep in mind all other personas. Hopefully, one of them is a bit like you.

Before a talk at a conference, I always ask the organizers about the audience. Even if the topic stays the same, the audience completely changes the story and the way I present it. I might tell the same user story differently to one of my team members, to the leader of another team, or to a chief executive. Differently internally, to a client or a third party.

When telling a story, contrary to a written story, you will experience an immediate feedback or the lack of it from your audience. You should go even further and shape the story based on this feedback.

Telling a story is an interactive experience. Engage with your audience. Ask them questions, and let them ask you questions as a start, then turn this into a shared storytelling experience, where the story is being told by all participants together (not at the same time, though, unless you turn the workshop into a UX carol).

When you tell a fairy tale to your daughter, she might ask you, why can't the princess escape using her sharp wits and cunning, instead of relying on a prince challenging the dragon to a bloody duel? Then, you might start appreciating the story of *My Little Pony*, where the girl ponies solve challenges mostly nonviolently while working together as a team of friends, instead of acting as a prize to be won. So, why not spin a tale of heroic princesses with fluffy pink cats?

Start with action

Beginning *in medias res*, as in starting the narrative in the midst of action, is a technique used by masters, such as Shakespeare or Homer, and it is also a powerful tool in your user story arsenal.

While telling a story, always try to add as little background as possible, and start with drama or something to catch the attention of the audience, whenever possible.

At the beginning of *The Odyssey* quite a few unruly men want to marry Telemachus' mother, while his father has still not returned home from the Trojan War. There is no lengthy introduction explaining how those men ended up in Ithaca, or why the goddess, flash-eyed Athena, cares about Odysseus.

The poem was composed in an oral tradition and was more likely to be heard than read at the time of composition. While literacy has skyrocketed since Homer's time, you want to tell and discuss your user stories. Therefore, you should consider a similar start (maybe not mentioning the user's mother or her rascally suitors).

Simplify

In literary fiction, a complex story can be entertaining. *A Game of Thrones* and its sequels in *A Song of Ice and Fire* series is a good example for that. The thing is, George R. R. Martin *writes* those novels, and he certainly has no intention of discussing them during sprint planning meetings with stakeholders. User story maps are more similar to sagas, folktales, and other stories formed in an oral tradition. They develop in a discussion, and their understandability is granted by their simplicity. We need to create a map as simple and as small as possible, with as few story cards as possible.

So, how big should the story map be? Jim Shore defines *story card hell* as something that happens when you have 300 story cards and have to keep track of them. Madness, huh? This is not Sparta! Sorry Jim for the bad pun, but you are absolutely right, in the 300 range, you will not understand the map, and the whole discussion part will completely fail. The user stories will be lost, and the audience will not even try to understand what's happening.

 There is no ideal number of cards in a story map, but aim low. Then, eliminate most of the cards. Clutters will destroy the conversation.

In most card games, you will have from two to seven cards in hand, with some rare exceptions. The most popular card game both online and offline is Texas Hold 'em Poker. In that game, each player deals with only two cards. This is because human thought processes and discussions work best with a small number of objects. Sometimes, the number of objects in the real world is high. Our mind is good at simplifying, classifying, and grouping things into manageable units. With that said, most books and conference presentations about user story mapping show us a photo of a wall covered with sticky notes. The viewer will have absolutely no idea what's on them, but one thing is certain, it looks like a *complex project*. I have bad news for you: projects with a complex user story map never get finished, and if they do get finished, to a degree they will fail. The abundance of sticky notes means that the communication and simplification process needs one or more iterations. Throw away most of the sticky notes! To do that, you need to understand the problem better.

Tell the story of your passion

Seriously, find someone, and tell them the user story of the next big thing, the app or hardware that will change the world. Try it now; be bold and let your imagination flow.

I believe that in this century, we will be able to digitalize human beings. This will be the key to both humankind's survival as a species and our exploration of space. The digital society would have no famine, no plagues, and no poverty. This would solve all major problems we face today. Digital humans would even defeat death. Sounds like a wild sci-fi idea? It is, but then again, smartphones were also a wild sci-fi idea a few decades ago.

In this chapter, I will tell you the story of something we can build today.

The grocery surplus webshop

We will create the user story map for a grocery surplus webshop. Using this e-commerce site, we will sell clearance food and drink at a discount price; this means food that would be thrown away at a regular store--for example, food past its expiry date or with damaged packaging. This idea is popular in developed countries, such as Denmark and the UK, and it might help to reduce on the amounts of food wasted every year, totaling 1.3 billion metric tonnes worldwide. We are trying to create the online-only version of WeFood (`https://don ate.danchurchaid.org/wefood`).

Our users can be environmentally conscious shoppers or low-income families with limited budgets, just to give two examples. In `Chapter 3`, *Journey Map - Understand Your Users*, we will introduce personas, and treat them separately; for now, we will only think about them as shoppers.

The opportunity to scratch your own itch

We have seen in the previous chapter that mapping will help you to achieve the most, with as little as possible; in other words, maximize the opportunity, while minimizing the outputs.

Let's refresh the mapping lingo: The outputs are products of the map's usage, whereas the outcomes are the results. The opportunity is the desired outcome we plan to achieve with the aid of the map. This is how we want to change the world. We should start the map with the opportunity.

The opportunity should not be defined as selling surplus food and drink to our visitors. If you approach a project or a business without solving the users' problem, the project might become a failure. In `Chapter 5`, *Remote and Lab Tests for Map Creation*, we will see the best way to find out what our users want, by researching them, through remote and lab-based user experience testing. Until that time, we need to settle for the second best solution, which happens to be free, the need to *solve your own problem*, in other words, *scratch your own itch*. Probably, the best summary of this mantra comes from Jason Fried, the founder and CEO of Basecamp:

> *When you solve your own problem, you create a tool that you're passionate about. And passion is key. Passion means you'll truly use it and care about it. And that's the best way to get others to feel passionate about it too. (Getting Real: The Smarter, Faster, Easier Way to Build a Successful Web Application)*

So, we will create the web store that we would love to use. Although, as the cliché goes, there is no *I* in *team*, but there is certainly an *I* in *writer*. My ideal e-commerce site could be different to yours.

When following the examples of this chapter, try to think of your itch, your ideal web store, and use my words only as guidance. You can create the user story map for any other project, ideally something you are passionate about. I would encourage you to pick something that's not a webshop, or maybe not even a digital product if you feel adventurous.

You need to tell the story of your passion. My passion is reducing food waste (that's also the poor excuse I'm using when looking at the bathroom scale). Here is my attempt to phrase the opportunity:

The opportunity is where our shoppers want to save money while reducing global food waste. They understand and accept what surplus food and drink means, and they are happy to shop with us.

Actually, the first sentence would be enough. Remember, you want to have a simple one or two sentence opportunity definition.

> *I ended up working for two tapestry webshops as a consultant. Not at the same time, though, and the second company approached me mostly as the result of how successful the first one was. It's a relatively small industry in Europe, and business owners and decision-makers know each other by name.*
> *I still recall the pleasant experience I had meeting the owners of the first webshop. They invited me to dinner at a homely restaurant in Budapest. We had a great discussion, and they shared their passion. They were an elderly couple, so they must have spent most of their life in the communist era. In the early 90s, they decided to start a business, selling*

tapestry in a brick and mortar store. Obviously, they had no background in management or running a capitalist business, but that didn't matter, they only wanted to help people to make their homes beautiful. They loved tapestry, so they started importing and selling it. When I visited their physical store, I saw them talking to a customer. They spent more than an hour discussing interior decoration with someone, who just popped by to ask the square meter prices of tapestry. Tapestry is not sold per square meter, but they did the math for the customer among many other things. They showed her many different patterns and types and discussed application methods. After leaving the shop, the customer knew more about tapestry than most other people ever will.

Fast forward to the second contract. I only talked to the client on Skype, and that's perfectly fine because most of my clients don't invite me to dinner. I saw many differences in this client's approach to the previous one. At some point, I asked him "Why do you sell tapestry? Is tapestry your passion?" He was a bit startled by the question, but he promptly replied: "To make money, why else? You need to be pretty crazy to have tapestry as a passion." Seven years later, the second business no longer exists, yet the first one is still successful. Treating your work as your passion works wonders.

Passion is an important contributor to the success of an idea. Whenever possible, pour your passion into a product and summarize it as your opportunity.

How to create a user story

The first step in story mapping is creating the user story cards, used to facilitate the conversation. They are atomic functionality pieces, which provide value to the user. It makes sense to use the same template for all user story cards within the same project so that you can easily compare them.

User story templates

In this section, I will show you the most common formats, but you are welcome to use any format to create your user stories.

The Three Rs or the Connextra format

The most common format for user story templates is what you have already seen in the previous chapter. It's called the Three Rs or the Connextra format (a team at Connextra developed this template).

As a _____ *[role -> persona]*, I want _____ *[requirement -> output]*, so _____ *[reason -> outcome]*. The third R (reason) part of this template is optional.

The grocery surplus e-commerce site example's first iteration: *As a shopper, I want to see the contents of my shopping cart anytime, including the total value, the number of items, and their combined weight, including the total shipping costs, so that I can make decisions on adding further items.*

This contains too many details, a common mistake. So, let's remove what's not a critical detail here: *As a shopper, I want to see the contents of my shopping cart so that I can make decisions on adding further items.*

Much better, but the third R part (*so that I can make decisions on adding further items*) can be omitted, and the user story will still work as intended. Not only can it can be omitted, but we should trim down any unnecessary text from our user stories to follow the principle of simplicity from the previous section.

The simplified example should read: *As a shopper, I want to see the contents of my shopping cart.* This is how a user story looks in the Three R format.

The big advantage of the textbook template for user stories is the fact that it's widely known and accepted.

Five Ws

The most basic information-gathering and problem-solving questions are who?, when?, where?, what?, and why?.

As _____ *[who? -> persona]* _____ *[when?]* _____ *[where?]*, I _____ *[what? -> output]* because _____ *[why? -> outcome]*.

Our previous example would transform to this: As a *shopper, during the process of finding additional items, in a dedicated view, I want to see the contents of my shopping cart,* because *I need to make decisions on adding further items.*

This version is clearly more complex and trickier to write or discuss than the previous Three Rs. I would suggest avoiding this or any template that goes against the principle of simplicity. Two additional fields add marginal value to this template. Instead, if needed, the answers to *when?* and *where?* can be incorporated into the *requirement* part of the Three R template.

Lean Startup

The **Lean Startup User Story** template is inspired by Eric Ries' book, *The Lean Startup*. It adds actionable (also auditable and accessible) metrics to user stories while dropping the role/persona/who from the previous templates altogether.

 _____ [feature -> *output*] will move _____ [actionable metrics]

View shopping cart will move shopping cart abandonment, related customer support queries, and shopping cart average value.

A start-up, especially in the early seed stage, should have only one persona. So, dropping the role is one of the benefits here. Replacing the reason (outcome) with actionable metrics is the real difference, unfortunately, for the worse. At the stage of considering a new project or discussing whether we should add new features to an existing one, we are far from measuring the effects of those features. If we add actionable metrics, senior management will ask for an estimate. For example, how big is the impact of the view shopping cart feature on the number of customer support calls? There is no sure way to have an acceptable estimate for changes in metrics this early before the development has even started, so it's pretty much a wild guess. At this stage, you can admit that it's possible that the effect will not even be measurable, or if it is, it can be within the margin of error. Alternatively, you could come up with a number. I suggest 42. Not just because I'm a sci-fi fan, but because when pronounced separately in Japanese, shi ni (four two) sounds like the word *death*. That's exactly what will happen to the project if you base user stories on wild guesses.

Kaizen-UX template

During the first few years of my consulting career, I have used the Three Rs template, with smaller or bigger modifications. The result of those learnings is the Kaizen-UX template.

 _____ [*outcome*~optional~] -> _____ [*output*] This is the first iteration. Extend or simplify as needed, through a continuous improvement process. The outcome is optional. So is the arrow. In other words: *Write the output on a sticky note, and add anything else you see fit.*

So, our example will be as simple as *I want to see the contents of my shopping cart.* This is something a client would say to a developer, and that's the beauty of it.

Wait, did I just write a whole section, just to say write the output on a sticky note, and add anything else you see fit? Yes, and that's the most important learning from this chapter. People love templates, and user story templates are also attractive.

I'm applying the Kaizen continuous improvement principle to all areas of UX and life. We reached the above template by removing waste from a user story card template. The only thing that is surely not a waste is the output, *the user story map is a structured collection of outputs.*

Some projects may require personas (we will get there in the next chapter) or some other additions to this template, for instance, edge cases, acceptance criteria, or even actionable metrics (hopefully, you will never get there in the planning stage). Those can be added to the cards, and the project's template can and should be improved continuously.

What's more important is what gets into the template. So let's meet the INVEST rules.

INVEST - the characteristics of a good user story

Bill Wake created the INVEST mnemonic, originally for the Extreme Programming agile methodology. Regardless of the methodology you use, you can benefit from following those six principles. For example, I used the principles successfully with both Kanban, Scrum and my methodology, the Kaizen-UX.

The principle contains the six main attributes of a good user story, as follows:

I for independent

Each user story should be self-contained. Ideally, each user story should be prioritized or eliminated without considering any other story. For example, seeing the contents of the shopping cart might seem to be dependent on many things. In reality, creating a shopping cart view is pretty much self-contained. Sure, you could argue that it depends on the existence of the add-to-cart feature, but it doesn't. Two developers could work on those two features at the same time, or one of them could be developed first. Although adding things to the cart helps the website, the view cart can be tested without that feature, with prepopulated shopping carts.

N for negotiable

The user story can be rewritten or even dropped as a result of a discussion or negotiation. For example, a 3D preview of the product box can be replaced with just a few images of the product as a result of the negotiation. The annoying popup asking for a newsletter subscription can be dropped (probably should) after discussing it. At this stage, we are capturing the essence of the user story, so there is infinite room for negotiation.

V for valuable

One of the agile principles is to deliver valuable software. We want to create something valuable for someone, ideally for both the user and the business. In reality, the UX expert needs to balance business goals with user needs. In the previous example, the shopping cart view is certainly valuable, and so is a 3D preview of the product, but the shopping cart view is probably more valuable. That's fine, that's why we have the discussion on negotiable user stories. Some of the value might get discarded.

E for estimable

How long will this story take to be implemented? The estimable principle leads to the most chaos misunderstandings when it comes to user story mapping. First of all, humans are terrible at estimating things. We usually estimate based on the best-case scenario, then add padding to handle the anomalies. Unfortunately, reality doesn't work like this. Unforeseeable things can and will happen, but that's fine. Estimates don't need to be accurate.

The shopping cart view should take less than half a sprint, depending on the team, while the whole checkout process might need to be split into multiple sprints. Always discuss estimates, with the development teams, even if you think you know them and their capabilities well enough.

S for small

A good user story should be small. That's obvious to most people. Small stories have many benefits, tying back to the previous principle that states the smaller our user stories are, the easier it is to estimate. More importantly, discussing small stories is easy, whereas large, complex ones will confuse people and ruin the communication. There is a term for large user stories: they are called epics. We will have a section of them in this chapter, mainly so you understand the term, then we will see how to break them down into user stories following the INVEST principles.

A story should be just big enough to solve an atomic problem for the user. This usually leads to user stories being buildable in a maximum of half the development time in a sprint. They should be built in a few days by the agile team. (Maximum 5 days for a 10 working day sprint.) If you aren't working on a software or aren't using an agile methodology, then the right size is the smallest size where you can't split it further, still conforming to the INVEST principles.

The shopping cart view conforms to the smallness principle, so is the pop-up newsletter subscription. The whole checkout process might not be small enough. However, I give you the most obvious, although often encountered example for a not-small-enough user story: *As a manager, I want to be able to manage my webshop's backend*. There are many issues with this user story, but the most obvious is the sheer size of it. Also, it does not contain the sub-tasks required, so the user story becomes terrifying.

T for testable

Even if you don't follow the test-driven development process, testable user stories will be useful. This is because if you don't know how to test something, it usually means that you don't understand it well enough. This also enforces the smallness, as smaller user stories are easier to test.

You can think about testability as *what would make you accept that user story as done?* How do you know it's working as intended? For example, we know that the shopping cart view works if it shows the contents of the shopping cart, including the unit prices, total amount, weight, and shipping costs. Moreover, it enables us to remove and change the quantity of the items, it leads to the checkout through a highly visible call to action button, while it also allows us to get back to our previous view. As you can see, this can lead to rather complex criteria. Thinking about that will be helpful when we create the Wireflows in `Chapter 4`, *Wireflows - Plan Your Product*. For now, testability helps to check whether we have a shared understanding or whether we just think we do.

Epics

Epics? No, not the purple drops in World of Warcraft. As I hinted previously, when we discuss project management or user experience, *epics are oversized user stories*. There is no universal right size standard for stories that all depend on the project and conversation.

If it's possible to break the story apart and still have a relevant and meaningful conversation about solving the atomic problem of the user, it's an epic. Epics should be broken down into smaller user stories.

Epics are in the way of a good conversation. Make the user stories simpler and conform to the INVEST principles. Breaking down epics can have additional benefits because smaller stories can reveal UX improvement possibilities you didn't think of when you looked at the epic.

I was genuinely overjoyed to lead a team creating a commercial content management system. It sounded like an amazing UX and project management challenge. It turned out to be a nightmare right at the beginning when we started to create the user stories. The impending doom sort of nightmare, where you feel that failure is imminent, and you should escape the project as soon as you can. Almost none of the user stories fit into a sprint, and even worse, for at least six months the new CMS would not be releasable. Our map was full of epics.
After a brief period of panic, we started rethinking the approach. We had to forget the workflow-based approach and started breaking down the epics we had. One of the most stubborn offenders was this user story: I want to add new pages for my site and edit them later. Splitting this into creating a page and editing a page would serve no purpose because the same code would be responsible for creating new pages and editing the existing ones, and both were essential anyhow. The problem arose from the fact that the page could be a contact form, a picture gallery, an article, a blog post, a FAQ item, or many other things. Then, we realized that there is a group of elements that don't depend on the page type.

Things such as the URL, the title, the meta description, and the status of the page (published, draft, deleted, and so on). We named them meta elements, although not all of them represent meta tags. This split created the following user story, passing all INVEST criteria: I want to create pages and edit their meta elements. This resulted in a backlog item that our senior Ruby on Rails developer could do in a day. It was testable and immediately usable in production because the early version had a text area below the meta elements, where you could put in any HTML code, which was then rendered below the heading. This text area was obviously replaced in the next iteration, but it was amazing for the **Minimum Viable Solution**.

The hidden benefit we discovered, when focusing on this user story, was that the user might not want to create the meta elements, so they should all have a default value. Moreover, the values should be linked, unless you broke that link. For example, you typed in the title, and the H1 element and the search engine friendly URL was generated from it:

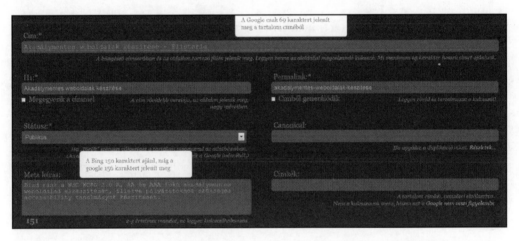

We even had time to add meaningful labels, strong validation, and inline help. For example, you could see that you have only 65 characters in the title, as our recommendation (the green underscores). At that time, Google showed 69, so we underlined characters 66-69 with yellow and anything above 69 with red. It was possible to add a title of 255 characters, but our inline validation actively discouraged it. That alone could have been a user story, something like I want to create and edit the titles of my pages, while always knowing the character limits of it. Another story could have been I want all meta elements to have useful defaults and where possible generated from the title. However, that only leads to the story card hell. Our CMS could have had thousands of sticky notes. Instead, we stopped at the point where the user stories became small enough to be developed in half a sprint tops, while still big enough to solve a user's problem.

The image for this case study is published with the blessing and written agreement of *Initiale Srl*. It shows a pre-alpha gray-on-gray view of the CMS. The UI was Hungarian only at that stage. The white boxes are tutorial messages to help the new user, whereas the light gray areas are the inputs.

Breaking down epics into good user stories

Always start breaking down epics by simplifying and splitting the outputs. Focus on what the users will see. Decide what is the result of their actions.

As we have seen, all story card templates contain the output. More often than not, the outputs of epics can be split into multiple, still meaningful outputs. If you are using the **Model-View-Controller (MVC)** software design pattern, don't worry about the model. Worry about your users. Try to create user stories which are simple and will translate gracefully into views. With less technical words, focus on what the users will see as a result of their actions, then create a user story for each of those results, if they solve a problem. At first, don't worry about actions that can result in a problem or nothing. If the user searches for a car in our grocery surplus webshop, that's their problem for now. Later on, we might want to help them, by suggesting something they can actually buy here. Maybe they were looking for carrot cakes, or we might start selling surplus car air fresheners if we identify a need for that. The point here is that it's much easier to have a great and actionable discussion on small and simple user stories than epics.

Have a specific user in mind and create their user story. This will help to break down epics efficiently. If something is useful to them, you keep that part. Otherwise, you rewrite the user story.

It's possible that different personas (more on them in the next chapter; for now, let's just treat them as a group of similar users) would want a different representation of the same data. In our grocery surplus web store, the accountant, the store owner, the warehouse assistant, and the buyer would want a different representation of the same order. It's possible to create a user story for each of those personas, but before researching the users, that's probably a bad choice. It's much easier to pick one user and solve the issues for them. Ideally, that user is you; remember to scratch your own itch.

There are many customer segments you can use to constrain your unruly user stories. For example, focus only on technically proficient users at first, from only one country, one language, probably from only one sector. This might create a narrow user base, maybe less than 1%. Like Wall Street stock traders, you can ignore the 99%.

However, this can be done only for your Minimum Viable Solution. Later during the continuous improvement process, you should start caring for all users or consciously create a product, which is not for everyone. Obviously, the latter is much better because it's impossible to please every possible user.

 After you have simplified and split most of the outputs and reduced the target audience to one person, yourself, you might still have some epics. This is when the project calls for a walking skeleton. No, not necromancy, but an atomic implementation of the system, performing a small end-to-end function, linking together the main architectural components.

Alistair Cockburn's walking skeleton definition can help you to reach to create something that can serve as a proof of concept or Minimum Viable Solution. Gojko Adzic and David Evans goes even further with a humorous twist on the walking skeleton, by suggesting to put the skeleton on crutches. This means that you can start with something the user can interact with, and don't worry about linking together the main architectural components. In other words, create a user interface and ship it as soon as possible. Everything else can be placed in future iterations. I love this idea, mostly because this way you can start testing with real users a few weeks or even days after discussing the project for the first time.

Worst case scenario at the walking skeleton step (with or without crutches) will be where we always ended up with no epics, just simple and easy-to-discuss user stories.

Now, we should have good user stories. However, how will you change the world with user stories? The deceptively simple answer is in the next section of this chapter. It's called the 3 Cs process.

3 Cs – the process to turn stories into reality

Ron Jeffries and his co-authors created a great summary of the user story process. The 3 Cs stand for *Card*, *Conversation*, and *Confirmation*. Going through those three steps in this order will enable you to deliver solutions to the users' problems.

Card

The size, the shape, and what's on the back of the card are all irrelevant. As long as it's writable and movable, almost any object can serve as a medium for your story. With that said, a stone tablet is a bit less practical than a sticky note (often called Post-it note after the famous brand), so most people prefer sticky notes for story cards.

The biggest advantage is that they stay on a vertical surface, like a wall. Also, user story maps are often created on walls. This has many benefits. First of all, it forces people to stand up. This creates much better discussion dynamics, while also shortening the average length of the meeting, forcing people to focus, and optimizing the communication. More importantly, my personal observation is that people will reach an agreement much faster when they are standing up and at arm's length from each other.

The other, more subtle advantage of using a wall is that most of the time you can keep your sticky notes there for a while. If not, you can take a photo of them. Some teams use a table. The problem with a table is that people might sit around it. This will create a situation where some people see the cards upside-down. If you are the storyteller, chances are that they will arrange for your comfort. This will lead to a one-sided conversation, the kind you want to avoid. On the other hand, when you all stand in front of the wall, everyone will be on the same side, literally. The ideal room for telling user stories has no tables and no chairs at all. Just some white walls and empty space, so people can freely move around and explore.

To write the stories to the cards, you could use one of the templates I have shown before, or create your own style. The only advice I have here is to use the same style or template for all cards. Contrary to Internet forums, all caps help the communication on hand-written story cards. Most of the time it's better to write only the keywords on hand-written story cards, instead of the full story. That will make scannability easier. Alternatively, you can use a highlighter to give emphasis to the most important keywords.

After you have created your story cards, it's time to invite people to the conversation. Don't forget to bring a few empty cards, or blank sticky notes to the meeting, because new user stories can emerge during the conversation.

Conversation

This is the key element. Everything we do in this chapter leads to improving the conversation. I would like to emphasize the conversation word. It should be an interactive storytelling experience. Other people in the room should ask many questions, and everyone should work toward the shared understanding.

The number of people in a user story conversation should be kept to a minimum. If you invite too many people to a meeting, it will turn into someone presenting, while the others checking Facebook on their phones. To make sure that you have a conversation, you want to invite five or fewer people. The other problem might be stage-fright. As a frequent conference speaker, I'm quite used to speaking in front of a large crowd; however, for some people, speaking to more than five is a torture.

Organizing large meetings in a corporate environment can be difficult. That's fortunate because large meetings are a total waste of time for all participants. Many of us have survived countless meetings, which could have been solved by an e-mail or a discussion among four people. Although it's great to involve the UX director in as many things as possible, I would have preferred to work on something meaningful during many of those 10-plus person mega-meetings, where nothing is actionable for me at the end. Those meetings are usually the longest. People get bored, and some of them might feel the need to say something, comment on something, and then if some people do, there is a peer-pressure, so everyone has to add some random stuff to the conversation. After three hours, nothing is decided or really discussed, and we agree to have another meeting in the near future.

A small group of people usually have an easy time organizing a meeting, even ad hoc. Those meetings are faster, and making them phone/video conferences is much easier.

> *Have you tried a video-conference with 20-plus people? At least half of it will be spent on fixing technical issues of the video-conference itself, with the other half suffering from the remaining technical issues. The best solution I have for those events is having my cat sleeping on the table in front of the camera. Participants can ask if it's a real cat or plush. That's my cue to wake the cat up, and bring some cheer to the totally pointless meeting, while some people reinstall Skype and the sound driver.*

Another extreme is when someone gives an expert analysis of the user stories, so everyone can avoid the meeting. This approach totally defeats the purpose of user stories. Without communication and knowledge sharing, there will be no solution and there will be no shared understanding.

The power of four amigos

Gojko Adzic named the solution to the conversation size problem the *three-amigo meeting* after the American western comedy from the 80's ¡*Three Amigos!*, a comedy showcasing the results of miscommunication in hilarious ways.

The three-amigo meeting involves the business representative, the developer, and the tester. I think that the UX expert should be the fourth amigo, to represent the users' needs.

The equation is simple. A business representative, usually a product owner, introduces the opportunity, the stories and optionally presents the initial scenarios, basically telling the other amigos what the business needs. Then, the UX expert will champion user needs, essentially representing the users in the meeting room.

The developer will bring the existing infrastructure and technical constraints to the table, often playing the devil's advocate. The developer will fight against adding unnecessary complexity to the software, eliminating ideas that might sound great, but would eat up precious development resources. The tester will consider how the story might be tested. Often, the tester will bring new scenarios or edge-cases, which will help to eliminate bad ideas that slipped through the other three-amigos.

Sometimes, the four-amigos can be three or even five; don't worry about the number. The key learning is to constrain the number of people to a handful, who can work together and discuss the project in a meaningful way.

When I worked as a consultant for a ride-sharing start-up (similar to Uber, but this was a different start-up); they always invited a domain expert, a guy who used to run a taxi company for years. He knew all about the taxi industry, regulations, and often came up with really clever scenarios. The three-amigo meetings had five people, and it worked great. On the other hand, for another start-up, when the two-amigo meeting was just the founder and me, the communication was much less fruitful--having a third person really helps. When I suggested inviting another senior developer, the founder (also being a full-stack developer) was not sure if that was needed. He thought that this would take developer hours from the other developer, hours for which he was paying from a very limited budget. After the first truly three-amigo meeting, he was convinced. As a side-effect, the senior developer was more engaged with the project and more enthusiastic. He still had the same share in the company as before, but now he felt that he could shape the future of it. This, among many things, contributed to the success of the app.

It's worth nothing that tech-amigos and business-amigos often have a hard time understanding each other. Moreover, business-amigos will not understand most of the techy discussion the tester, the developer, and the tech-savvy UXer will have. They might feel excluded and start finding excuses to avoid the amigo meetings. This goes the other way around too if you have a business domain expert, a business analyst and another business representative, the tech-amigos will be bored, and they will feel that the discussion had little or no actionable items for them, rightly so. For complex projects, you might need two, focused discussion groups, instead of just one. There should be a person present in both groups. Ideally, this person is the product owner, but not necessarily. The goal is to have the two discussion groups working in sync to create a great product.

Confirmation

So, you have put your story on cards, and you have discussed it. How do you know the story is put in practice as intended? What would make you accept the story as completed? Simply put, how do you know when it's done? Those questions lead to the third pillar of user stories, the confirmation.

Request for Comment (**RFC**) e-mails are probably not what we are looking for, neither is asking the developers. The solution is agreeing on *acceptance criteria*. They have a less scientific sounding name, which tells us what they really are: *story tests*.

A hidden benefit of thinking about how we will test a story is finding gaps in our story and our reasoning. This is also why we invited a tester to a four-amigos meeting.

Don't worry if your story tests are not perfect. At this stage, they don't need to be. When we create Wireflows (more on them in Chapter 4, *Wireflows - Plan Your Product*), we will have a much more detailed understanding and communication about the story; therefore, our acceptance criteria can be refined.

The narrative flow

How do the stories create a map? You simply need to arrange the cards. As we have seen in the previous chapter, by nature, people understand that *a card above another card means a higher priority.* Where the left-to-right writing pattern is dominant (most of the world, excluding Arabic and Hebrew and a few other written languages) if you *put a card to the right of another card, people will understand that the story is told after the previous one in the flow.* To reinforce this, some people add an arrow pointing to the left, but that's unnecessary. The user story represented by the card on the right of the first card is told after the first card, and so forth, while the rightmost story is told as the last. If possible, try to follow the natural order of events, as they happen with the user interacting with the product.

The narrative flow means organizing the cards in a map left to right, each story put after the previous story in this left to right order. Combine this with the vertical order, where a card above another card means higher priority and you will get a two-dimensional map.

For example, a user story related to product search surely happens before the user story related to checkout, for example, entering your home address. *Manually entering your home address* and *using an automatic address finder based on postcode* seem to be part of the same story, but manually entering your home address is a critical, very important feature, while the postcode-based finder is a nice-to-have one. Therefore, you should add the postcode finder story below the manual entry story.

Events (tasks)

Arranging the cards alongside the narrative flow could be a challenge. To help with that, *each column of the narrative flow will be an event.* Each event will contain one or more user story. Remember, user stories are atomic solutions, and we tried hard to make them as small as possible for a given project. For our web store *shipping* is an event. The user needs to enter their shipping details. One user story is: *I'd like to enter my address (manually).* Another user story is: *I'd like to enter my postcode, then select my address from the possible addresses on the given postcode.* A third one is: *I'd like to select the shipping method.*

Many authors, including Alistair Cockburn and Jeff Patton, use the term tasks for what I call events. The problem with that term is that it leads to misunderstandings because planning the creation of a product means creating development and testing tasks for your team. Moreover, they are not always tasks in the most common sense of the word, as in a piece of work to be done. Events can be simple thoughts that cross the user's mind or as complex as viewing the home page for the first time. Usually, events can be associated with things happening while the user interacts with the site. For example, in some turn-based card games, for example, Hearthstone, observing the opponent's turn is certainly an event, but it would be a bit odd to call it a task, as the player can't actively play until it's their turn.

It's often not possible to tell the order of events. For example, we can start our activities in the webshop by searching for the desired product, or by browsing the site, going from categories to subcategories to products. It's also possible that we start with one method, then switch to another. Please remember that the order of cards is the order of the narrative flow, the order in which we will tell the story, not necessarily the order in which the user might perform their actions. However, it certainly makes sense to align the narrative flow with the user's anticipated actions as much as possible.

Milestones (activities)

Most of my user experience maps depict possible paths the user might take to fulfill the opportunity. Milestones of my maps group all events which lead to a common goal. They are more than just simple aggregators. *Every achievement the user has on the road to reach the opportunity is a milestone.*

Some authors tried to coin the term *activities*, but I prefer to call them milestones. Most of the time, the card used to represent them is the same width as the common user story card, for the simple fact that few people carry around oversized sticky notes for this purpose. Events in a milestone usually share the thought processes of the user. For example, checkout is an obvious milestone for a webshop. When they reach this milestone, the user's mindset changes, and they will start to react to triggers differently.

Milestones are usually named after the common goal the events share. Our webshop's user story map could start with the planning milestone, but there is nothing to develop there at the moment. It's certainly part of the whole experience, but unlike most other milestones, planning happens outside of the webshop. It contains things such as searching something in Google, finding an item sold in our shop on Facebook, or reading an article about our site (obviously, we wish to get into mainstream media). It's mainly a thought process when you plan to buy something, and ideally (for our site) this could conclude in reaching our site.

Instead, we will start with the research milestone. This milestone contains the events happening when the user reaches our site, but they don't immediately start exploring what's available. Instead, they would want to make sure that it's safe to buy from here, understand what grocery surplus is, and might have other questions related to the site or buying here. Those can lead to many different user stories. One user story in this milestone could be *I want to live-chat with someone to get answers to my questions.*

The user story map on the wall

Now, you are fully equipped to create the user story map for your dream project on the wall. It may or may not look something like this:

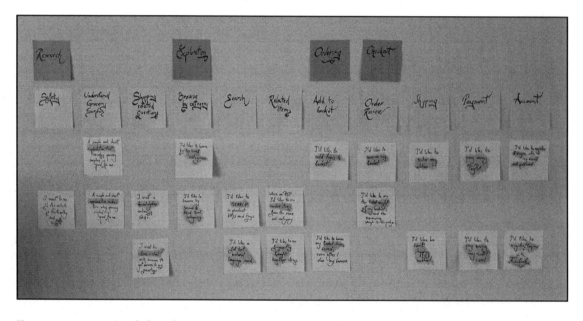

I'm sure you noticed that there are gaps on my example. This is because I like to order my story cards vertically by release. The first row is the Minimum Viable Solution, the smallest release I can make to research the idea and learn from it. It could enable me to fail early, instead of failing late with massive investment. Moreover, if successful it can be developed further into the second row, the public beta. The third row contains everything that will not fit into the public beta, but will be part of the release.

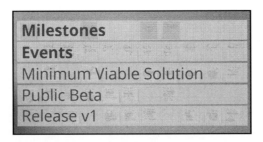

What fits in which row is obviously something you need to discuss with the amigos. Try to have many rows and few cards in each row, so user stories for a release can get a proper focus, and you can have a fast release cycle. I stopped at release v1, but you are welcome to add more future releases. Want a 3D product view? No problem; add it to release v3.

In the next section, we will explore a neat web app to create your user stories digitally.

Creating user story maps digitally

You can use any software to create a map digitally, even Microsoft Word as we have seen in the previous chapter. You should pick the software you are most familiar with. In this chapter, we will use an online tool, *StoriesOnBoard*, available as a web app at `http://stori esonboard.com`. You can try the tool for free in the first 30 days. This tool is great for creating and discussing user stories with remote team members because it has real-time collaboration capabilities. It was a new tool at the time of writing this book, released on May 30, 2016; it is very promising, though.

Creating a new board

Similar to real life, you need a wall for your sticky notes. While in the real world building a wall inside the office might be problematic, digitally it's just a few clicks. First, you need to register to be able to use the product, but I assume that you will have no difficulties with that. After registering, you will start with a view where you can create a new project using the **here** link.

It's likely that this will change in the future, as that's clearly terrible user experience and onboarding. However, don't worry, the rest of the app has a better UX.

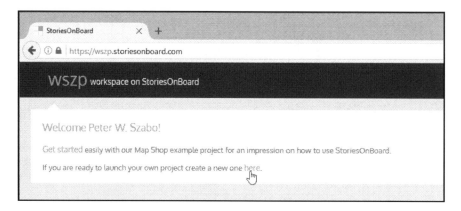

Naming your projects is always important; try to give the board a meaningful **name**. You may want to enable **Viewers can comment on cards**. Remember that we are doing this to get feedback on our user stories, so comments should always be welcome. You can safely skip the rest of the **Name and description** page for now. Simply click on **Save and go to storymap** and start creating your story map.

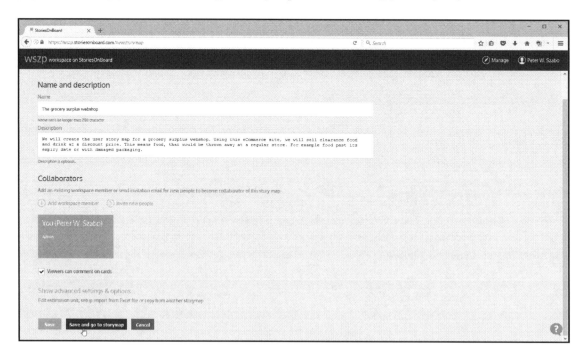

Now, you have a wall where you can put together your User story maps.

Adding cards to your board

I have no idea why a new map doesn't start with the first card added, but hopefully, they will fix this in the near future. Until that time, you can click on another **here** link or press the *N* key on your keyboard.

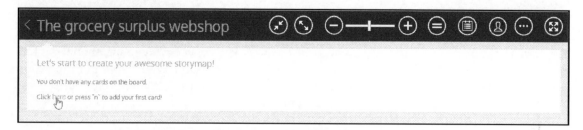

You can start typing in the title of your card. You can use markdown in the titles of your card. This lightweight markup language enabled the creators of this app to skip adding a rich text editor, and it makes the app and your work much faster. You can simply type in the text, and you don't need to worry about markdown if you don't want to.

The only markdown you will probably use in your card titles is **bold** and *italic*. To make something italic, put it between * (asterisk) or _ (underscore) characters. To make something bold, put them between double * or _ characters. For example, I typed in **Research** to end up with **Research** in the title.

The app has a simple zoom feature, which you can use with the + and - keys, or you can use your mouse to click on the zoom buttons:

You can add a new card with pressing the *Tab* or the *N* key on your keyboard, then drag the card to the right location. Alternatively, you can click on the subtle blue arrow pointing down below your card. This will automatically create the card placeholder at the right position, as an event of your **Research** milestone.

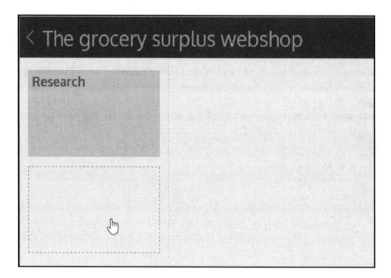

Clicking on the placeholder will enable you to add a title to your card.

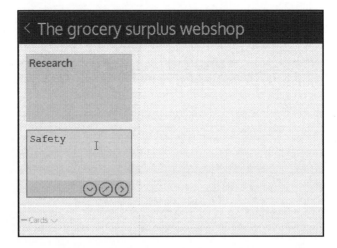

When you hover over a card, you can see arrows in circles; those add cards to the left or below the card:

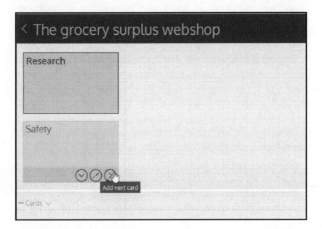

If you want to add a card in the position where there is a card, and don't want to overwrite the given card, you can select the card by clicking on it, and then press the *Shift* and *N* keys together (as if you wanted to write a capital N.) This will add a card at the selected position, moving the cards to the right.

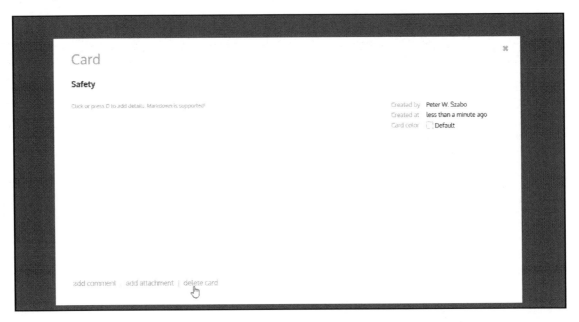

Clicking on a card will select it, giving it a thicker border. Clicking another card will open the card editor modal. You can use this modal to delete the card, add more details to it, make comments on it, attach files to it, or edit any of its properties. Actually, for deleting the card, you can simply select the card and press the *Delete* button on your keyboard.

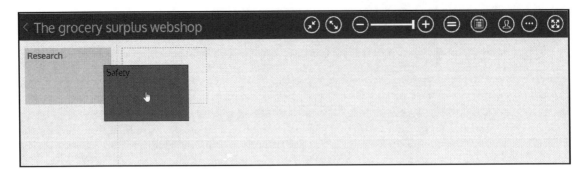

You can rearrange your card by mouse drag and drop.

> For simple maps, you don't have to group your events into milestones. To do this, switch to a two level board with the icon showing two horizontal lines.

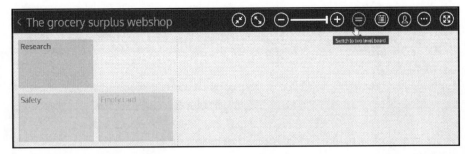

> If you need, you can switch back to the default three-level board with a three horizontal line icon in the same place.

Next to the share icon, there is the **More...** menu (⊚), containing every other menu item, which didn't fit on the top menu row. Using the **Manage releases**, we can create the rows of the user story map, in other words, the releases like Minimum Viable Solution or Public Beta.

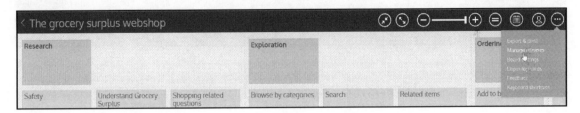

We can add, move, and delete releases in the **Manage releases** modal editing the layout of our map. Later down the road, when your map starts to get too many user stories, because of the zillion releases you had, you can start archiving old releases from this modal.

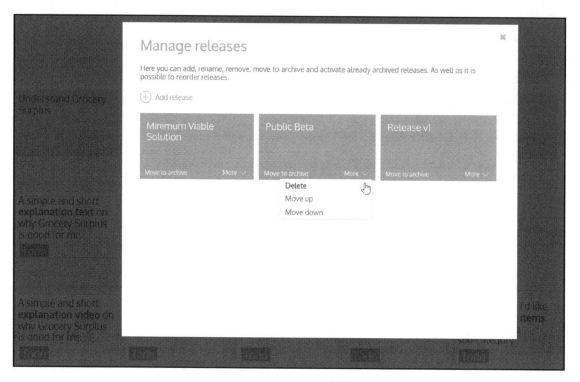

Now, create the user story map for your dream project; have fun! On the following screenshot, you can see my example:

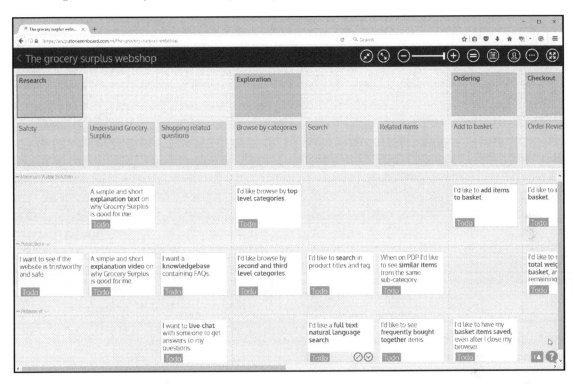

Now, you need to have a conversation. When you click on the share icon , you will be able to share this with the four-amigos (and anyone else you wish) from the appearing modal:

The problem is, some business stakeholders don't want to access yet another app. In the **More...** menu (), you can find a menu item titled **Export & print**, which opens the **Export & print** modal.

In the **Export & print** modal, you can create a PDF or PNG, which enables you to print this, converting it into a low-tech paper map, or an attachment in your next stakeholder digest e-mail:

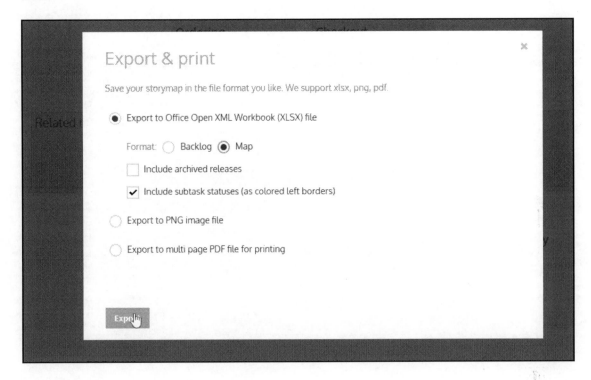

However, the most exciting feature is the (currently) first option, to export the map as an Office Open XML Workbook (XLSX) file, or with simpler words, an Excel spreadsheet. You can obviously open this file with Google Sheets, OpenOffice.org, LibreOffice, or any other software capable of opening XLSX files. In the following screenshot, I have used Microsoft Excel 2016:

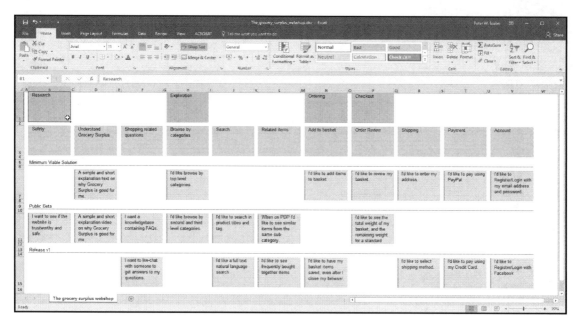

Your map on an Excel spreadsheet

Enjoy mapping your product, and remember, you need to share it with three or four-amigos to take the first step in fulfilling your dream (and becoming a billionaire as a side-effect.)

Summary

The user story map tells the whole story of a solution to the user's problems or needs. It is composed of *cards* containing user stories and atomic functionality pieces that are valuable to the user. The user stories should be **i**ndependent, **n**egotiable, **v**aluable, **e**stimable, **s**mall, and **t**estable: INVEST.

The map is used to facilitate the *conversation*, achieving shared understanding with the power of four amigos. With the help of the narrative flow, you can create the map easily on a wall with sticky notes, or digitally with any software you prefer. Story tests will be your reality check, the *confirmation* of the user story map.

In the next chapter, we will gain a deeper understanding of our users, create personas for them, and finally a journey map, one of the most iconic user experience deliverables.

3
Journey Map - Understand Your Users

In this chapter, we will build a journey map for a game. For this, we need to understand our users and model their tasks.

 A journey map is a tool, that helps us to understand and communicate users' behavior as they progress through a route by means of interactions, as they try to accomplish their goals.

To be able to do this, we will create the following:

- Personas, made-up characters, representing a group of your users with similar goals:
    - To create personas, we will use the 3i method: investigate, identify, and imagine
    - We will learn how to use Smaply to create our personas
- Task models, a story of what our personas do at each milestone of their journey:
    - Set the milestones
    - Create an evaluation diagram
    - Use Adobe Illustrator to create task models
- Design the user's journey and distill the design into a map:
    - We will learn about interactions
    - Finally, we will build the final deliverable for this chapter in Adobe Illustrator

Journey maps are all about finding the treasure in product development. This treasure is called understanding and communicating user behaviors. This requires empathy for user needs and understanding their behaviors.

If you haven't got a plan, you don't have a map. If you don't have a map, you'll never find the treasure.

-Richard Templar

Journey maps they have one of the most popular user experience deliverables, and they have widespread usage among UX experts. Nowadays, a broad range of maps are commonly called journey maps, and laymen might call all user experience map types journey maps. Hopefully, this book will show that there is more to UX maps than journey maps.

The line can be blurred between different UX maps; this is why we defined the journey map by its focus on a route through a solution, usually our solution.

 It's also a good idea to create journey maps for our competitors' solutions. We can learn from that, and it will often serve as a reality check. Competitor benchmarking is something you should do as often as possible.

With that said, in this chapter we will create a journey map for our demo solution. As in the previous chapter, I encourage you to find a different dream and realize it.

F2P FPS (an example from the gaming industry)

Free to Play First First-Person Shooters (F2P FPS) are popular nowadays. Think about Team Fortress 2, World of Tanks, or Dirty Bomb. The true king of the genre is CrossFire. In 2014, it earned global sales of $1.3 billion. It is still successful; revenues from January 2016 to November 2016 were $1.1 billion. Moreover, the *Fast & Furious* producer, Neal Moritz, is working on the movie version of this highly acclaimed game. In this chapter, we want to create a better game than Smilegate, without copying them. We will map an F2P FPS and earn user experience knowledge worth billions.

MechWarrior Online, Hawken, or Titanfall (1-2) are good examples of the fact that first-person gamers love piloting huge walking machines. It doesn't matter whether we call them mechs, titans, or something else. As long as they are somewhat humanoid, robot-like walking weapon platforms, the concept will resonate well with our target audience. We will call them juggernauts, so they don't violate any copyright and still sound cool. This leads to our working title, *Project: Juggernauts*, the next big F2P FPS hit for PC (possibly for Xbox One and PS4 as well, but let's focus on the PC platform first).

The opportunity is that our players want a unique free-to-play first-person shooter, where they can fight on foot, or pilot a huge walking weapon platform, called a juggernaut. They want to pay for customization and avoid the grind (repetitive gameplay to unlock items), but they don't want microtransactions to give them a competitive advantage (we should not make this a pay-to-win situation).

We will create the journey map for this game. Since not everyone is lucky enough to work in the gaming industry, in `Chapter 4`, *Wireflows - Plan Your Product*, I will show a different journey map as a starting point for our wireflows. This will also showcase the differences and similarities between journey maps from different industries.

Personas

User journey maps are always based on one or more personas. Even if there is no mention of personas, when it was created the cartographer must have had at least one persona in mind. That's why it makes sense to add the persona's name to the map itself, to make sure that it's never detached from the map. Now, it's about time we defined personas.

Personas are fictitious characters, representing a group of your users with similar goals. Personas should be rendered as a short, shareable, and easy-to-understand character sheet containing the behavior patterns, needs, and emotions of a target group. Personas will help you focus on your users and have empathy for them.

When Alan Cooper introduced personas in his book *The Inmates Are Running the Asylum*, the concept drastically changed UX (and he is also the reason why they are called personas, not personæ.)

Nowadays, It's almost impossible to talk about user experience without personas. That would mean assuming that all computer users have the same goals, skills, and behavior patterns, or at least they are willing to adapt to what's given to them. That was true to a degree in the late 80's, but fortunately we evolved and left behind the digital stone-age.

3i: How to create personas

Develop a precise description of your user and what he wishes to accomplish.

-Alan Cooper

For creating personas, I have developed a simple three-step process, which I named *3i: investigate, identify, imagine.*

Investigating (potential) users

We need a source of information about our potential users (obviously including our existing ones if we have any). As we will see in `Chapter 6`, *Solution Mapping Based on User Insights*, the best source for that is remote or lab-based user research.

 Create personas based on user research, but don't try to find testers matching your personas.

If, however, your budget or time constraints don't allow the luxury of that, you can get away with some other persona sources. Even if you do have the time and money for user testing with real users, you can complement that with the following methods:

- Interviews (usually the most valuable, apart from remote or lab research)
- Existing user database
- Analytics
- Surveys
- Social network (usually the least valuable)

Interviews

From the list mentioned in the preceding section, the interviews are usually the most valuable, and they are listed in descending order of value, in my experience. Most of the time, interviews are a must have for your UX projects. Simply put, talk to people working on the product, and more importantly individuals who know the product's target audience. For example, customer support staff are always a great source of personas, but so is management. Conduct as many interviews as you can, not only to create personas but also to understand the challenge much better.

Don't make the interviews formal because you don't want to hear the formal view of the company about their users. If you have a chit-chat about the users, you will learn much more about them. This also means not taking notes and relying on your memory, but that can also be an advantage. If the same issue keeps coming up repeatedly, you will remember it. If you forget something about that one user about four years ago, that's not a major issue.

The main things you are looking for during the interviews are user pain points, as those are the hardest to guess. The project owner should have a fairly good idea about what problems the project solves, and for whom, but if possible don't rely on just one person's understanding of the users.

Existing user database and analytics

Any data about your existing customers can help creating with some of the personas. The main reason this is not higher in my persona source priority list is because user experience is not only about existing users. We should always strive to get new users, ideally from new user groups, who were non-existent or underrepresented previously. If our data suggests that 80% of our users are males, we should find ways to make our product more appealing to females. If almost all our users are from the UK, we should understand why we don't have more business from other countries, and so forth.

This doesn't mean that we should have token personas from other countries. Please don't make your Irish customer a redhead poet, whose favorite passtime is getting drunk. This kind of approach can completely derail your personas (*a few years ago a multi-million dollar corporation had a persona image of a cartoon character wearing a sombrero, while riding a donkey with tequila in its hand.*)

Surveys

Truth to be told, I'm not a big fan of surveys. Users find them boring, and they are notoriously inaccurate, even when done with a generous budget and with a scientific approach by the best social science experts. For example, just three days before the 2016 United States presidential election, a survey was published by the Princeton Election Consortium. They claimed that Hillary Clinton has a 99% chance of winning the election over Donald Trump. Three days later Trump won the presidency with 306 electoral votes to Clinton's 232 votes.

Obviously, a little quantitative information can ground your personas in reality, and some senior managers love surveys. Just remember to always take the results with a grain of salt. Quantitative information can be measured and written down in numbers. Usually, it is an answer to the question: how much? On the other hand, qualitative data can't be written down with numbers, and it's mainly concerned about the reasons, usually answering the question: why?

Social media

It's interesting to see what content resonates well with your existing users. What do they share, and how many likes do different posts get? You can also use social media to recruit participants for remote or lab user testing, or interview your superfans. Some of your customers will use Twitter or other social media channels to vent their frustration about a bug or (lack of) a feature. Social media only demonstrates extreme feelings, such as extreme frustration and extreme support, but it rarely has a trace of the middle ground, so I would avoid creating personas only based on social media alone. With that said, social media can add some details to existing personas.

Some UX consultants add fluff to personas by finding a social media profile resembling it as much as possible. This approach leads to way too detailed personas that most people will simply not read. I'm a big fan of simple personas, which can be used to enhance communication, and only contain details relevant to the business. Although it's fun to include the number of cats the person lives with, it's probably irrelevant for a website selling handcrafted jewelry. However, if you are selling cat food, the number of cats becomes one of the most important attributes.

Identifying behavior likelihood

After you do your research, you need to summarize the behaviors relevant to our solution. In `Chapter 6`, *Solution Mapping Based on User Insights*, we will discover some ways to summarize user research. As a simple example for our demo project, let's assume we have discovered five key behaviors and needs.

 Always try to rate behaviors on a scale of 0-3, in plain-English words, from very unlikely, to unlikely, then likely, and very likely. Most of the time it's impossible to create a finer grading. The scale lacks a neutral point because that doesn't help our purposes. If we can't identify how likely a behavior is for a user, it's better to mark it as no answer or not available, maybe a simple "-".

For *Project: Juggernauts*, we have identified microtransactions as the most important behavior for our business. In other words, would the users spend small amounts of real money for virtual goods for their in-game characters? Our business model relies on the in-game store, where users can purchase virtual goods via micropayments. Since the game itself will be free to download and play without limitations, this is the only revenue stream for us. If you are not familiar with the gaming industry, nowadays microtransactions are a common and highly profitable revenue source. They are found in many games, but some gamers have a negative attitude toward this business model. To determine the score, we need to find out how many games they played where they spent real money on microtransactions. If the number is relatively low (1-2), we need to look at the amount spent in total. Using the following flowchart, we can determine this score for all testers:

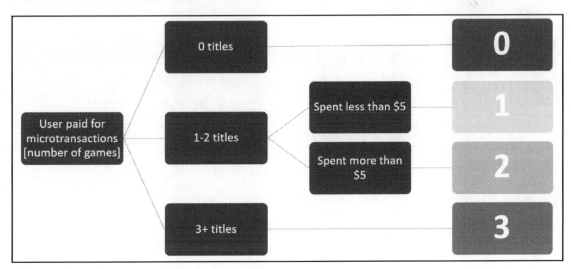

The other behaviors can be benchmarked in a similar fashion:

- **Current hardware**: This is the specifications of their PC, where 0 means that their hardware at the time of release is unlikely to run our game. (For example, they have a 3-year-old, low-end laptop and are not planning to buy a new one in the next two years.)
- **FPS skills**: This means how experienced they are with FPS games, ranging from people who have almost never play one to pro players who regularly stream their amazing skills on Twitch for others to learn. This is their skill when they start playing our game. Hopefully, they will become better after our tutorial, and while playing.
- **Social aspects**: These are probably the hardest-to-identify behavior set. It relates to how important certain features, such as VoIP, clan wars, chat, forums, events, and so on, are for a player. It's actually the summary of many loosely related factors. This simplification is necessary to avoid overly complex, thus hard to communicate, personas, and also to keep the number of personas in check.
- **Customizability**: This is becoming more and more important in FPS gaming. Nowadays, players can change many things about their characters. Almost all AAA FPS titles have custom skins for your character and your weapon, and many weapon choices with different attachments and other customization options. This is important for our business model. We don't want to sell better weapons or playable characters; we want to sell different-looking character, weapons, and juggernaut skins. Moreover, we can also sell cosmetic attachments, such as a parrot sitting on the character's shoulder, or a huge sword on the back of the juggernaut.

Behaviour	Tester																																							
	1	2	3	4	5	6	7	8	9	10	11	12	13	14	15	16	17	18	19	20	21	22	23	24	25	26	27	28	29	30	31	32	33	34	35	36	37	38	39	40
Microtransactions	3	2	0	0	0	3	0	1	0	0	1	3	3	-	1	2	1	2	1	1	1	1	1	0	2	2	2	2	2	2	2	2	0	0	2	2	2	2	1	0
Current hardware	3	0	0	1	1	3	2	0	0	0	3	3	3	1	2	3	1	1	3	3	3	3	2	1	1	2	3	3	3	3	3	0	3	3	3	3	3	3	3	3
FPS Skills	0	0	0	1	1	1	1	1	0	2	3	1	3	1	1	3	1	1	3	2	3	3	0	0	1	1	2	2	3	3	2	2	0	3	2	2	2	2	2	3
Social aspects	3	3	3	3	3	1	0	3	1	0	0	2	0	2	2	2	2	2	2	3	3	0	0	3	2	3	1	3	0	1	3	2	2	3	3	3	3	3	0	0
Customizability	1	1	0	0	0	-	0	0	1	0	3	3	3	3	3	2	3	0	0	0	0	0	0	0	0	0	3	3	3	3	3	3	2	0	0	0	2	3	2	3

Users who have a zero at both microtransactions and current hardware are people who are very unlikely to play our game, and at the moment there is nothing we can do about it. We will not develop for them, and no persona will be created to represent them. For our purposes, they simply don't exist. They are represented in the red columns in the preceding table. They probably represent more than 95% of the Earth's population, but our pre-qualifying criteria were related to being a gamer, not simply being a human. That's perfectly fine, we don't try to get everyone and their cat to play our game. Note that if someone has a zero microtransaction score, they can still download the game and play it without investing any amount of money. One of our goals will be to convert some of those players, without annoying them.

Imagining the characters

Now we have lots of numbers, but numbers are terrible for communicating and planning development. It would quickly become cumbersome to repeat that we have X percent of players who are new to FPS games. Instead, we will imagine a character who is new to the genre with some basic FPS skills at level 1 (they are unlikely to be good at FPS games when starting with our game). This will be their primary attribute. We obviously need to know what their goals, motivations, and behaviors are. Probably, customizability is important for them, but not very important:

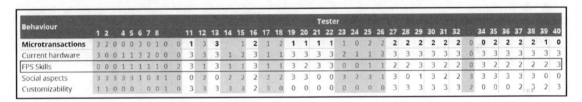

Behaviour	Tester																																			
	1	2	4	5	6	7	8	11	12	13	14	15	16	17	18	19	20	21	22	23	24	25	26	27	28	29	30	31	32	34	35	36	37	38	39	40
Microtransactions	3	2	0	0	0	3	0	1	0	0	1	3	3	1	2	1	2	1	1	1	1	0	2	2	2	2	2	2	0	0	2	2	2	2	1	0
Current hardware	3	0	0	1	1	3	2	0	0	0	3	3	3	1	2	3	1	1	3	3	3	2	1	1	2	3	3	3	3	0	3	3	3	3	3	3
FPS Skills	0	0	0	1	1	1	1	1	0	2	3	1	3	1	1	3	1	1	3	2	3	3	0	0	1	1	2	2	3	3	2	2	0	3	2	2	2	2	2	3
Social aspects	3	3	3	3	3	1	0	3	1	0	0	2	0	2	2	2	2	2	3	3	0	0	3	2	3	1	3	0	1	3	2	2	3	3	3	3	3	3	0	0
Customizability	1	1	0	0	0	0	0	1	0	3	3	3	3	3	2	3	0	0	0	0	0	0	0	0	3	3	3	3	3	3	2	0	0	0	2	3	2	3

In total, 47% of the testers left in the pool after removing people with 0 scores both in microtransactions and hardware fall into this group. By looking at the most common behaviors, we can set the numbers for our persona by finding the most common or most likely association. For example, people with 0 and 1 at FPS skills have an average score of 1.4 at microtransactions. We also assume that they are more likely to spend money on games they are more familiar with, for example, MOBAs. Hence, we assume they have a 1 microtransaction score, so they are unlikely to spend money on our game at this stage. Hopefully, we can change that.

For their current hardware, the average is 1.5, so they will be able to play the game on low settings as the worst case scenario, while some will have better hardware. I try to avoid rounding the numbers up or down; instead look behind the number and try to understand what it means. I will give them a 1 because that was the most popular number (7 out of 16 testers fall into that category). Following the same logic, the social skills score will be 2.

Now, customizability can give us a hard time. Although the average is 0.93, oddly enough there are many zero and three scores, while 1 is rare. That's normal because the player's skill in a game has probably no correlation with their love for customization. Although they might love customizability, that adds another layer of complexity to the game they don't master. So instead of giving 1, we give them 0, and ensure that we will have a persona with a 3 customizability score, to make sure those needs are well represented.

This leads to the final scores for our new player persona. However, a persona is much more than just a bunch of scores. It's a fictitious character, and as such we need a name and gender. We know that probably more than 75% of our player base will be male, but we would love to get more female players. We will definitely have a female persona, but not this one. One of the personas will be a casual player, and we will set her gender to female. It's perfectly normal that some projects have more male or female users. For example, our grocery surplus web store would have three female and two male personas.

The name should be easy to remember. I would not name a persona after a tester. Testers are not personas, and many tests with different testers will be distilled into personas. I have named this persona *Ohforf, the Noob*, as a tribute to Gianna Masetti's amazing webcomic htt p://thenoobcomic.com/. New players are often called noobs in online multiplayer games. Because the term can be a bit derogatory, I will use my photo for the persona in this book. For real-world personas, you can use a picture from the Internet with **Creative Commons** (**CC**) license or a stock photo, which represents a member of the persona's demographic. Don't use your face for any persona. (You can use mine if you wish.) Although some books, such as *Smashing UX Design* by Jesmond Allen and James Chudley, suggest using pictures of friends and acquaintances, I would avoid that. Not only because that's morally debatable, and some people from the production team might know them, but mainly because it will influence you. If one of the personas has your daughter as a photo, that persona might become the most important one for you, even if not selected as a primary persona (more on primary personas in the next section).

In an ideal world, you would have photos of your persona reflecting user behavior, as well as gender, in their natural environment, while encountering the problem we will solve, all this while they still feel real, and not a stock photo or overly posed. In the real world, that's usually too much effort, and overworked UX consultants just pick the first picture that's fairly acceptable for a persona.

The preceding logic can be used to create other personas with all bells and whistles. You can specify their age, nationality, occupation, marital status, religion, and shoe size, just to make them more real, but if those are not relevant to their behaviors that's just extra work on your part, creating extra clutter, so I would avoid that.

Try to keep the number of personas as low as possible. I always aim for two to three personas, then if I must, I create four to five, but rarely go above five. More than five personas are against my principle of simplicity in user experience design.

The exact opposite of our noob is *Wiktor, the Pro*, named after one of the most successful FPS players Wiktor "TaZ" Wojtas. He won over $400k, participated in 100+ official tournaments, and may or may not be interested in playing our game. That doesn't really matter. We don't want to find the exact match for our persona, but we want to turn this game into an eSport with real money prizes at professional tournaments. For that goal, we need the serve the needs of the best players.

Alexander, the Socializer, named after Alexander Garfield, the founder of the North American eSports organization Evil Geniuses and CEO of GoodGame, is a representation of the players who mainly want to interact with other players. By interaction, we don't only mean shooting them (that's something all of our players will do), but instead creating guilds/clans/teams, playing together, chatting on voice chat, and in-game text chat. Those are the players who will write the bulk of the forum and Reddit posts, share our game on social media, and most importantly, invite their extensive player network to the game if they like it. If we meet their expectations, they might save us millions of dollars in marketing.

The final persona represents those who take the game lightly maybe play 8-10 hours a week, not per day like the pros. They might socialize a bit, and definitely enjoy customizing their players. Since their playtime is limited, those are the players who might buy time-saving items, such as XP boosts from the in-game shop. I named her *Suzy, the Casual*. She will be our female persona, as hinted before.

Create your personas to help you make design and business decisions. They will also put the users first, always reminding you that real people will use your solutions in solving their real problems. Only create as many as needed, and keep them as simple as possible to enhance communication, not hinder it.

The primary persona

Not all personas are created equal. *Ohforf, the Noob* will be our primary persona. Everyone will be new to our game at the beginning of their experience with it. This is also the most crucial time for them. If the experience is terrible when they start the game, most people will abandon it and the project will fail.

We will create our user experience with the primary persona in mind while making sure that it works for the others. When we need to prioritize features, we always prioritize based on what's important for our primary persona, and we will try to balance our business goals with the needs of this persona.

HAL 9000 will not use your app

I have seen a product team adding a *system* persona with a picture of HAL 9000's menacing red camera eye from *2001: A Space Odyssey*. Obviously, product development has many tasks, which are invisible and obscure to the end user. Switching from MongoDB to another database might be the most urgent and most stressful task for some team members, but adding it to the user story map will not help, quite the contrary. Business stakeholders and most UX experts will have no clue what that really means. *Is switching the database a higher priority than moving all static assets to Amazon S3 buckets?* That's a real question, but it's not something that can be answered with a user journey map. Sometimes, those tasks creep into the backlog because someone wanted to account for the utilization of development hours or some other similar idiocy.

In reality, such extremes will help you lose your best and most dedicated full-stack developers, and then you will remain with people who are in it for the money only. They will find extremely clever ways to account for every minute of their work day, while your product fails miserably in every imaginable way. As a person who works with developers directly or indirectly, you should have a bit of understanding of their work, and respect them. Give them freedom and flexibility. This will almost guarantee outstanding success if you picked the right people to work with.

Creating persona documents with Smaply

We will use `smaply.com`, a great start-up created by a small team in Innsbruck, Austria.

Microsoft Word and PowerPoint are more popular as a persona document creation tools, but Smaply makes the job easier and faster. Richard Caddick and Steve Cable have a good tutorial on creating personas using Word and PowerPoint in their book, *Communicating the User Experience: A practical guide for creating useful UX documentation.*

After signing-up, you need to create your first Smaply project by clicking where the arrow points (**Create a project**):

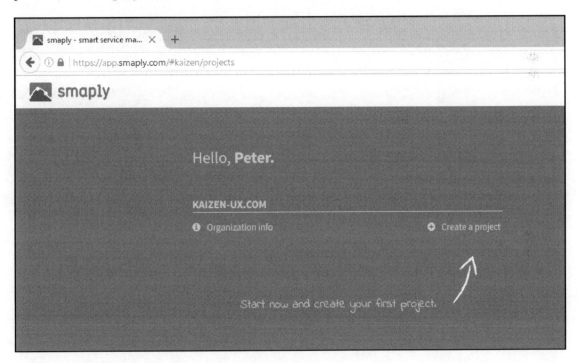

Try to find a meaningful project title and paste the "Opportunity" in the **DESCRIPTION** text area. We will use the same project throughout this chapter, not just for personas, so make sure that you create a project you will enjoy working on:

After the project is ready, we can invite additional users to it from the right side of the screen. On the bottom, we can create **PERSONAS**, **STAKEHOLDER MAPS**, and **JOURNEY MAPS**. We will get back to stakeholder maps in Chapter 10, *Ecosystem Map: A Holistic Overview*:

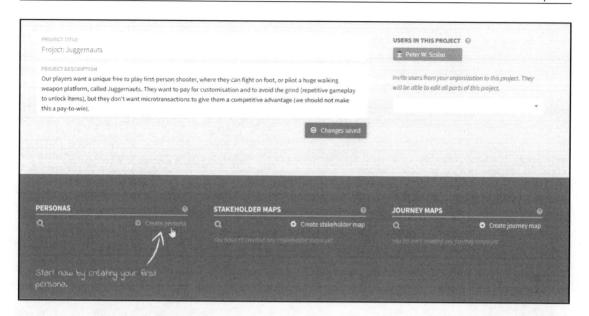

Now, let's start with creating the personas, as they are essential for a good journey map. Clicking on the **Create persona** link a modal lets us introduce the name of our first persona:

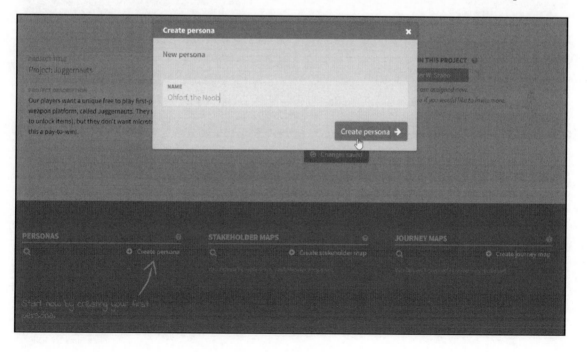

I tend to give long and meaningful names to my personas, such as **Ohforf, the Noob** for our primary persona. If you follow suit, I suggest also creating a **SHORT NAME**. We can save lots of space and reduce clutter by using short names to reference personas:

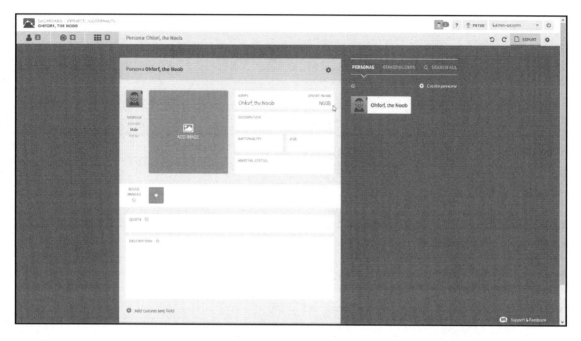

Details of a persona

Adding a picture is as simple as clicking on the **ADD IMAGE** placeholder:

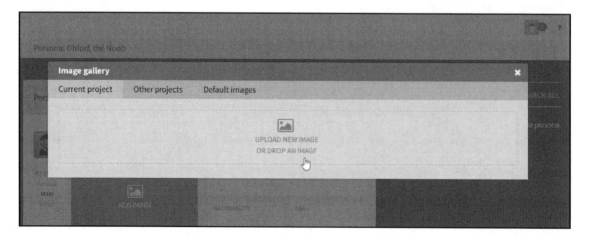

You can also crop the image from the modal to a square by dragging the anchor points (small squares around a dashed line), so don't worry about finding square persona images or pre-cropping them in Photoshop:

After uploading the persona picture, you want to specify the persona avatar icon, a small picture, which can be just a resized version of the persona, or even better a graphic. Again, this will be helpful when we get to journey mapping. You should pick something that will make you recognize the persona easily. Color coding is also important. Ideally, you want a different color for all your personas; just think about what is the most logical color choice. *Being green* usually means inexperienced, so I have picked green for the noob:

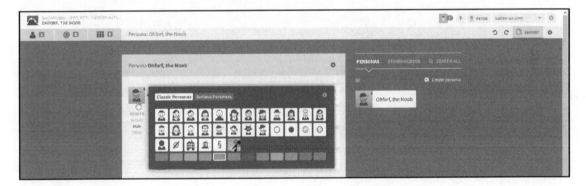

Quotes are important for personas. They help with building empathy with the persona; moreover, they anchor them in reality. They can also highlight one of their pain points. For Ohforf, we could use; *So, this means no artillery. I thought 'no art' means no paintings or statues*:

> QUOTE ❓
>
> So, this means no artillery. I thought 'no art' means no paintings or statues.
>
> DESCRIPTION ❓

Long persona descriptions are often ignored and never read. A few bullet points are enough here. The most important thing is to list the **Key goals and behaviours** as identified during our research. We can list some reminders too, things we should create and other things we should not create during development. This usually leads to three or four heading structures (some experts separate goals and behaviors). In Smaply, select the text you want

to convert to headings and click on the **heading** icon (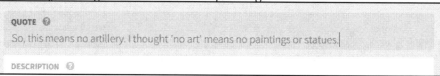). With the bullet list icon ( ), we can create lists below our headings. You can use bold and highlight in a similar fashion (select and click) to emphasize certain parts of the text:

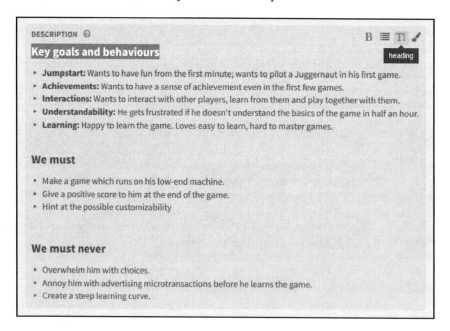

In the following description, you can see a link titled **Add custom text field** (

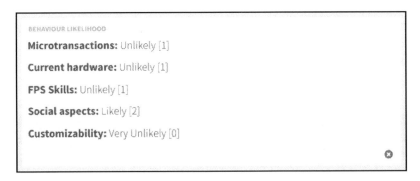

). This will come in handy when adding our behavior likelihood numbers for each persona. Custom text fields work in a similar fashion to the description:

BEHAVIOUR LIKELIHOOD

Microtransactions: Unlikely [1]

Current hardware: Unlikely [1]

FPS Skills: Unlikely [1]

Social aspects: Likely [2]

Customizability: Very Unlikely [0]

It would be great if Smaply had better support for visually representing numerical values, but we can always use some old-school ASCII characters (or rather UTF-8 characters). I have used U+25FB and U+25FC Unicode characters for this example. You can use the O and * characters from your keyboard, or _ and # if that's easier for you.

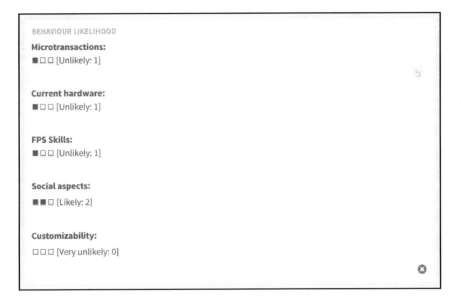

This concludes our primary persona. We are ready to export it as a PDF and share it with stakeholder. To do this, click on the **Export as PDF** button below the persona (

):

The primary persona

Now, you need to create the remaining personas. The benefit of using a primary persona is that you don't need to detail the remaining personas as much if you don't have time:

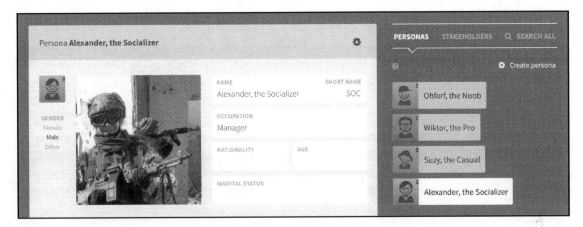

Creating a journey map with Smaply

We can continue with Smaply and create a new map from the **Journey maps** tab ( ) on the left side, by clicking on **Create new**:

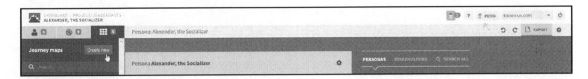

You need to name your journey map. A large and complex project may have many journey maps. For this exercise, we will focus on the most crucial journey, the new player journey. It will contain the first interactions of a new player with our game until the first microtransaction (our conversion goal).

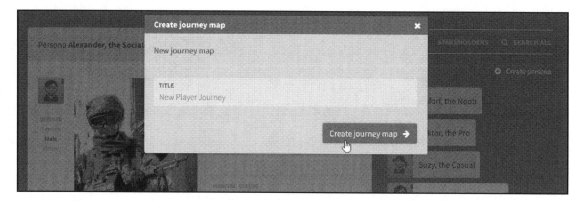

Now, we should add the personas we created in the previous section, by clicking on the **ADD PERSONA** button:

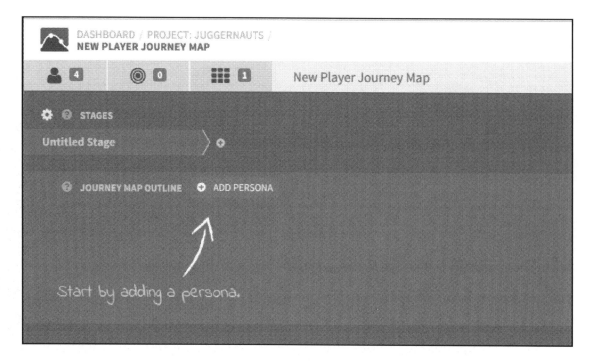

Experiment with creating journey maps and task models with Smaply. For the rest of this chapter, I will continue with Adobe Illustrator, due to the current limitations of Smaply. You can follow along with Smaply. If you do, you can share your results with me on my Twitter account: @wszp.

Task models

A task model is a story of what our personas do at each milestone of their journey. The user journey map is based on the task model, providing a specific route through our product as a solution. In other words, the task model is the question asked by the persona. We will answer this question with the user journey map.

Fortunately, the same research used to create the personas in the previous section will enable us to design the task model diagram for them.

Creating the task model in Adobe Illustrator

When you launch the software, you will start with a new document, a blank canvas. While it's possible to create task models without personas, usually they become too complicated, too generic, or both.

I usually start the task model with a header, which includes the persona, the project title, the task model's title, and if available the project logo or logo placeholder. If you use Adobe Illustrator, Photoshop, or an other layer-based software, it makes sense to make all major elements of your map a different layer with a descriptive name:

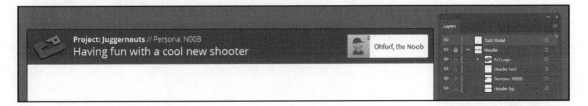

 I usually create task models using Adobe Illustrator. For the examples in this book, I will use Adobe Illustrator CC 2017 (version 21). You can use any software to create evaluations, including Microsoft Word, Adobe Photoshop, or the free and open source GIMP. The idea is to represent different, often unrelated thoughts the user might have in a milestone.

A task model is a map of tasks, which helps you to design your solution based on this understanding of the users' mental processes. We represent each task with a circle. This convention will help us when we create a journey map, because the interface elements supporting the mental processes of the user can have rectangular shapes.

Milestones (stages)

Milestones group all events that lead to a common goal. Each achievement the user has on the road to reaching the opportunity is a milestone. Milestones give structure to the journey map and allow easier organization and communication.

If you created a user story map (refer to `Chapter 2`, *User Story Map-Requirements by Collaboration and Sticky Notes*), you should already have the product-related milestones, but not all of the milestones required for a task model are product milestones.

In some sources and software products (such as Smaply), milestones are called stages; others call them phases or activities. They all mean roughly the same thing, but the user experience terminology is still evolving. Hopefully, in a few years, user experience will have a unified and clear vocabulary.

The origin story

Always try to capture the big picture of the experience. Thus, for task models, it makes sense to start with a milestone before the persona's first interaction with our solution. Usually, this first milestone is called the origin story. This is when the persona encounters something that requires a solution, usually a problem or an idea. *Alexander, the Socializer (SOC)* might hear about a new F2P FPS from a friend. He will only play games he can play with friends. If some of his friends have already played it, that's a good incentive for him to try playing it. *Suzy, the Casual (CAS)*, might be bored with her current games and want to try something new, without the need to spend money on it.

The origin story tells us how a persona starts using our solution for the first time. It answers the question of why this persona will use our product. This is usually the first milestone of our task model.

The origin of the story can go deep, but to maintain simplicity, we will start from the current state of things for the persona (exposition) and the emotional triggers and problems encountered. Then, we will see what the persona does as a result of the emotional triggers. How do they intend to solve the problem? Donna Lichaw calls this a *rising action*.

Rising action can take many forms: asking or hearing from friends or on social media, Google searches, seeing an advertisement or reading a review. Some personas will take many actions during this event. For example, *Wiktor, the Pro* (*PRO*) might see our game in Steam's *Today's Highlighted Deals* but only decide to download it after checking the reviews and seeing that a member of his eSports clan has already played it. (A clan is a group of players playing together in an organized way.)

The end result of this milestone is the persona getting in touch with our solution. This can be a landing page, our homepage, or maybe our game's page on Steam.

 Some authors, such as Jesmond Allen and James Chudley, call origin stories entry points.

While it's possible to create a map for the origin story, for a task model we want to summarize it as the first landmark on our map.

Milestones of a task model

I prefer using the simple but versatile **Type Tool** (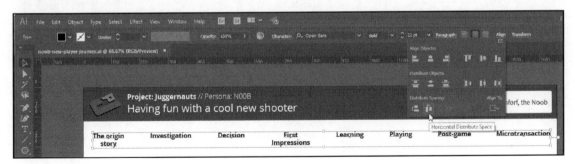) to add milestones to the map. We will start with the origin story, and add the relevant milestones found during our research, including our conversion goal. The milestones for the N00B's first encounter with our product could look like this:

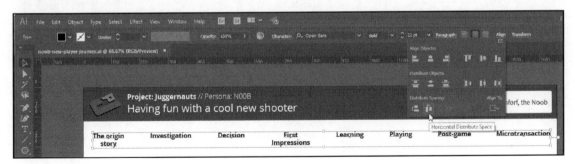

I have used Horizontal Distribute Space from Align as you can see from the screenshot to achieve even spacing between the milestone titles. To do this I had to select all titles with the Selection Tool ( ) by dragging over the milestone titles.

Evaluations

Evaluations occur when a persona has different needs, which need to be fulfilled to progress through a milestone. If the decision is non-binary (more complex than proceed or abandon, yes or no), we have an evaluation. This is where the user will take a conscious action. In the journey map, we need to support that action. For a task model, we need to identify the thought process behind the evaluation.

Evaluations are usually represented by a large circle containing the emotional needs and content requirements for the decision-making process. Even if we only provide one solution to the evaluation, we should think about all thought processes our persona will have, not just the ones leading to our solution. This will help us understand the users. Obviously, we can't hope to please each and every user, but we need to understand why we are not providing the right choices for some. The task model can have one or more evaluations, but you should avoid more than one evaluation pin for each milestone.

For example, choosing the juggernaut is a clear example of evaluation. The user might consider the stats of different juggernauts, how they look, their own playstyle, what clan members and other players suggest, and search the Internet for answers (what forums, guides, and streamers suggest). As game designers, we would want our players to choose their juggernauts based on their playstyle, and make all juggernauts look awesome. A playstyle can be defined with a group of questions about our players' gameplay preferences or battlefield roles: Do they prefer long distance engagements or close quarters? Artillery barrage or high precision lasers? Mobility or heavy armor? We group all of those thoughts into *playstyles*. As stats go, obviously we want balanced stats, and many tests, to make sure that no juggernaut is overpowered (OP in gaming slang), but some players will always look for the *best, most OP* variant.

Creating an evaluation diagram

First, you need the **Ellipse Tool**. If you hold down the *Shift* key while dragging the cursor, you will create a perfect circle:

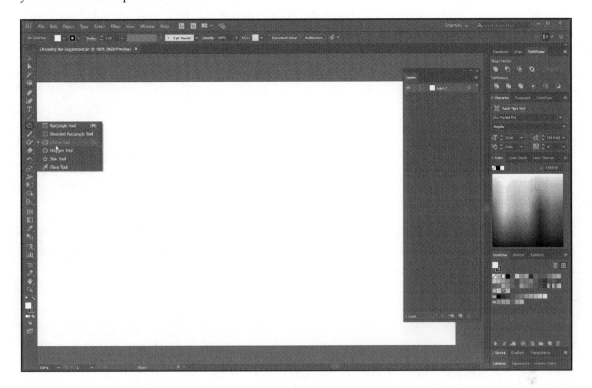

Selecting the Ellipse tool

Now, let's create a scaled down copy of our circle to serve as the path for the title text of this evaluation. Make sure that your circle is selected, then go to the **Object** menu, then **Transform > Scale...**:

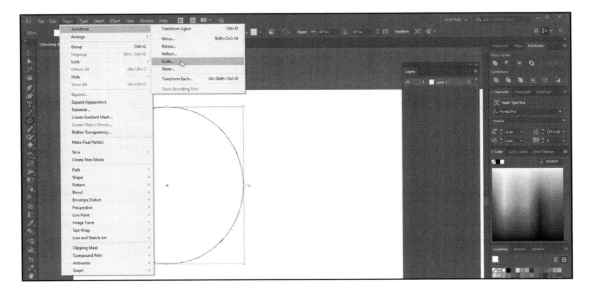

Scaling down the circle

Depending on how big you want your title text, you can set the uniform scale to about 70-80% of your original circle:

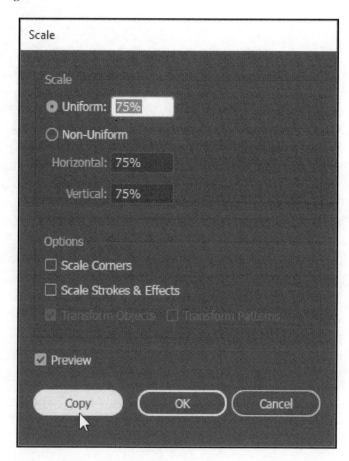

Now, you need to use the **Type on a Path Tool** to add text in the inner circle:

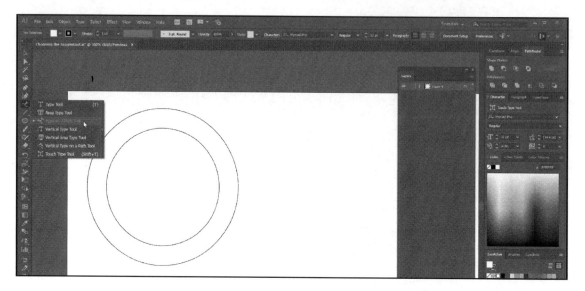

Use Type on a Path tool to add text

Position the pointer on the path, then click (illustrator automatically removes stroke or fill attributes from the path after you add type on it, so don't worry about those). Now, type or paste the title of the evaluation:

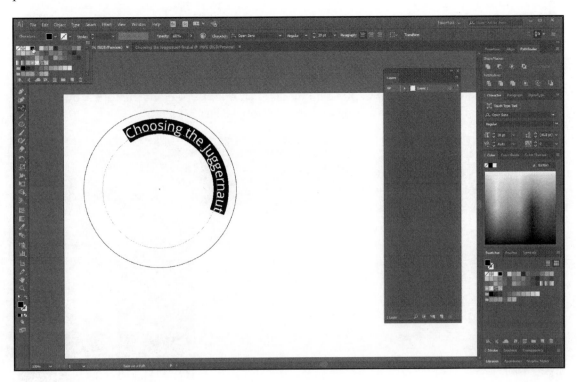

Adding text, following a path

You can select a colour for your text from the character color selector, swatches, or the color panel using the **Eyedropper Tool** (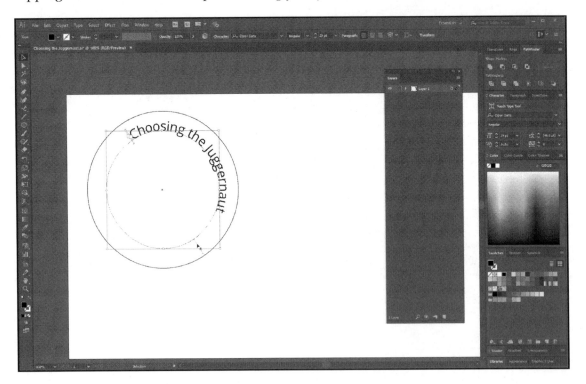). The text might not be in the right place along our original path, like in my previous screenshot. To remedy this, you move (or even flip) text alongside a path. When the path with the text is selected, a vertical line (bracket) appears at the beginning of the text, at the end of it, and at the midpoint between the start and end. If you move your mouse cursor over the type's center bracket, a small icon ( ) will appear. Now, you can drag the midpoint to make sure that your text is in the desired position. Holding down the *Ctrl* key (the *Command* key on macOS) will prevent the type from flipping to the other side of the path, making your job easier:

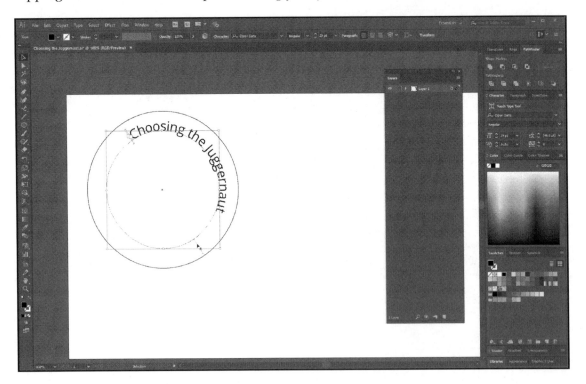

Placing your text in the desired position within the circle

Don't worry, this is one of the most advanced things we will do with Illustrator in this book. My aim here is not to make you an Adobe Illustrator guru, but to show how to create good-looking maps with different software, using simple commands and common features.

Now, we need to add smaller circles into our big circle to hold different thoughts or decision criteria. We can use the **Ellipse Tool** as before, but now the inner circle should be the same size as the outer one, so we will use an even faster way to duplicate our circles. For this, you will need the **Layers** panel to be open. If it's not visible, go to the **Window** menu and select **Layers**.

In the future, we will use the common > shorthand for menu items. This example would become **Window** > **Layers**.

Alternatively, you can press *F7* on your keyboard to reveal the **Layers** panel.

You may need to expand your current layer by clicking on the arrow before its name ( ). You can see the contents of the layer, including your new ellipsis. That should be the top-most object because new objects are at the front when they are created. Now, drag and drop this layer into the Create new layer icon ( ) at the bottom of the **Layers** panel. This is a fast way to duplicate any object when you want the copy to appear in the exact same spot as the original.

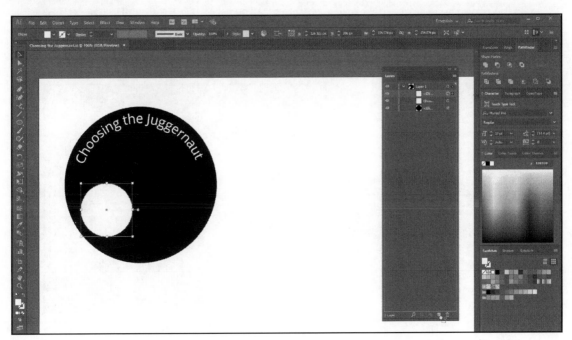

Using Layers panel for duplicating an object

Now, select the **Area Type Tool** and click on the path (aim for the border of the circle, not inside it):

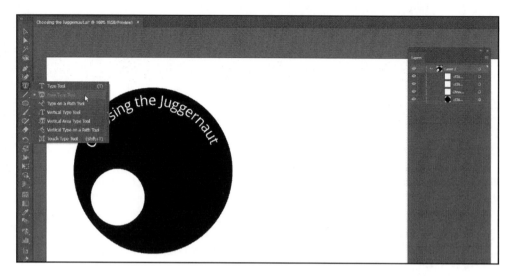

Type in the thoughts you want to represent here. What would influence the user's choice?

Automatic hyphenation helps with fitting text into non-rectangular shapes. You can turn that on from the **Paragraph** panel (**Window** menu > **Type** > **Paragraph** OR *Alt + Ctrl + T*):

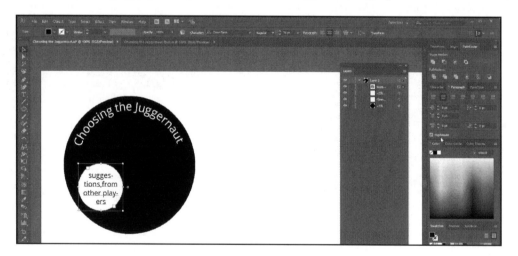

Adding content to the inner circles

With this technique, you should be able to finish the evaluation diagram. It may look something like mine, or even better customized to your liking. I usually highlight the most important factor for the given persona. For our N00B, that's how the juggernaut looks. He doesn't want to spend much time at that milestone, but wants the most awesome looking piece of metal on the battlefield.

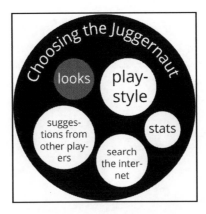

This evaluation diagram can be reused for our other personas, but only as a starting point. For example, *Wiktor, the Pro* would have a harder time choosing the juggernaut. The look is almost irrelevant, heavily outweighed by the other four thought processes, so I would fade that out, or even delete it. For the Pro, it's important to find a juggernaut that has the best stats relevant to their playstyle. Wiktor will spend time trying to understand the connection between stats and playstyles, before making a decision. I have used the **Line Segment Tool**

(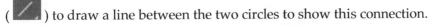) to draw a line between the two circles to show this connection.

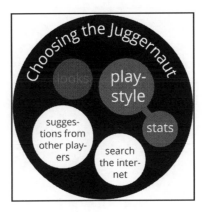

The simple techniques we learned when creating the evaluation diagram can be used throughout the task model and journey mapping processes. I started with the most complex element of a task model. The rest will be even easier. Just draw circles and add text to them.

The finished task model

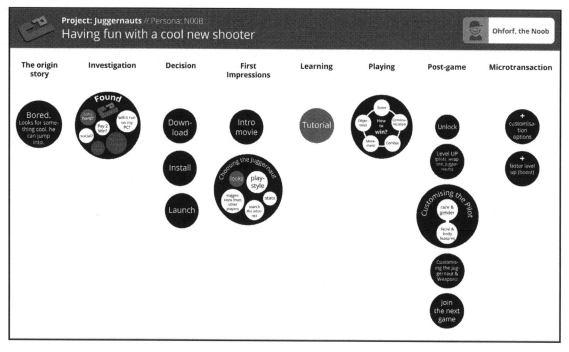

The task model map

Some authors suggest adding connections (usually arrows) between different tasks. While it's okay to do that for linear task models, such as the checkout for an e-commerce site, in my opinion they just add visual clutter. For complex scenarios, such as our game, the tasks are rarely in a linear order, and always necessary. For example, download, install, and launch must come in that order, but the player will not always level up or unlock a new thing after each game. It's also likely that the user will start customizing the pilot, then go to a microtransaction, buy new camouflage, then go back to customization.

The finished task model will serve as the foundation of our user journey design, which will be communicated as a journey map.

Designing the user journey

The path through a system is a user's journey. This path is composed of many interactions. It should be designed to maximize the opportunity while minimizing the outputs.

Usually, you want to design your first journey map early, before any interface elements are designed, before a single line of code has been written. Then, you should revisit, improve, or even redesign the journey from time-to-time, to make sure that it stays relevant and fresh.

 As a visual representation, the user's journey can be distilled into a journey map, reflecting the behavior of a persona.

One of the reasons for creating task models is that they serve as a base for our user journey. We will create our journey map on top of our task model from the previous section, literally.

To do this, make sure that you have the task model open, and the **Layers** panel open (**Window > Layers**). Now, click on the **Create New Layer** button ( ) at the bottom of the panel. Initially, this will be called *Layer 2* or something similar, but double-clicking on this automatic name enables us to rename the layer.

Now, you need to move all elements not part of the header or the milestones into this layer. With the object(s) selected, you can click the name of the desired layer in the **Layers** panel. Then, choose **Object** > **Arrange** > **Send To Current Layer** from the top menu. Alternatively, you can drag and drop the objects from one layer to another, as shown in the following screenshot:

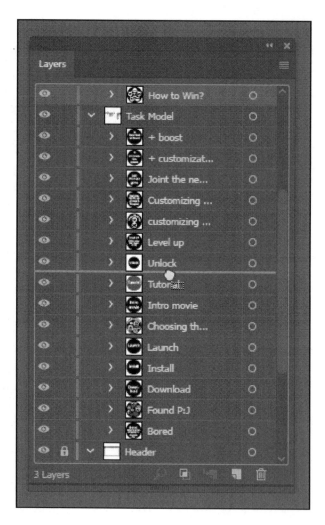

When you have everything arranged into layers, create a new layer for the journey map. You can copy the milestones by dragging the whole layer onto the **Create New Layer** button ( ). Then, you can hide the task model and the original milestone layer by clicking on the eye ( ) before the layer's name. If you have a large monitor, you can keep the task model visible and create the journey map below it. I have hidden the task model to avoid clutter on my screenshots, but have kept the PNG export open next to the Illustrator window.

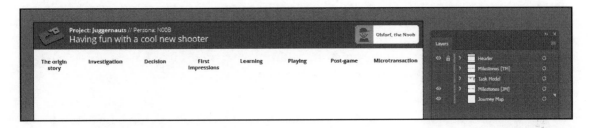

Why do we need to duplicate the milestones? Journey map milestones can be different from task model milestones, and even if they are not, the elements below them will be different, so their placement can change quite a bit. For example, a journey map might have a different width, because the text in rectangles takes less space compared to the spherical elements of a task model.

Interactions

Interactions are the basic building blocks of a journey map. To ease communication, we mostly map pages or views as interactions on a journey map, instead of atomic interactions, such as clicking on a button or filling an input.

As UX design conventions go, we use rectangles for visually representing the interactions.

The **Rectangle Tool** ( ) will be useful here. Just click where you want to draw the rectangle, then drag to adjust its size.

> Holding the *Space* key before finishing the shape allows you to move the rectangle around. This trick works with all the line and shape tools in Illustrator.

Starting from task model's origin story, think about what happens with our N00B when he is bored. How do we capture his attention?

For simplicity's sake, let's say we will do *digital advertising*. Sometimes, it makes sense to split digital advertising into different channels, ad-sources, campaigns, and such. You can even create the journey map for the origin story alone, but we just simplify everything into one board interaction category: Ohforf viewing digital advertising about our game. Social media posts, Google organic searches, or a Twitch stream showing our game can also be the first spark that ignites the N00B's curiosity.

Not everything we map is something we can create or directly influence for example, Ohforf talking to one of his friends. It's also perfectly normal to have overarching interactions, spanning across two or more milestones. The previous example, Ohforf, talking to a friend, can be both the origin story and the investigation. The N00B might trust the friend enough to download the game and start playing on his word alone. (This is why word of mouth is such a powerful way to acquire new users.)

 For overarching interactions, I simply draw a rectangle wide enough to fit under all needed milestones. If most interactions are overarching between two milestones, you should consider merging them into a single milestone.

Early in my career, I created a journey map containing only five interactions and three milestones. Then, I spent 2 days trying to find additional interactions and milestones. I managed to add 10 more interactions and 2 more milestones. I exported the map as a PNG and sent it to the client. Due to some random luck, or maybe subconscious influence, I attached the first export, the one with five interactions. The client loved its simplicity, and we created a straightforward user experience based on that journey map. Yes, I wasted two days on something that was never even shown to the client, but I learned something important about journey mapping: *simplicity beats any efforts you make to please the client with the amount of work you put into the project.* There is no ideal number of interactions, especially no maximum or minimum number, but never add additional interactions just to please the client. Keep it simple!

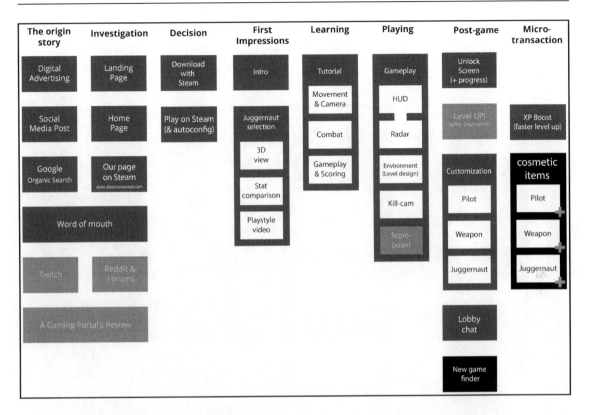

Adding arrows is the last, optional task, depicting the path the persona should take according to our design. You can use the **Line Segment Tool** ( ) to draw lines. If you press and hold the *Shift* key, you can constrain the line to a perfect horizontal or vertical line.

When you have your line, use the **Stroke** panel (**Window** > **Stroke**). In this panel, you can set the weight of the line, create a dashed line, and add arrowheads. If the selected arrowhead is too big, you can also scale it down. For example, I used the 3-pt line weight and **50%** scaled down Arrow 2 arrowhead for the final map of this chapter:

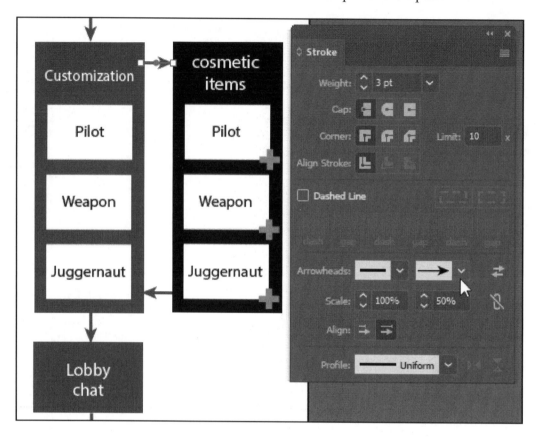

The following is a screenshot of the completed journey map for your reference:

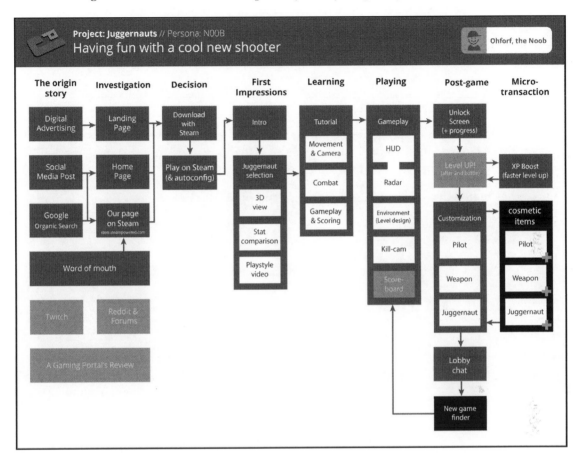

Summary

The journey map is the plan we create to guide users through our solution, to solve their problems with a series of interactions. To be able to create such a path, we need to understand the needs of different user groups.

For this reason, we create personas. To create them, you can use my three-step process, the 3i: investigate, identify, imagine.

After creating our primary persona, we created a task model. Starting with the origin story, we grouped all events that lead to a common goal into milestones. The final task model, with complex evaluations, served as the base for our journey map.

The journey map will serve as a base for a more complex map in the next chapter. Join me for that adventure!

4

Wireflows - Plan Your Product

The next logical step to enrich journey maps is to add the screen designs to key interaction. We will use wireframes to design those views. You can read more about wireframes later in this chapter, as they are the building blocks of our wireflows.

 Wireflows are journey maps where key interactions are represented with wireframes of the relevant views. They allow you to create, explore, communicate, and improve the interactions. You can achieve this with only a map, without having to commit resources to coding or visual design.

To create wireflows, we will need the following things:

- An opportunity--an AI-driven customer support chatbot is my choice. What's yours?
- To create wireframes. To do this, we need to understand:
    - Whether we want colored or grayscale
    - High or low-fidelity wireframes
    - How to create the wireframes using Balsamiq Mockups
- To link the wireframes together, creating a wireflow.
- To discuss and improve them, through a Wireflow Improvement Workshop.

I have been creating wireflows for 10 years now, but until recently I have called them *linked wireframes*. In December 2016, Page Laubheimer from the Nielsen Norman Group coined the term wireflows. I really love that name. I'm also quoting Laubheimer's definition here:

> *Wireflows are a combination of wireframes and flowcharts. They can document workflow and screen designs when there are few pages that change dynamically.*

> *- Page Laubheimer (source:* `https://www.nngroup.com/articles/wireflows` *)*

The customer support chatbot

Similar to all chapters of this book, we will solve a real-world problem with user experience mapping. This chapter's problem is getting detailed customer support, as fast as possible.

Imagine getting instant help from the most qualified, and always cheerful, support personnel. No more waiting in support queues or getting short, hard-to-understand replies. This is possible with an incredible AI and a stunning wireflow. I have no idea how to create this artificial intelligence, but I will try to show you how to create a wireflow for a customer support chatbot. Don't worry about how this will work behind the scenes. Just think about artificial intelligence, machine learning, neural nets, and every other hot buzzword that comes into your mind. Obviously, this decreases the size of human customer support teams, saving money for our customers, and the companies who want to provide support.

 The opportunity is *our users want to get helpful, detailed support for their problems as fast as possible.* We will create a customer support chatbot to give quick answers to the questions and queries typed in by the users as a minimum viable solution.

As before, try to think about a different opportunity, and follow this chapter by creating a different dream. Truth be told, I have picked an opportunity that leads to faster and simpler wireflowing. The examples from our previous chapters can be turned into a wireflow, but we will need to create many complicated wireframes for the key interactions. That's a fun but lengthy exercise. I encourage you to do it, but to keep the book short, simple, and impactful, I have picked *faqAI, a customer support chatbot.*

Wireframes

Developing and communicating a plan is traditionally done as a drawing--think about floor plans, blueprints, or engineering drawings. The same approach is also used for designing user interfaces, and in a broader sense, digital experiences.

 Wireframes are used to define user interface requirements for digital solutions. They represent the UI skeleton of a single view or a single page.

Wireflows don't need to cover every single view or screen from a digital solution. We aim to showcase key interactions and templates, from which the remainder of the solution's UI skeleton can be extrapolated. So we usually start with one or a few wireframes and then create more only when needed.

 Create the first wireframe for your solution alone:
Even if you are relatively new to user experience or UI design, you have seen and used countless apps, websites, and other digital solutions. You should have a strong judgement. Ideally, you have seen users during your tests, or you can trust your instincts.

The goal is to sit down and finish a wireframe alone. Design by a committee for wireframes usually fails, and it's a waste of time. When it's done, you need to ask as many people as possible, and even validate your wireframes with real users. It's vital for your project to be seen from many diverse perspectives, but only when there is something to be seen.

Wireframes and color

Some experts suggest wireframing in grayscale. That's not a bad idea, especially if you are new to UI design. Even seasoned UI gurus can benefit from the lack of color. If you add any color to a wireframe, that might lead to a discussion about color choice, color theory, and the psychology of colors. Those discussions should be left for later stages of the project. The problem with grayscale wireframes is that sometimes you really want that button to be green or that link to be blue. The exact shade of blue can be picked later, but a hint of color can make your wireframe look better and communicate better. (As long as you make sure that it still looks like a concept with color added, and not confused with a UI design.)

One of our first clients at Initiale needed a clear call-to-action for his company's new site. At that time, I had to be self-sufficient. Although I already had two employees, I had to work on this project alone, and the client wanted to see the first wireframes in 2 days. It was based on my hunches, as there was no time or money for user research. This sounds like a recipe for disaster, doesn't it? I was nervous during the meeting, and not without reason. The mostly grayscale design had a small purple logo, and an enormous purple button as the call to action on every page. I kept explaining to the client over-and-over that this is just the first draft, to serve as a base for the conversation. Two weeks later, the first draft of the visual design was presented. Turns out, the client loved the big purple button, and now it was smaller and strikingly orange. The button looked much better with the rest of the design, being an integral part of it. The client wanted the big purple button. I disagreed. A simple AB test was quickly created to compare the two buttons. The big purple button won, and I learned to trust my instincts. This reinforced that sometimes color is beneficial in wireframes. You should also trust your instincts, then verify them.

Long story short, if you have a meaningful color choice for some UI elements, you can include them in the wireframe, especially if it is not just a simple style or color preference, but somehow meaningful in the bigger picture of user experience.

Low-fidelity versus high-fidelity wireframes

We will compare the two wireframes, lo-fi and hi-fi, in this section. When the wireframe shows little resemblance to the look of the proposed product, we call it a lo-fi, or low-fidelity wireframe. When the aim is to show visuals close to how the final product will look, we create a hi-fi, or high-fidelity wireframe. An example of both is shown in the following screenshot:

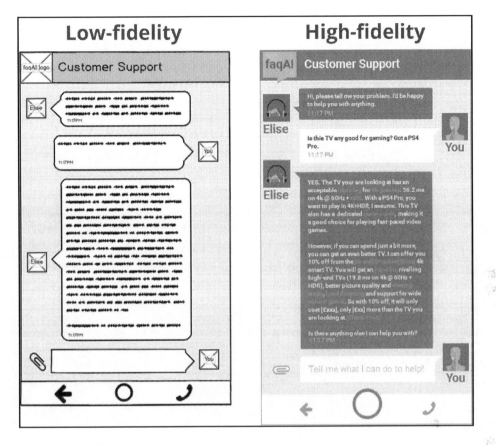

Let's now take a look at low-fidelity wireframes in detail.

Lo-fi wireframes

Low-fidelity wireframes often have sketchy looking rendering, but that's not a necessity. The lack of detail and visual design elements is what defines lo-fi wireframes. When creating them, we often replace visual design elements with placeholders. The alignment, spacing, font, and icon selections are often accidental, and there is no emphasis on those. Since they are usually created early, even in the ideation phase of the digital solution, they lack refinement, but that can be a good thing.

One of the obvious benefits of lo-fi wireframes is speed. You can create a low-fidelity wireframe in a few minutes, even during a discussion. You can sketch them on paper, on the whiteboard, or even digitally on your tablet or laptop. As this can happen in parallel with the discussion, chances are you will not forget critical details, and stakeholders can give immediate feedback.

Learning a lo-fi digital wireframing solution is much easier. Just take a look at the user interface of my favorite lo-fi tool, Balsamiq Mockups. (The following screenshot is from version 3.5.9, but I don't think Balsamiq has any intention to make their tool more complicated or harder to learn in the near future):

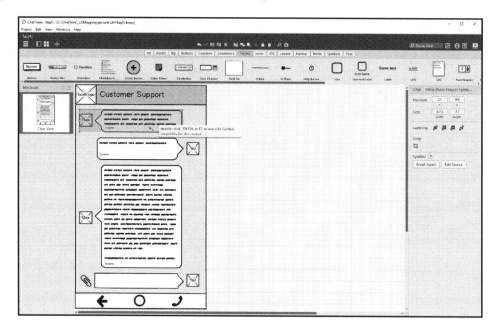

Balsamiq Mockups 3.5.9

Since lo-fi wireframes lack the details and finish, usually opting for a sketchy look, people will find it easier to comment, critique, or suggest a totally different direction. They are fast and easy to create, so those who work on them will not feel attached to the design, and they can easily accept such suggestions. Overall, the low-fidelity has clear communication benefits. This approach also keeps your options open. If you don't waste time on creating a visual language or style, choosing a font or fine-tuning design elements, you can focus on what's really important from day-zero: the user and creating outstanding user experiences.

You can also skip the real content. You use add *lorem ipsum* instead. *Lipsum* is a filler text commonly used as a placeholder, derived from Cicero's *De finibus bonorum et malorum.* You can also copy and paste some random text from the Internet, or add some scrambled lines. That later is the default representation of a block of text and line of text elements in Balsamiq. Worst case scenario, you could leave the space empty, but I wouldn't recommend that, as it can create misunderstandings later.

Anyone can participate in creating lo-fi wireflows, or adding things to them. Even people without design, UX, or software development backgrounds can help to crystallize the idea. We will see the importance of this in the *Wireflow Improvements Workshop (WIW)* section of this chapter. As I said before, I love to create the first wireframe alone, but for subsequent versions, it can be helpful if people can simply draw their idea, even free-hand, on the printed wireflow.

Low-fidelity wireframes are also much cheaper, thus being even more helpful to a fail-fast approach. Lo-fi wireframes usually lack color and branding elements, but that's not always the case.

Low-fidelity wireframes are ideal for the early, ideation phases of a project. They can facilitate communication and experimentation. Often, a team is familiar with a type of design or some UI/UX solutions. They know how to implement that easily, but that might not be the solution that is the best for the users. At this stage, lo-fi wireframes create the perfect environment for experimentation and clashing of different approaches or solutions.

Overall, low-fidelity wireframes have many clear communication benefits. This approach also keeps your options open. If you waste time on creating a visual language or style, choosing a font or fine-tuning design elements, you can focus on what's really important from day zero: the user and creating outstanding user experiences.

Hi-fi wireframes

If you keep adding more details and refinement, you create a higher fidelity wireframe. There is no sharp division line between low and high fidelity; they are two extremes. The highest fidelity wireframe would look exactly like a screenshot of the finished product. For practical purposes, high fidelity wireframes don't use sketchy rendering. Instead, sharp lines, well-defined boundaries, layouts, and alignments are used. High-fidelity wireframes are usually in color, instead of grayscale, and when available, branding elements could be used instead of placeholders.

They take considerably more time and resource investment, and generally, they are harder to create. Arguably, more skill is needed for them, and often high fidelity wireframes are created by a team of visual and UX designers working together with brand, frontend, and any other relevant teams. They also require different, more complex software solutions. Some people use Adobe Photoshop, Illustrator, Experience Design, Sketch, or Axure RP.

For this section's high fidelity example, I have used Axure RP (version 8.0.0.3323) to recreate the same solution. High-fidelity wireframes are also higher-cost wireframes. A considerable amount of time is required to create them. Creating the hi-fi example for this section was five times longer than the lo-fi one. Probably, I spent too much time with the dialog between Elise, the AI, and the user. Then again, you need to be prepared to spend a lot of time on fine details when creating hi-fi wireframes.

A high fidelity wireframe example, created with Axure RP 8

When you create a high fidelity wireframe, you want real content, or content as close to real as possible. If you really can't get real content, lorem ipsum will do, but most stakeholders will prefer real (looking) content for hi-fi wireframes.

If they have so many cons, why do people create high fidelity wireframes? The main reason is probably the same as for the existence of architectural 3D rendering: people want to see how things will look. A low-fidelity wireframe requires a considerable amount of imagination and visual thinking. A high fidelity one can be sent to the client in an e-mail, saying that it will look pretty much like this. You will leave little to the imagination. This facilitates communication, and non-technical people are much more likely to commit to a project after seeing hi-fi wireframes.

High-fidelity wireflows are best when created in the later phases of a project, before rapid prototyping. With a rapid prototyping software, such as Axure RP, you can convert your high-fidelity wireframes into high-fidelity prototypes. You can even use the same software to create both the wireframes and the prototypes, thus saving time and making the transition effortless. No need to worry about importing bugs, resolution, alignment, converting text, color space differences, and other issues that might arise when importing hi-fi wireframes created by another software.

Overall, high-fidelity wireflows are best created once you have a clear understanding and plan for your solution. Regardless of the fidelity, you should always focus on your users and create outstanding experiences for them.

I had a bad feeling when a good friend of mine approached me to create high-fidelity wireframes and a prototype for a super urgent and important app project they were working on. Truth be told, I never encountered any project that was not urgent or not important for some people, but this was a genuine case of urgency. Naturally, I started with a user story map, then, we created personas, task models, and a journey map, which was quickly accepted, with minor suggestions. The only real suggestion for those was to move faster with the project. During the same meeting, I had presented a few sketchy looking low-fidelity wireframes. My friend asked me, when can they see the "real thing", although the deadline was five weeks from that point.

I always try my best to avoid sacrificing long-term value to please a client. It was obvious that my friend wanted some UI design fast. As there was enough time left, I asked a member of my team to create a high fidelity wireframe, based on the seemingly accepted low-fidelity wireframes, for the next meeting. This became Variant A. Fortunately, the deadline was in the far future (in our line of work, five weeks is a generous deadline), so I continued with low-fidelity wireframes. I named this side project Fork B. We worked hard on Fork B, continuously improving the lo-fi wireframes, as we found out more and more about the users from real user tests, competitor benchmarking, and some contextual research. We agreed on the project's budget beforehand, so my friend was a bit puzzled by this approach, and privately told me that my standards are unreasonably high, and not start-up like. I took his comment as a compliment.

My friend was genuinely happy when he got the working prototype for Variant A almost

three weeks before the deadline. My initial strong judgement and good instincts lead to an acceptable UI for a hunch-based user experience. However, I promised a much better version before the deadline. He compared the lo-fi work-in-progress wireframes of Fork B with the finished hi-fi clickable prototypes of Variant A; Variant A won. My friend was inconvincible at that point. He wanted to start, so his team immediately started working on the project based on the Variant A solution. A day before the deadline, I presented him the high-fidelity wireframes of the fabled Fork B. He thanked me and then hid the files in a dark and damp folder, where abandoned projects go to die. I learned that high-fidelity wireframes are likely to beat low-fidelity ones, even if the lo-fi ones provide a superior user experience. This could have been the end of this story.
Miraculously, after a successful release, Fork B was released from the aforementioned dark and damp folder. My friend started working on the second version of the app. That version was based on Fork B, improved with the learnings from the first version.

Wireframing with Balsamiq Mockups

Balsamiq Mockups is a great digital tool for sketchy looking, low-fidelity wireframes. You can focus on your vision, and priorities, without being lost in the details of the layout, contents, images, navigation, or technical possibilities. It's probably the closest digital approximation to hand-drawn sketchy wireframes--the ones you make during a meeting or on a napkin in a pub.

Most common UI elements can be found in the UI library on the top of the screen. If you can't see the stripe with UI elements, you need to open it, by clicking on the **Show UI Library** button ( ). Alternatively, you can press *Ctrl + L* (*command + L* on Mac) to show/hide the UI library.

Balsamiq comes pre-packed with quite a few UI elements, but you can download more from **Mockups To Go** at `https://mockupstogo.mybalsamiq.com`. Mockups To Go is a repository for community-created interface libraries and templates that can be used in Balsamiq Mockups. You can also construct your own reusable symbols (we will get there soon) from basic building blocks. The most basic of those is the **Rectangle** (Canvas, Panel) UI element.

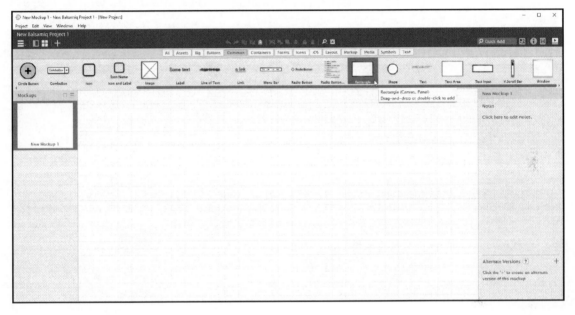

Adding a rectangle element

For our starting view, we could mock-up a whole site, just to show the **faqAI** button, or we could just suggest the site behind it. To follow the idea of simplicity in communication, we will, of course, just draw a hint of a website using the **Window** UI element. You can find that in **Common** UI elements, or type `Window` into the **Quick Add** field on the top right of the interface. Most interface elements are customizable from the inspector on the right side of the Balsamiq window (if not visible, go to **View** menu and choose inspector). For example, you can add a vertical scrollbar, buttons, drag handles, and title to your Window element.

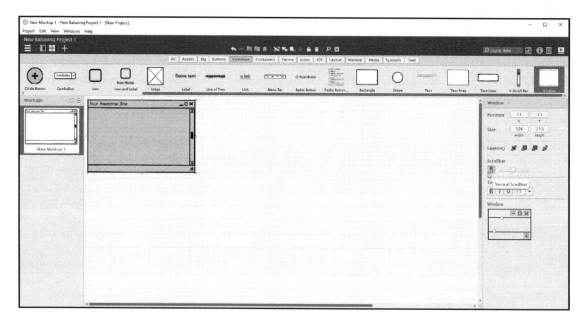

Customizing the Window element

As I mentioned before, we will just give a hint of some content on the site, below our sticky chat button. If you are interested in the technical side, our chat button will be fixed bottom, right, as the topmost element (z-index: 999). In other words, it will always be visible. To give a hint of content behind, we will add a **Scratch-Out** (easy to find with **Markup** filter from the UI library). With the **Opacity** slider, we will decrease the Scratch-Out's transparency to almost invisible.

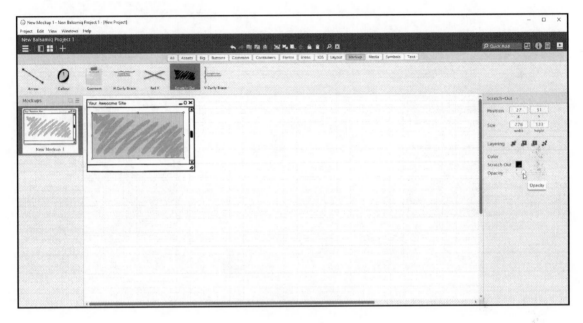

Using Scratch-Out

Then, we add a **Button**, a regular one; other button types can be found using the **Buttons** filter of the UI library:

From the inspector, you can find an icon for your new button. If you are not sure, you can even type in generic terms, such as chat, and Balsamiq will give you a few icon choices from the Font Awesome Icon Set. With the slider below, you can set the size of the given icon from **XS** (extra small) to **XXL** (extra extra large):

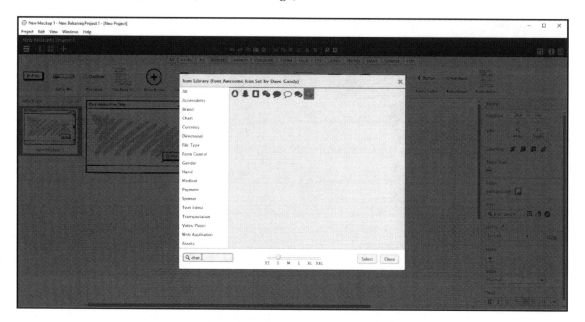

You can edit the text of any element by pressing *F2* or *Enter* while the element is selected. For many elements, double-click will also edit the text, but for some elements, double-click has a different function; for example, double-clicking on the image element will select the image.

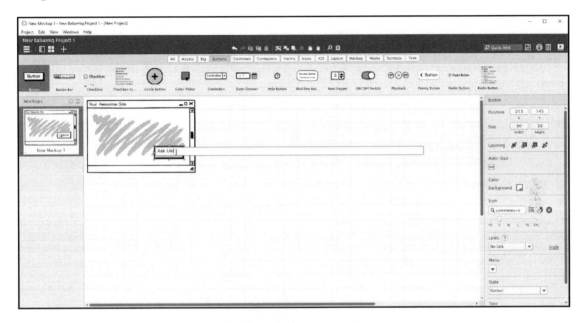

Editing the text in the element

When an item like a button is selected in Balsamiq, it will have eight squares around its border. Those squares can be used to resize it. When you click on one of those handles, the cursor will change. Balsamiq will automatically snap elements relative to other objects on the canvas using smart guides when you move or resize them. This is really helpful when you want to align elements and will result in better-looking layouts.

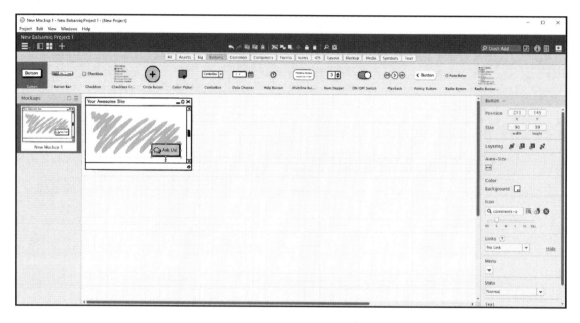

Aligning elements

However, sometimes you just want to freely move or scale items. You can temporarily turn off snapping, by holding down the *Ctrl* (*command* on Mac) key while moving or resizing.

Beyond the first wireframe

When creating a wireflow, I usually create one mockup for each wireframe, then a final one, where I add all mockups. To do this, first, you need to rename your **New Mockup 1**. On the left side of your screen, there is a navigator with all mockups. Double-click on your active mockup and then the rename model will appear.

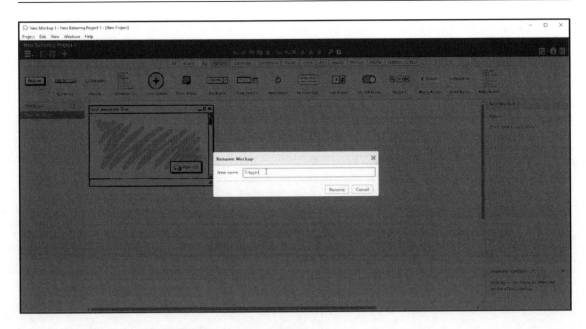

Renaming the mockup

A project is essentially a collection of mockups, assets, and symbols. It goes without saying that you need to save your project. You can do this from **Project** > **Save Project**, or by pressing *Ctrl + S* (*command + S* on Mac). In the **Project** menu, you can see **Auto Save Every Change**; I would suggest leaving that checked, so you don't end up losing any changes due to your laptop battery dying, or a cat stepping on the power button for eight seconds.

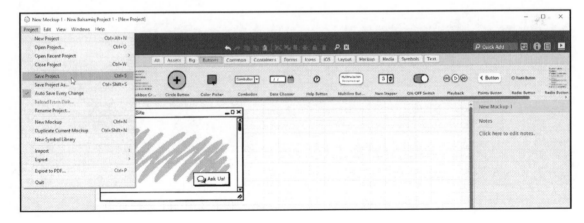

Save your project!

After saving the project, add a **New Mockup** for our next wireframe in the wireflow. You can do so from the **Project** menu (**Project** > **New Mockup**) or by pressing *Ctrl + N* (*command + N* on Mac).

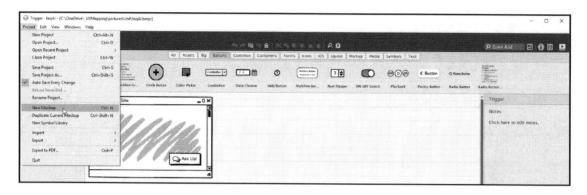

Creating a new mockup

For the chat view wireframe, we need a new element type, the **Image**. By default, it looks like a box with an X in it. You can add text to explain what will be there. To edit the text, press *Enter* or *F2*.

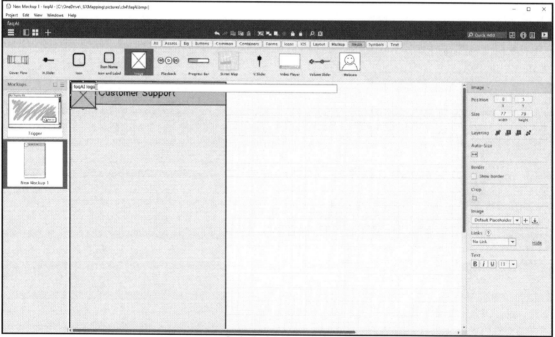

Starting the chat view wireframe

However, the best feature of the **Image** UI element is that it can load a real image into itself. From the inspector, you can click on the **Import from Disk...** button, or you can double-click on the element on the canvas to select your image file--for example, the logo of your app.

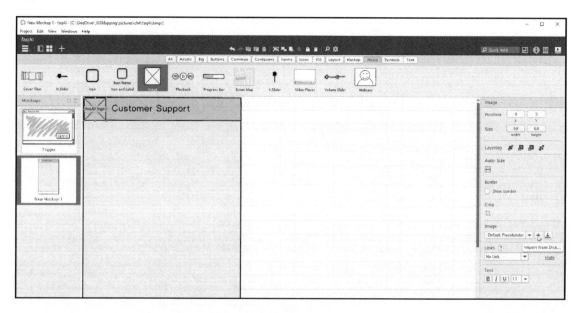

Adding an image element

This will replace the square with an X with the image you just loaded. You can use PNG files for logos with a transparent background, like I did.

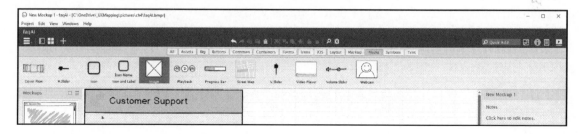

Replacing the X with a real image

Now, you probably see, that this colorful, high-resolution logo is out of place in our sketchy-looking grayscale wireframe. To remedy this, we can turn any image into a sketchy-looking grayscale one with a simple click on the **Sketch it!** checkbox in the inspector.

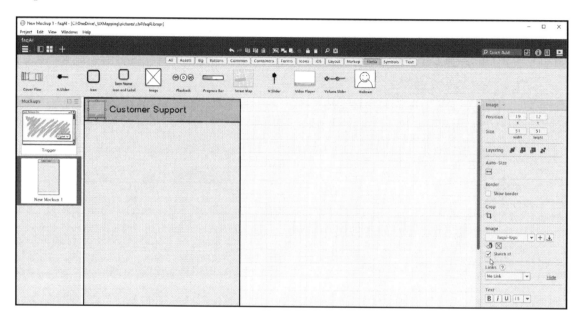

Converting the image to grayscale

Do experiment with other UI elements. For example, chat bubbles were made with the **Popover** element from the iOS filter group, by setting the **Popover** position and Point Position in the inspector. Remember that our goal with lo-fi wireframes is to give the viewer an idea of what we want to achieve, not exact design or precise layout.

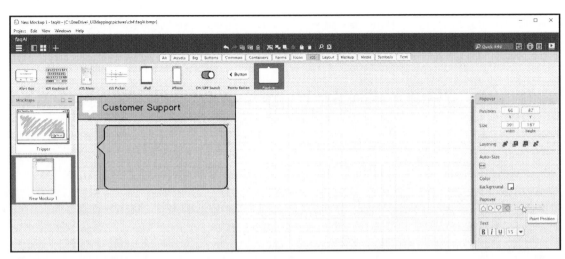

Adding chat bubbles using Popover element

In the preceding section, we saw that one of the benefits of lo-fi wireframes is that you can safely skip adding real content. Instead of lorem ipsum, I prefer the scrambled line look of Balsamiq. The default of the **Block of Text** element will produce that until you add some real text to the elements.

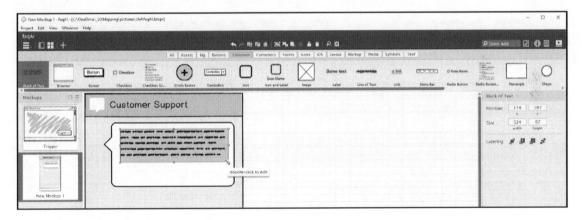

The Block of Text element

If you want just a scrambled line, not multiple lines, you can use the **Line of Text** element instead.

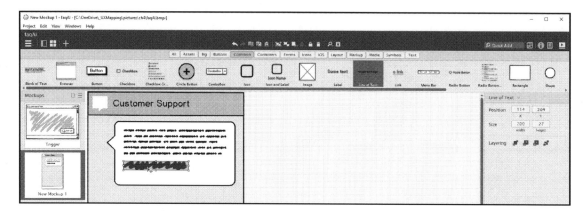

Use the Line of Text element

If later on, you decide to add the real text to any of those elements, you can double-click or press *Enter* or *F2* to edit them. After that, they will show the text you entered into them. This is a pretty good fit for our continuous improvement process.

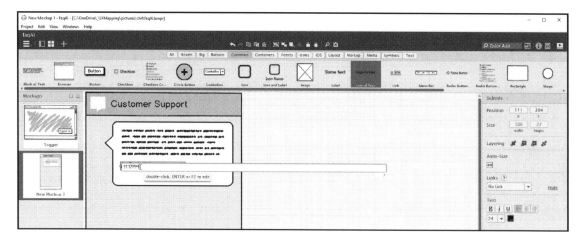

Adding real text

For graphic element placeholders, you can also use the **Icon** UI element. In the inspector, you can search for what you wish to add, and change the default look from the rounded

rectangle to the chosen icon. With the Rotate 90° button (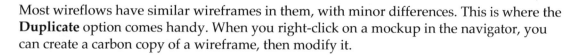), you can rotate your icon. I hope one day Balsamiq will have free rotation for all elements, like Adobe Illustrator or Axure RP has.

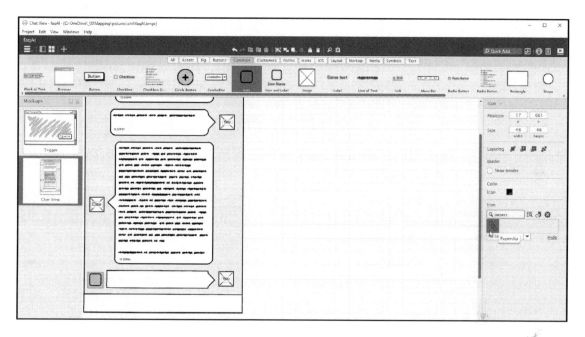

The Icon UI element

Most wireflows have similar wireframes in them, with minor differences. This is where the **Duplicate** option comes handy. When you right-click on a mockup in the navigator, you can create a carbon copy of a wireframe, then modify it.

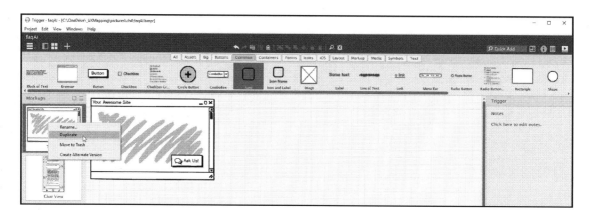

Duplicating your wireframe

For example, it's easy to create the second trigger, which is more visible to the user, shown after they have been idle for a few seconds. Later, we can look for other behavioral clues for a user needing help, such as going in circles on the site, switching between tabs, or scrolling up and down a few times. This delayed trigger can be bigger, so we can show a happy and helpful human face, larger button, and, of course, a close option. (For the happy face, I have used the **Media** > **Webcam** UI element.)

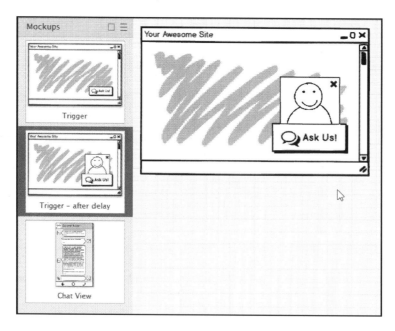

Creating symbols

A symbol is a reusable group of elements, which we create to speed up the creation of wireframes. Symbol is a common name for this feature, but also misleading, because in some software, such as Adobe Animate CC 2017, symbols work differently. They are more powerful, nestable, come in multiple types, and so on. The beauty of Balsamiq lies in its simplicity, and this also applies to symbols.

For creating wireflows, I usually convert each wireframe into a symbol. To do this, select everything in the wireframe by dragging the selection box from one corner to the opposite.

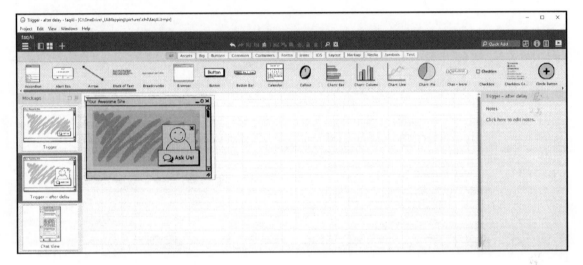

Selecting the contents of a wireframe

Once everything is selected, you need to group the contents of the wireframe. **Edit > Group** or *Ctrl + G* (*command + G* on Mac)

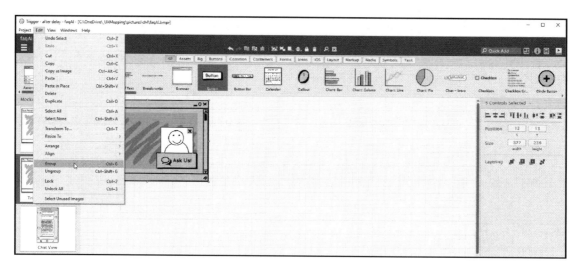

Grouping the contents

After being grouped, they turn to a bluish color. In the inspector, you can name your new group, then click on **Convert To Symbol**.

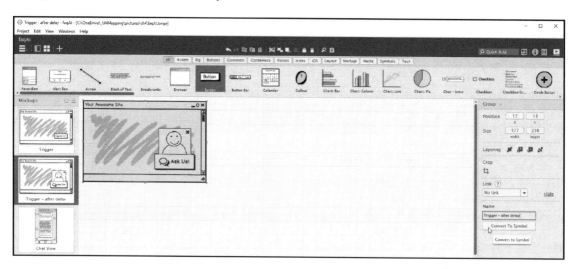

We can convert a group into a Symbol

After you converted something into a symbol, it will appear to be greenish, instead of blueish. Moreover, now you can see it among the Symbols in the UI library, probably, as the first and only symbol, if you were following my example.

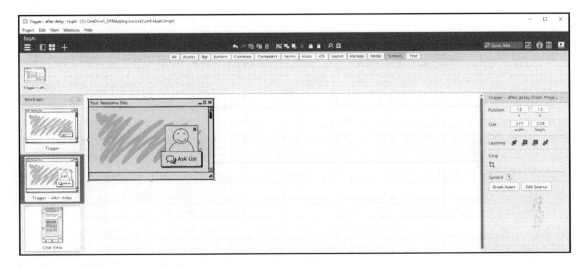

A wireframe converted into a symbol

The after chat survey

Another important view we need to wireframe is the after chat survey. We want to get feedback from the users after finishing the chat, with the intent of improving our solution. People hate long surveys, so we should make this quick, easy, and not like a survey. Our other intent is to provide a fall-back to human support in case faqAI failed to solve the user's problem.

People understand star ratings from real life, digital reviews, or many other sources. So, we will go with the 1-5 star scale. Manually spacing out the stars created with the **Icon** element would be quite challenging, but fortunately, when we select all five, we can see some alignment options in the inspector; the most useful here is Space Out Horizontally:

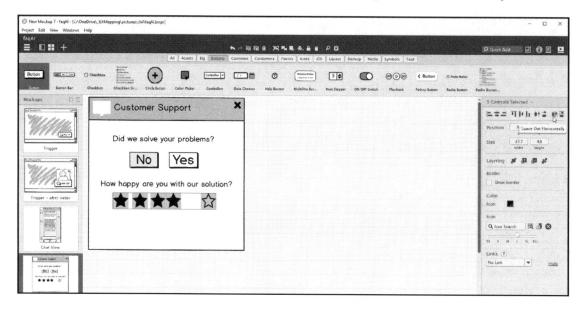

Spacing elements horizontally

Balsamiq doesn't support opacity for most elements, such as buttons. To fade a button, I just place a rectangle with a white border and fill color and set it to 75% transparent with the **Opacity** slider:

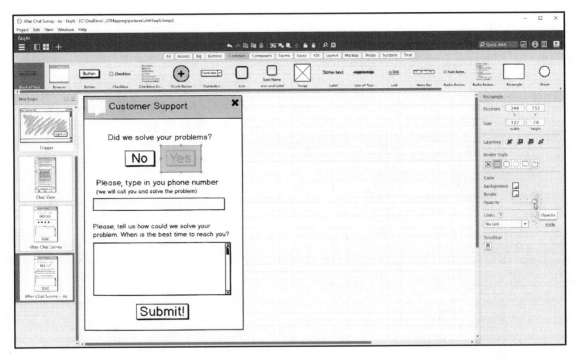

Fading a button

A common issue, especially for people used to other software, where Symbols are nestable, is the disabled **Convert to Symbol** button. To solve this, we just need to edit the contents of our group, by double-clicking on it:

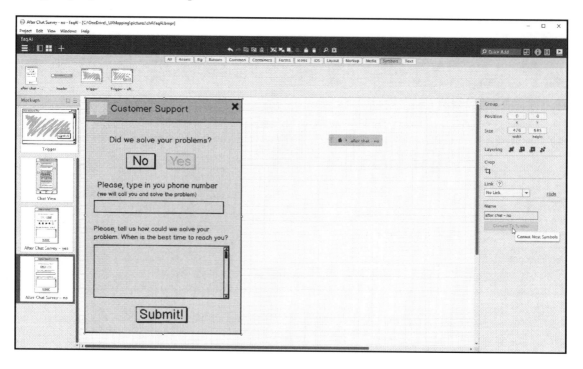

Editing the contents of the group

When editing the contents of our group, we need to find all the symbols inside, then click on the **Break Apart** button. When our group doesn't contain any symbols, we can convert it to one.

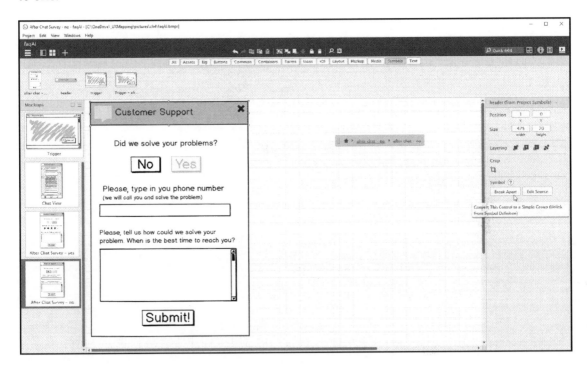

Breaking symbols apart, converting them to a simple group

Creating the wireflow

Now, we have some great wireframes. It's time to create the path leading the user through our solution. After you have a symbol with the contents of each wireframe, you need to put them all together to create this path.

To be able to see the whole wireflow, you might need to **Zoom Out** from the menu (**View** > **Zoom** > **Zoom Out**), from the Zoom icon (see the screenshot), or using the *Ctrl + -* keyboard shortcut (*command + -* on Mac).

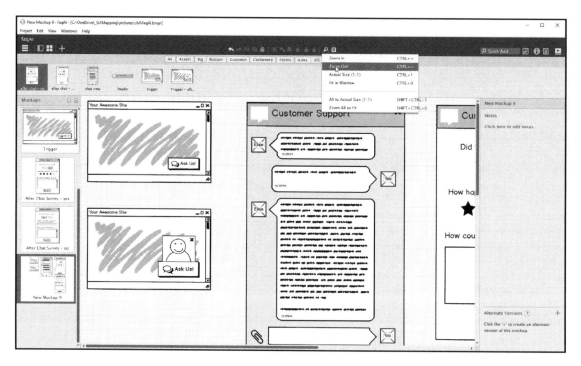

Zoom out to see the whole wireflow

After you have arranged the symbols, you can connect them using the **Arrow** from the **Markup** UI filter group. You can specify stroke style, opacity, add labels, and arrowheads. It has three handles--beginning, end and midpoint handle. The latter is useful to add curvature to the arrow.

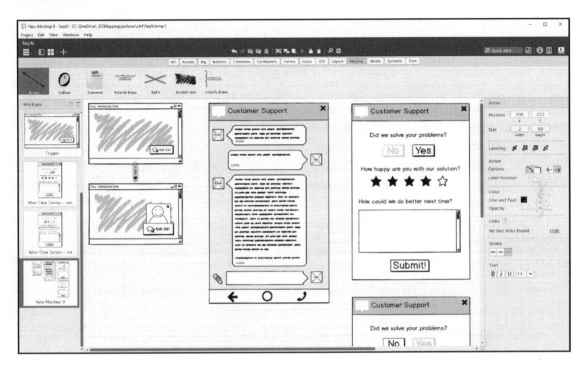

Adding arrows

Sometimes, adding annotations to the wireflow helps with understandability. For example, I have used **V.Curly Brace** to specify when the trigger transforms into a more visible one. Besides the curly braces, **Comment** and **Callout** can also be used to annotate our wireflow.

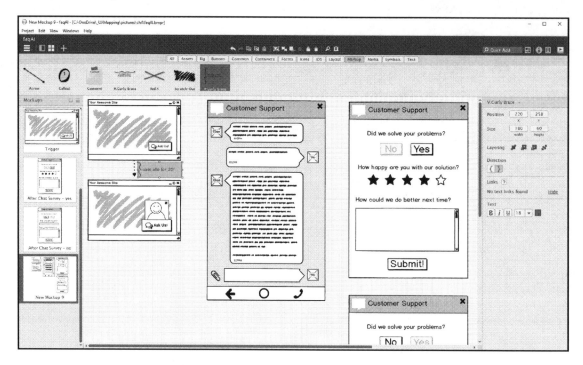

Annotations for the wireflow

Finally, when you create the arrows, you can select all of them to give them a unique color using the color picker in the inspector. This technique can be used to change the style of many elements with just a few clicks.

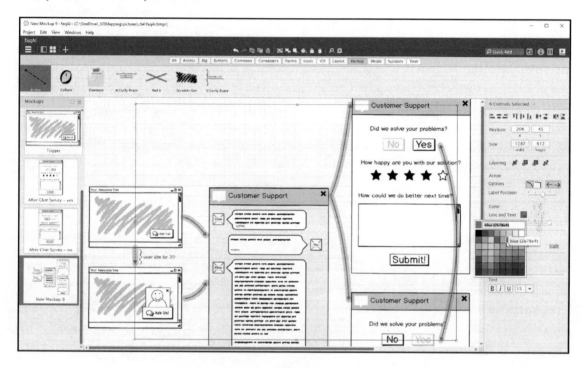

Coloring the arrows

Now, we created the final wireflow for our solution. By now, you should have planned your product. It is ready to be explored, to be talked about, and to be created.

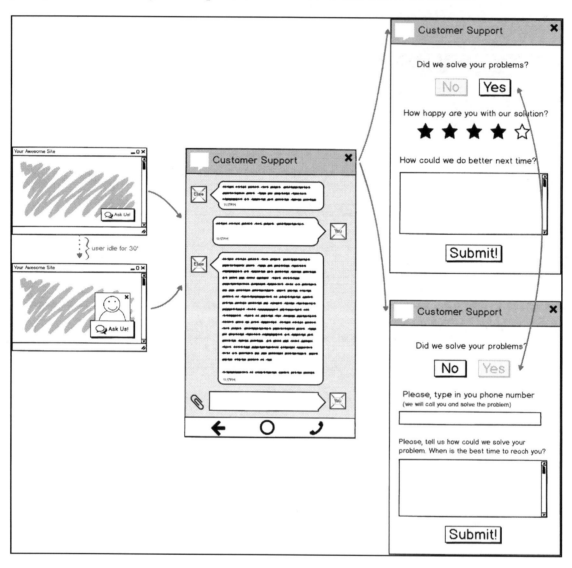

The finished wireflow

If you decide to go with a less sketchy look, maybe as a step toward hi-fi wireflow, you can change Balsamiq's rendering style from the **Project Information** page. You can view that by clicking on the **Show Project Info** icon (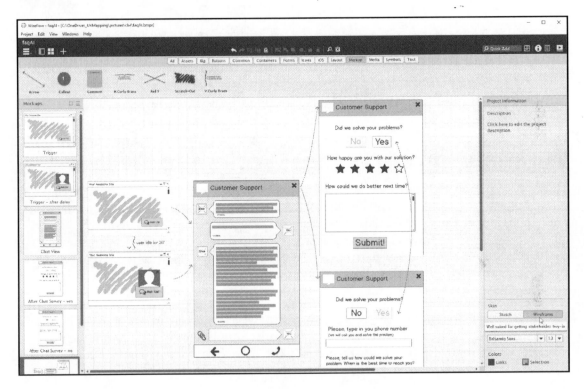) on the top-right corner of the Balsamiq window. Alternatively, you can access it from the menu (**View** > **Project Information**). This pane can be used to add the project description, set default font face and size, and specify link and selection color. However, we are here to set the **Skin** or rendering style of **Wireframe**. Go on, try it. You need to find out which style resonates better with your stakeholders.

The Project Information panel

Finally, export your wireflow mockup to conclude the wireflowing. I recommend the PNG format. Go to **Project** > **Export** > **Current Mockup to PNG...** (alternatively, use the *Ctrl + R* or *command + R* keyboard shortcut).

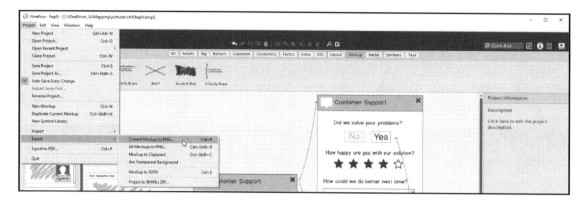

Wireflow Improvement Workshop (WIW)

The best validation and source of improvement for wireframes is to test them with real users. In the next chapter, we will create test designs and run the tests with real users. More often than not, we can't run as many user tests as we would wish. Testing with real users takes many resources, time, and money. If we are limited in any or all of those resources, we could skip testing our wireflows, or at least the first iteration of them, and run a **Wireflow Improvement Workshop** (**WIW**) instead. If you can do a lab or remote user test, that can serve as a base for a WIW. You only have to gain from running such event.

The WIW is a collaborative meeting session, during which we focus on the current iteration of the wireflow, with the intent of considerably improving it. This is also communication exercise, where many ideas of improvement can be shared, discussed, and evaluated.

Why should you run a WIW?

Improved wireflows can transform the project and lead to better user experience. Just discussing the wireflows with people can be beneficial, even during a five-minute chat. However, to truly get inspired for the next version, I would suggest a WIW. The WIW might build consensus. This workshop can also make participants feel heard and their ideas considered, making them more committed to the project.

Owing to the apparent communication benefits, there is no real reason not to run a WIW, especially because it's a low-cost workshop. You just need a printer, a few felt tip pens, and a room. You can also run it online with some adjustments.

Running a WIW

Organizing a WIW and running it is rather fun and easy, even if you are an external consultant or contractor. You can go through the following checklist or keep it entirely free-form, but the most important thing is to keep the atmosphere informal, where communication thrives and new ideas can easily emerge.

1. **Invite participants**: You should invite at least the key people of the *four amigo* meeting from `Chapter 2`, *User Story Map-Requirements by Collaboration and Sticky Notes*. If you have the business representative, the developer, the tester, and the UX expert, you can think of adding more people. Adding more people can lead to more ideas, but will certainly make it longer and harder to schedule meetings. It's also helpful to invite someone who has a fresh pair of eyes, usually someone not involved in the project, maybe an intern. If you have more than 10 people, it will be hard to get everyone involved. My ideal number for a WIW is seven people, but by all means, I won't hold a grudge if your WIW works better with six or nine people.

2. **Prepare the wireflow**: Send everyone a copy of the wireflow through e-mail and have at least two copies printed per person. The e-mail allows people to see it beforehand, while the printed copies will be drawn over during the WIW. No, I'm not trying to contribute to deforestation, but trust me, you will need two printed copies for each participant. It goes without saying, but you might want to distribute some writing tools too. Felt tip pens are probably the best, especially colored ones if your wireflow is grayscale. You should pick a color that is not present on the wireflow. Alternatively, you can just have cartloads of pens, and let people pick their favorite shade.

3. **Introduction**: It's important to emphasize that there are no wrong answers. Everyone should participate and communicate as much as possible. We do the WIW for a common goal, so explain the opportunity again. If you have a whiteboard, write the opportunity in big letters, and leave it there. (We will not need the whiteboard for anything else.) Most likely at this stage, everyone has heard the opportunity a few times, but rehearsing it again anchors the WIW to the opportunity. Also, tell people how WIW works, if someone is unfamiliar with it (see the next items in this list).

4. **Main task**: Tell people the most important or most common task, which can be done with the solution. Everyone should work individually and mark how they would interact with the solution. This should be quick and easy for everyone. If people are puzzled about doing something, it's a sign that an interaction needs improving. What seemed easy and straightforward for the wireflow creator might not make sense for the users, so it needs improvement. A task could be as follows: *find and buy the washing machine you would genuinely want, then ask a few questions about it from support* or *imagine you have ordered some flowers for Valentine's Day, they haven't arrived, and now it's the 15th of February, and you want a refund. The chatbot wants to resend them instead.* Marking the steps could be as simple as drawing a circle where you would tap. This is probably the most important step; this step can validate the wireflow, or find major shortcomings of it.

5. **Secondary task**: Now, tell everyone the second most common task, and ask people to mark the interaction on the same paper, with a different color if possible. If your solution is geared towards one straightforward task, you can still add some variety or spin to it. For example, if you try to improve the checkout process, you can give a second task similar to this: *Imagine that after reviewing the basket, you changed your mind and instead of buying the same shirt twice, you only want one of it. Buy all the items, except the extra shirt.*

6. **Discuss the interactions**: Focus on how the interface feels. Try to involve every participant by asking relevant questions, such as how does the interface respond and act to user inputs? What do the users expect to happen? How could the interface design be clearer and better structured? Is there any technical limitation for this? All this discussion quickly leads to identifying missing features, interactions or even views.

7. **Add what's missing**: Now, ask participants to take the second copy of the wireflow, and add what's missing. You need a second copy to avoid clutter, and to be able to design a better interaction for the same tasks.

8. **Simplify**: Then, ask the participants to remove what's not essential; a simple scratching out will do. You usually want to combine steps 7 and 8 into one individual work phase. Adding missing elements and removing extras should take about 5 to 10 minutes of individual work.

9. **Discuss the improvement**: After everyone has had a chance to create their improved version, you need to discuss this. Ask people to explain their solution in 180 seconds tops. Be diligent about time, otherwise, the meeting will become way too long, and people will simply avoid subsequent WIWs. After everyone has had a chance to talk, you can discuss how all those ideas could be merged into a final improvement plan. You don't need to create that on-the-fly; it's perfectly fine if you create it later, and that becomes the next version of the wireflow.

10. **Commit to actions**: The most important commitment is a date and time for the next wireflow version. Other commitments should be related to suggested improvements or particular areas of discussion. For example, if people are not sure about technical possibilities, an action could be to investigate those.

Don't forget to collect the papers at the end, and use them as a base for the next wireflow version.

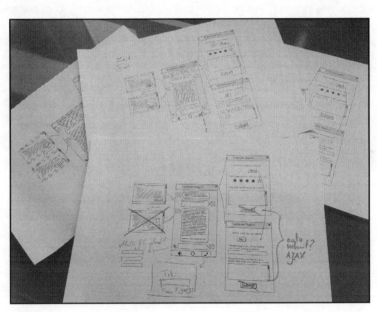

It's a bit hard to run WIW without an actual wireflow, but it's possible to do so before the first iteration is created. In that case, you just hand out empty papers, maybe with a few frames representing a browser window or a phone's screen, or whatever your solution will run on. The participants will quickly sketch the wireframes individually for the first task, based on the journey map and task model, if those were created. Then, they can improve the sketch, so it works for the second task as well. You should give about 10 minutes for the first sketch, and five more for the improved sketch based on the second task.

Summary

Wireflows are the plans of our product. They are an enriched journey map, and they're based on a good understanding of the users, their pain points, and behaviors. We create wireframes for our UI solutions and link them together with arrows.

In the early phases of the project, we can create low-fidelity wireflows, continuously improving them during WIW. Later, before rapid prototyping, we can build a high fidelity wireflow, as a close-to-real representation of our solution.

However, the best way to understand our users and to improve our user experience maps is testing with real users. In the next chapter, we will conduct *Remote and lab tests for map creation*. So, let's get closer to our users!

5
Remote and Lab Tests for Map Creation

To understand our users better, we need to watch them while they use or struggle with our solution and similar solutions. The techniques we will discover in this chapter can help you to design and run any user test. Even if you don't intend to create a map from the results, user testing is the silver bullet to better product design.

 User experience testing is the process of understanding real users. By watching them, while they interact with a solution, we gain an understanding. This understanding leads to better maps and better experiences.

In this chapter, we will do the following things:

- Discover the problem to be solved with real user testing. We will run the test on Samsung's UK website.
- Define test objectives. We will also get together for yet another four amigos meeting--this time, to define test objectives.
- Decide whether we want to test in a lab, remotely, or the guerrilla way. Don't worry, UX guerrillas prefer a pub or the kitchen over a jungle.
- Set the number of users for our test.
- Find the right users for those spots. We will target devices and talk about the ever so elusive target audience.
- Discuss private panel and moderated versus unmoderated testing.
- Set the scenario, in other words, craft a one-sentence background story for this epic adventure called user testing.

- Write the test script for our smartphone buying journey. Just some tasks and questions, but this will become the life-essence of our test design.
- Learn what's a pilot test, and why it's important. Note that no airplane pilot was harmed during the creation of this book.
- Put all this into practice. Set up and launch a test with the `WhatUsersDo.com` remote testing platform.

Let's jump-start this chapter with one of the essential questions of modern product development: *How to create better user experiences?* My friend, Lee Duddell has the perfect answer for this:

"To build better User Experiences we need to understand people's behaviour. Insight helps us understand"

-Lee Duddell

Alternatively, if you prefer stronger wording, take a look at Jakob Nielsen's:

"Shut up and listen to users!"

-Jakob Nielsen

Contrary to what the name implies, user testing doesn't mean testing the users. It's important to make sure that the users are also aware of that. We work together with the users to create a better product for them. User testing is just one aspect of that. We want them to follow a set of instructions. We give them some tasks, they would normally do, when interacting with our solution. We want them to speak their thoughts and verbalize what's happening in their minds. Their words combined with careful observation of their behavior will lead to the understanding we seek.

 There are two sentences I always tell the users at the beginning of most tests: *Please make sure that you follow every instruction and speak your thoughts as you do so. Remember, we are testing the site, not you.* Those two sentences summarize what user testing is about, and it will tell the users what we expect from them.

User experience researchers, design thinkers, and product owners want to understand what people do and why they do it. This chapter and the next will help them understand the users. Remember that we don't test to create maps. We create maps to understand and communicate the results of our tests, and to provide a visual representation of what needs to be changed in order to create a better solution.

Samsung's 2017 redesign

In the previous chapters, we solved problems by creating something new from scratch. However, now we will do something completely different--we will test an existing site. Then, in the next chapter, we will create a map based on the results, and see how we can action the map, resulting in a better site, or even a new product.

Samsung's UK website from January 2017 is the base for our redesign project. If you visit `http://www.samsung.com/uk/` while reading this book, the site might look different:

The opportunity is that Samsung's potential customers want an easy way to get a new smartphone. They want to learn more about Samsung's products and want a fast and secure way to buy them. If we understand the users, Samsung can increase the conversion rate of the website, creating a more straightforward path for the users. This can result in more sales.

Don't get me wrong, Samsung.com is not a bad site, far from it. It is created and maintained by smart and dedicated people. By choosing it, I want to demonstrate that any website can be improved by applying the learning from a few user tests. Even if it would be a terrible website, the intention of user testing is always to learn from it and improve, never to bash someone.

Samsung is a multinational conglomerate, with many products from ships to image sensor, from cranes to smart TVs. They have insurance products and hospitals, too. In the UK, they are best known for their smartphones, that's understandable. I have a Samsung TV, a Samsung dishwasher, and maybe some other Samsung gadgets that I completely forgot about, but my Samsung phone is always with me, and this is the device most people associate with Samsung.

Sometimes, you want to test competitor websites, just to see how the users use those, and hopefully learn what works there. By doing competitor testing, you can avoid the usability mistakes your competitors made. Learning from the users is probably the cheapest way to gain a competitive advantage. You become a trendsetter, instead of a copycat.

For the test itself, it doesn't matter whether you are testing a competitor or your own website. I would even encourage you to test both sites with the same techniques, same users, same test design, and most importantly, based on the same analysis criteria and guidelines. This will create an unbiased view and the learning will lead to better user experience.

Test objectives

Before deciding anything else about our test, we need to clearly define our objectives. Arguably, this is the most important step in test design. A well-defined set of objectives will make most test design decisions easy, if not obvious. It will help you to decide where and how to test, what kind of users to invite, and what tasks to give them; it goes even further. It will help us in the next chapter when you will create the analysis guidelines, find and summarize user insights, and communicate them in the form of a map.

The objectives are the base for designing, analyzing, mapping, and communicating any user test. The highest level objective for all user tests should be to gain a better understanding of the users and their behavior.

Besides the better understanding of the users and their behaviors, you will also need to have lower-level objectives--objectives that are specific to the test you will be running. *Test objectives should always be rooted in our the opportunity.* The first question you should ask yourself or your team is what do we want to test? What is fundamental to be understood? What do we already know, but want confirmation and clarification about.

Another important question is the purpose of the test. *The purpose is never to make a map. The map, any kind of map, is just a tool.* Another common mistake is to run a test, just to try a new testing platform, a new panel provider, a new prototyping app, a methodology, or any similar "meta test". All tests should be focusing on the users. If it doesn't, it's probably a waste of time and resources.

Think about what's problematic for the users. What are your hunches? Where are the pain points for the users? Moreover, what do we want to avoid testing? This can happen because we already tested parts of the solution, know the issues, but haven't fixed them yet. It can also happen because parts of the solution are not prototyped, not done, or just temporary. It's a terrible thing, but there are areas that we know are bad for the users, but we can't change. Legal compliance, brand, or the highest-paid person's opinion might prevent us from changing that or changing it now.

Our objective is to test how the users interact with Samsung UK's current website, and how we can improve the end-to-end journey of getting a new Samsung smartphone.

You can test many things, including hypotheses or simple hunches. You can test to find reasons behind stats from analytics or to gather hard proof for anecdotal evidence. User testing can even be run without well-defined objectives, although I would recommend at least some sort of goal or vague objective set.

The amigos run user tests

The ultimate secret weapon to define objectives is to have a kick-off meeting. It can be similar to the four amigos meeting from `Chapter 2`, *User Story Map-Requirements by Collaboration and Sticky Notes*. The product owner or business representative will start with higher-level business objectives. For example, *ensure that the new nav is performing effectively for users enabling excellent findability of products.* Another example would be to *evaluate the new feature pages to ensure that they increase engagement and influence product purchase.* The user experience expert will balance those with user needs. The user testing expert will design the test and facilitate it if needed. They will usually provide input on testability and help with choosing testing platforms, panels, users, and tasks. We also need a developer.
Besides needing them to test something that needs to be developed or prototyped first, their input is also necessary to conduct a test, which results in actionable insights. We need to focus on things we can easily fix or build.

With your amigos or alone, you are ready to test with real users. But where? In a lab, remotely while the users are at home, or in a pub? The choice will be made in the next section.

Lab, remote, and guerrilla testing

When doing user research, you could take multiple paths. In this section, we will explore the benefits and disadvantages of each approach. The choice, though, is often a matter of budget. If I had an enormous budget and a generous deadline for a project, I would run both lab and remote user experience testing to reap the benefits of both. Actually, I would just hire someone to do both, probably while petting my cats onboard a yacht floating on warm international waters. On the other hand, if I had zero budget and a deadline for tomorrow, I would ask around in a pub in Bromley and call it guerrilla testing. Real-world projects tend to fall between the two extremes, so we need to choose. Let's take a look at our options.

Lab testing

The oldest and most obvious testing place for rats and users is a lab. The user testing lab is usually a room with a table, where the user sits, in front of a device. There is a camera pointed at the user's face, while another might record the hands, to capture gestures on touch devices. Next to the user, usually quite close, sits the facilitator. We will get back to moderated tests, where there is a facilitator versus unmoderated, where there is no facilitator, but nowadays most lab tests tend to be moderated. The rooms usually feature a two-way mirror, and on the other side of the mirror, there is an observation room. In the darkness of the observation room, people can watch the test live. Most observation rooms have big screens, showing the live video feed from the lab. It's also possible to have a lab without a two-way mirror, just cameras.

How often do you use a website with at least two cameras pointed at you, and a stranger sitting next to you? For most people, that's a quite an unusual scenario. This unnatural environment can change user behaviors, which will be immediately obvious if you run the same test both remotely online and in a lab:

The most obvious drawback is the cost. The time investment is also considerably higher compared to remote testing. Planning a lab session is also more difficult. You need the lab, either in-house or from a third party, recruit participants, make sure that they turn up, provide food for everyone, and so on. Please don't use the food as a reward, that's for testing rats, not people.

You will only get participants within reasonable distances, usually restricted to the same city where your lab is. This limits the possible testers, especially compared to national and international panels, which most remote testing companies have. The lack of geographical diversity will also skew your test result unless you are testing an app or site aimed specifically at a local audience.

So, why do people bother with a lab? That's the most convenient way to test hardware solutions. The team can create one or two working physical prototypes and use those during the lab session. Creating a small initial batch and shipping them out to the remote testers is more costly and sometimes even impossible or not legally acceptable.

Lab testing has benefits for software solutions, too. Sometimes, you can only create a prototype that runs on a specific device or you are not legally allowed to host the prototype online. For example, you might be developing a game for a hardware, which is not yet available or common among testers. Alternatively, it may lack optimization, so it will only run poorly on older machines.

Lab testing is real time. That can be important for some tests, and it is always great to be able to ask questions from the user, right when things happen. You can also fix technical issues, or help your users overcome some difficulties much easier with lab testing. For example, if the user runs into a bug, it can derail a remote test, even if it is a moderated remote test. In a lab, a good facilitator will get some valuable feedback beyond observing the bug.

If someone is in the observation room, we can be sure that the person will get some exposure to the users, although sending a link doesn't always result in the videos being watched. In my experience, labs attract more interest from some stakeholders than remote testing videos. Lab tests might also look more professional and trustworthy.

Lab tests can be cheaper than remote tests if you can set up a lab in-house and if the facilitator, the analyst, and the panel recruiter are also part of your team. In other words, the lab is cheaper, if someone from your team or even you can simply run the lab, and you get the room for free or at a low cost. More often than not, the UX team will be overloaded and not experienced in things such as panel recruitment or test facilitation. However, that's OK, remote testing will solve those issues, without skyrocketing your costs.

Remote testing

Remote testing uses a software product to record how the users use a solution without the need for anyone to be present. No testing method is perfect. Although I'm a remote testing evangelist, it's only fair if I list the drawbacks of this testing method. However, no, I don't mean that it must be insanely hard to do remote testing with rats.

For humans, the most often cited issue with remote testing comes from its very nature--because no one from your team is present, things can go wrong. Technical issues can complicate things on both ends. The users can have problems recording the audio or their screen. They might be distracted or totally put off-track by unforeseeable things. If you don't use a dedicated remote testing platform, this is even more prominent. Although it's possible to run a remote test with a simple screen sharing software, such as Skype or WebEx, you really need to know what you are doing to attempt that. *I still haven't found a way to remote test with rats, but to be honest, my cats are more interested in rat behaviors than I am.*

You also need to be extra careful with your test design, wording, and understandability, not to mention the software running on the users' machines. Most of the time, you will have no idea about browser settings, add-ons, extensions, firewall rules, and other details about the user's digital environment. Obviously, you could ask them to use a specific browser, even to install some add-ons, but this will subtract from the natural nature of the test and might exclude testers who are less technically sound.

Remote tests don't lead to similar levels of involvement and commitment as lab tests do. Getting together in the observation room, watching users, and discussing the solution is a great internal event by itself.

Confidentiality is also harder to ensure. The users can take screenshots or even take a photo of their screen. In extreme cases, they could even reverse-engineer your solution before it hits the market.

If the remote test is unmoderated, like they usually are, it's harder to ask questions to the user or understand why they are doing certain things, if we haven't prepared for that eventuality in the test design.

The positive aspects of remote testing greatly outweigh the negatives listed above. The most important reason is the cheaper cost and the ability to conduct a more natural test. The users can use your website, app, or other digital solution at home, or wherever they would normally use it.

The test can happen in the moment when the need arises and certain behavior patterns emerge. For example, it's possible to remote test a recipe website with users who are about to cook a meal and would normally use a similar site. This can go even further, and the remote test can accompany the user to their kitchen, while they cook.

Recruiting testers is much easier and cheaper. You can recruit anyone from the whole country and even internationally. The testers can enjoy the comfort of their homes, cuddling with their cats. They can test your solution after working hours, even during the wee hours of the night. This flexibility leads to a greater diversity at a lower price-point. There is no travel involved and the tests can take 10 minutes or less, rarely going over half an hour. This means that it's easier to get busy people into remote tests. This is important for B2B solutions, where you are testing with business users, who tend to be crazy busy.

A common misconception is that you can test only websites with remote testing. You can test any software, app, or digital solution. Although it can be a bit difficult, you can also test TV programs, games on gaming consoles, or even physical products. British Gas even tested their printed bills using the WhatUsersDo remote testing platform.

If you are after larger user numbers in a short time, remote is usually the only solution. I believe that in the next few years remote testing will evolve even further, effectively eliminating lab and guerrilla testing from day-to-day user experience testing practices.

Guerrilla testing

Informal user testing is often called guerrilla, undercover, or corridor testing. This is an umbrella for anything you can do to test a solution quickly with a shoestring budget. You can grab a device and go down to a pub. If you work at an agency, ask some colleagues working on different projects. If you find your volunteers, give them some tasks and watch what they do. The test designs are shorter, and most of the time, the tests are not recorded.

Guerrilla testing obviously lacks the balance and rigor of a more formal testing. This can often lead to false assumptions, even sidetracked projects, based on undocumented anecdotal evidence.

User recordings essentially bring the user into the meeting room. Without a formal approach and recorded user testing video, you will only have your word. Even if you are the founder of an early seed start-up, you don't need to convince anyone. Do you really want to make a decision based on watching a few people navigating to your site?

The participants will be selected from amongst those who are easy to reach and willing to test the solution. Most people use friends, family, or coworkers for guerrilla testing. Those people will try hard to please you. They will praise your software. This can do wonders for your ego, but it's probably misleading. Remember, your mum is not a valid test market. Craig Brewster even named his UX consultancy after this golden rule.

You can also use your own devices for the test. This can lead to a participant seeing your incoming e-mail notifications, browsing history, visited links from previous tests, and so on. You may want to clear your cache and turn off all notifications for the test if you don't have dedicated testing devices.

The best thing about guerrilla testing is that it's free, or very cheap. You may want to buy some beers or cookies for the participants, but you can avoid pretty much all costs associated with remote or lab tests.

Guerrilla testing is also quick. A test is generally 5 minutes, and the whole testing session can happen during a lunch break.

Testing in suboptimal environments can have advantages. If the background noise is high and the light conditions are low, you can see how the users react to such situations. For example, if you are testing a taxi app, your users might be a bit tipsy, sitting in a pub at 1 AM, and looking for a cab. That is quite hard to accurately reproduce with remote or lab testing, but you can certainly go into a pub and ask a few patrons to test the app. You can offer free taxi rides in exchange.

Cennydd Bowles and James Box in Undercover User Experience Design suggest keeping a sense of humor for undercover testing. Things will go wrong. You're after quick input, not perfection. Undercover testing is the quickest way to learn something about the users, just take the results with a grain of salt.

Why run both lab and remote testing

Remember the yacht on international waters? Even if your budget is not that big, but not super tight either, you can run both lab and remote testing. However, why would you combine? Why not just maximize the number of remote tests and live a happy and easy life. It would mean much less administration, setup, and obviously much less time investment.

The main reason why I run both for larger projects is to reap the benefits of both solutions. In a lab, I can interview the users, ask questions, and see their facial expressions and hand movements. I can understand better why they do or expect certain things, and explore the subtleties of their behaviors. I can invite the stakeholders to sit in the observation room during the lab testing days. The lab itself adds an aura of professionalism and credibility to the whole research. Meeting face-to-face with users often give ideas on how to flesh out personas and model tasks and create better maps.

Remote testing will enable me to test with a much larger number of users, find many issues, and create priority lists. Usually, the users behave a bit differently in a lab compared to the remote tests they do at home. Watching and understanding both will lead to a closer understanding of the real behavior patterns. Remote and lab testing can complement each other and can lead to a deeper understanding of the users.

Rapid Iterative Testing and Evaluation (RITE)

RITE is the fastest way to create outstanding digital experiences. RITE is a testing method where you improve the prototype being tested between tests. In other words, you test with a user or a few users, and then update the solution being tested for the next test. This testing method was originally developed by Microsoft Studios, the video game production wing for Microsoft. Since 2002, it conquered quite a few industries and development teams.

You can use remote, lab, or guerrilla testing with RITE. I prefer remote testing for RITE because if you work with a company, featuring a larger panel, such as `WhatUsersDo.com` or `UserTesting.com`, most of the time you can get back the first videos within half an hour after launching the test. You can watch the video, improve the prototype with rapid prototyping methods, upload the new version, and test it again during the same day. If the changes are bigger, then you simply work some more and maybe continue testing the next day or the day after.

I prefer to launch the tests right before the end of my work day, so we can watch the videos first thing the next morning and start working on the next iteration. This is the fastest way to improve a solution, but it is a fairly advanced technique, and you need some routine in user testing and obviously rapid prototyping skills. Sometimes, you can even do RITE with a test version of a live site, updating the frontend code between tests. Some dedicated frontend developers might be needed for this.

RITE with remote testing, or RITER, is a perfect fit for the Kaizen-UX process. You can read more about that in `Chapter 11`, *Kaizen Mapping-UX Maps in Agile Product Management*.

 Instead of a RITER log, I have a RITER story. People prefer stories over logs for most purposes. Sysadmins might be notable exceptions. Now, if you are not a sysadmin, let me tell you my favorite RITER story. Back then, I was leading a consultancy. Now, if you are the director of a UX consultancy, you rarely have the luxury of running the full RITER process. Mainly, because it can be time-consuming and it might require your full attention for days. However, sometimes the project is so much fun that you can't resist. That's how I ended up running RITER for a large retailer's website redesign. I created the prototype in Axure and tweaked it between watching user testing videos with three of my new recruits. They were eager to learn, and I love teaching UX. Iteration after iteration, we modified the prototype, seeing how the users react. The RITER process took almost 2 weeks. The client was happy, and we called it a great success. The next project, for a smaller site, also required a prototype. We created it, then after watching just five videos, we started improving it. After two and a half days, the next prototype was done. At that point, one of the junior UX designers pointed out that the difference between the two prototypes of this project is much bigger than after the whole RITER process, which involved many prototype versions and took much longer. She was right. The thing is, UX projects are not measured by the number and scale of changes. They are measured by the impact those changes make. Sometimes, many microscopic changes will considerably improve the overall experience. Sometimes, you need to throw away what you have and rethink the whole approach. For the latter, RITER is still usable, just the first step will be much longer. If you have the time and budget, RITER is an amazing process, and good investment into the future of your solution, that is, improving the user experience.

RITE will not work for the example of this chapter, as redesigning a complex website is quite a long process. Even if we could use RITE, it would result in a very long chapter and quite a boring one. RITE is quite fun to do, but looks rather repetitive and boring if you read a log of a full RITE process.

How to test Samsung UK?

For this chapter's example, we will choose remote testing not only for simplicity's sake but also because we want users from all corners of the United Kingdom, not just within a reasonable distance from central London. We want our users to be in the same or similar environment where they normally are when searching for their next smartphone online.

If you don't want to spend a dime to test your dream solution with real users, most remote testing providers have some form of trial. Alternatively, you can just create a similar test design, but run the test the guerrilla way.

Remember, what matters the most is getting genuine feedback from real users. Any means and solutions to get feedback are great, as long as they lead to a better understanding of user behaviors and ultimately a better product.

How many test users?

When you have decided among lab, remote, and guerrilla testing, you face another tough decision: the number of testers.

One of the most debated questions of user experience testing is the number of test users needed for a test. In *Rocket Surgery Made Easy,* Steve Krug recommends three users in each round of testing. He claims that the first three users are likely to encounter many of the most significant problems related to the tasks you're testing. In *Don't Make Me Think!,* Krug compares one test with eight users, and two tests with three users. In the first case, he found five issues, whereas through the two tests with three users, he found nine problems in total.

In 2015, I conducted a remote user experience research experiment with 375 user testing sessions on the same website. User testing at that scale is a gargantuan task and an expensive one. However, that was the only way to make sure that we got a sample big enough to contain all user experience issues, even minuscule ones.

The bad news is to find all ($\approx$99.99966%) possible UX issues for a fairly complex e-commerce site, you need 250 tests. To be honest, that's only true for the exact website we tested, at that exact time. Since Q1 2015, both the website and the user behavior changed significantly.

The good news is in the real world you can get away with a lot less. I have calculated that just 46 tests will give you $\approx$93.3% of insights. This was a complex journey, touching many parts of a live website. If you test just one part of a website or a rather simple journey, you will need fewer tests for similar numbers.

I have demonstrated that you get diminishing returns on user tests if you go to a higher number. Although 46 tests gave us roughly 93% of the issues, we needed 76 for roughly 99%. So, with 30 additional tests, we found relatively few new issues.

My dedicated team found a total of 3,823 user experience issues after analyzing 375 videos. They ranged from minor annoyances to serious conversion blockers. Most of them were caused by a few core problems, and they were essentially variations of the same few user experience issues. Now, if you find so many issues, it's likely that you will only solve a small percentage of them in the next few weeks or months. While running many tests can help you to create a clear priority list, and focus on what's important, going above 75 is rarely justifiable. In fact, I would not recommend doing more than 46 videos in one sprint/iteration for each site or app you are testing.

46 users walk into a lab

However, 46 is still a much bigger number than 3 or 5. So, were Steve Krug, Jakob Nielsen, and numerous others wrong? Their claims are based on simple journeys, usually from around 2000, when websites were less complex. Back then, websites were only viewed on desktop computers. Nowadays, there is a wide range of devices from tiny smartphones, phablets, tablets, laptops to 40 inch+ 4K smart TVs.

When you run lab tests, the number of users is limited by your budget and time. In my experience, it's almost impossible to run more than five lab tests a day, with the same team, and the same lab, even five is a stretch. I usually aim for two in the first day, as a pilot. Then, three or four on the next days, depending on the complexity of the test. I will get back to pilot tests later in this chapter, but it's essentially a trial of the test design with the aim to improve. Lab tests are expensive and time-consuming. If you need an external agency to run your lab tests, you could easily end up paying £25,000 or more for a week's worth of testing and the subsequent analysis, with about 15 users. However, there are agencies asking for a 100-1000 or more for a week in a lab. So, lab testing with 46 users would be really costly and time-consuming. This leads to remote testing as the usual solution when you want to test with a bigger number of users.

 The number of tests you need depends on the complexity of the journey, the number of devices you target, and how many issues you can fix in a sprint or for the next version of your solution. The number of test users is the biggest factor to the time needed for analyzing the results. It's pointless to run a test with 50 users if you don't have time to watch and analyze all 50 videos.

In an ideal world, you would solve a few issues, then test again after they got fixed. So, you would keep the number of tests in each iteration low, improve, then test again. In reality, there can be weeks or even months between finding an issue and solving it, especially at larger corporations. The UX teams can be miles apart from the product team (sometimes even continents apart), and communication can be challenging. There are numerous occasions when you want to find as many issues as possible and warn the organization about them. For example, if you are an external consultant, contractor, or you need to build a strong business case to ignite action. Moreover, sheer numbers can and will provide justification and validity while certainly looking great. Imagine a business case where it is written that *one out of five users tested could not use the date picker*. Compare this with *for 19.46% of the users, the date picker was a conversion blocker based on a remote user research; sample size 46*. Which would resonate better with senior management? Which is more likely to result in an immediate action?

A small sample size can also be a trap. Three users can find UX issues that are conversion killers for only a handful of users in the real world, and you might miss other issues that are a lot more common. This leads to wrong prioritization and can even shake the belief in UX or your abilities as a UX expert. Finding and solving critical user experience issues can bring a measurable increase in conversions and mean more money for the company. Treat user experience tests as an investment in the future of your solution.

In the early phases of your project, you can run some quick, small sample size tests, with five to ten users. This should be enough for a basic understanding of the users and to validate your initial idea. You can create the user story map before this and update it based on the findings from the test, or right after this small initial test.

> *In 2011, FatFace.com observed an increase in mobile traffic. They redesigned their e-commerce site to be responsive. The new, redesigned version was live in Q1 2012, and the mobile conversion rate dropped. Smartphone users were less likely to buy anything from the mobile-friendly web store. The people behind Fat Face were stunned by this. However, they did the right thing: remote user experience testing. The very first WhatUsersDo video solved the puzzle. It showed a guy trying to pinch-zoom to see the details of the jeans he was about to buy. Pinch-zoom didn't work, so he was not able to see any details, any larger view. Obviously, he was not comfortable buying a clothing item he couldn't clearly see. In the following screenshot, you can see a frame from the video, showing the user's fingers on his phone, trying the usual gesture in vain:*

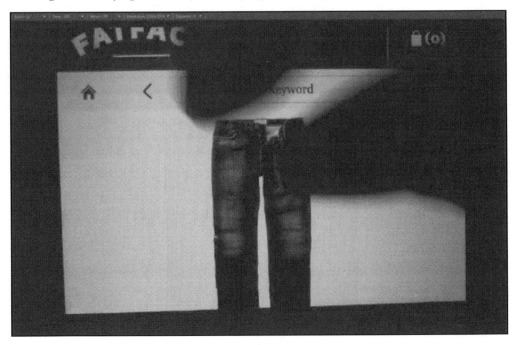

Sometimes, just one video is enough to find the most critical, most pressing issue. The subsequent videos showed this issue again and again. The users were so frustrated that they paid little attention to more subtle issues. There is little point in watching more users struggle with the same obvious conversion killer.

Fix the critical issues and then order some more videos to uncover other issues masked by a few striking conversion killers.

Finding the right users

After deciding the number of users, you need to select your users. You can use an external recruitment company or your existing users, but the easiest, most convenient, and often the best solution is to use the tester panel of your remote testing provider. Most big platforms, such as WhatUsersDo.com or UserTesting.com, have panels with thousands of users, essentially guaranteeing that you will quickly find 10,20, or 40 users matching your criteria. If you are using a small start-up as a testing solution, or your own remote-testing hack with a communication tool, such as Skype, then jump to the private panel section of this chapter. A private panel will enable you to use your existing users among other sources. For now, we assume that you are using the panel of your testing platform.

 Don't try to find users matching your personas. Personas, as we have seen, are fictitious characters, and they simply don't exist in the real world. Some testers still try hard to find close representations for them among the test users; that is a mistake.

Try testing with a broad audience and try to find as many usability issues as possible. You might even end up improving the personas after the analysis of the tests. Remember, personas should be based on real user testing. Real users should not be recruited based on personas.

Devices

At first sight, the question of devices is simple. For iOS apps, you only need to test on iPads and iPhones, maybe Apple Watch or iPod touch. The logical answer seems to be to test on every device on which your app runs. Most of the time you want it to run on as many devices as possible, within the resource limitations of the project.

The problem escalates for websites, web apps, or when your solution runs in a browser. A few years ago most people browsed the web on a computer screen. Most of the time, there were two or three dominant browsers. Most people had a landscape monitor with a horizontal resolution from 800, but more likely from 1024 to 1920 pixels wide. We never really cared much about the vertical resolution, because vertical scrolling was easy, especially when all mice started to gain a vertical scroll button. Yes, we wanted to put things as high as possible, to make sure that people will be able to see it without the need to scroll. We called this made-up area *above the fold*. Studies proved that there is a low chance people will see things that are below the fold, and even if they do, they will consider it less important.

Nowadays, there is a wide variety of devices and screen resolutions people use to interact with our website or web app. Some people even use their smartwatches to browse the web and some others use a 70 inch or bigger smart TV at 4K resolution (3840×2160). I firmly believe that the number of devices we use to access the Internet will increase in the next decade--maybe head-mounted augmented reality devices, large screens on our smartphone, hopefully self-driving cars, or something completely different. Moreover, we can already use a great variety of input devices: the traditional keyboard and mouse combo, a game controller, touch screens with gestures, and obviously our voice. I believe that soon we will be able to use our mind to control computers. The technology is already here, just impractical and expensive for widespread use. This will change in a few years.

So, why do remote testing providers restrict the device choice to three categories: desktop, smartphone, and tablet? The first reason is simplicity. Most people think in those categories when talking about websites. Frontend developers also target those device types first. Most of the time there will be no special rules written for other devices. For example, in 2016 4K displays became more popular, but they were rarely targeted by CSS media queries or other means to create device-tailored experiences.

The other reason is to protect the researcher from a common mistake, that is, being too specific with device targeting. For example, if you are looking for users owning a Samsung Galaxy S7 edge smartphone, you might miss issues that are only present on older Android devices or iPhones. Getting a random sample of devices can lead to the discovery of bugs and glitches that the developers never encountered.

 Remote user testing is not meant to be a replacement for a device lab, or the solution to test a site for most devices, but it can still reveal bugs. It can provide a strong business case to have an on-site or external device lab with as many devices as possible.

Another reason is panel size. While most remote user testing companies have a panel of thousands of users, if you restrict it to a specific device type, such as Nokia Lumia 920, the number of users might be low, maybe lower than the number of tests you want to run. Alternatively, you can look at a more popular and broader category, such as any Samsung smartphone user. You can follow with specifying an age range. Then you can continue with a pre-screener--a question the users need to answer before being admitted to a test. For example, you can screen for users planning to buy a new phone in the next three months. At that point, you will still end up with lots of users. The problem is, who are you missing out? You will certainly miss those users' voices who had other brand phones, outside of your specified age range, or who don't plan to buy a new phone during the next 3 months. Is their opinion irrelevant? Would they be able to contribute to a better user experience? The results of their tests lead to a better map, and ultimately a better product.

If you need to test users having a specific device, you can screen the panel for the users of that device. If it's a really uncommon device, you might want to test with a private panel and recruit testers who own the device or run a lab test. In some extreme cases, you might even ship out the device to the testers. I would not recommend a lab test where the users see the device for the first time unless you test the device itself. For example, if we want to test Samsung's website on a Windows Phone, it would be much better to recruit Windows Phone users, instead of inviting someone into your lab and giving them a Windows Phone.

Target audience

Nowadays, everyone and their cat has a smartphone, so finding the right users seems trivial. Just ask everyone, right?

Well, that would be everyone from the UK, because we are testing Samsung UK. Samsung's American or South Korean site can and should be different than the British one. Even beyond the possibly different language and currency, experiences are different from one country to another. It is possible to create a high-level "global" journey map, but the execution should be tailored based on country-specific research, a research with real users from the given country.

Unless you have a good reason to do so, I would not run a test with only one gender, or a really restricted age-range. You want the audience to be as broad as possible. Even if you are selling women's clothing, running the test with 16 women and 4 men can be beneficial. Some men do buy women's clothing. Not just those who want to wear them, but maybe as a gift or because their significant other asked them to do so.

British panel recruitment agencies and remote testing platforms, such as WhatUsersDo, tend to have another user categorization: socio-economic grouping. This demographic classification is based on the occupation of the head of the household. The grades are then grouped into ABC1 (middle class) and C2DE (working class). Around 2% of the UK population can be identified as upper class, and they are underrepresented in remote testing panels. To be fair, if you are an upper-class citizen, it's unlikely that you would spend your time testing websites for a few quid. This doesn't mean that you can't find some who will do it for fun. Most of the time, ABC1 is a good group to test even luxury products. For example, WhatUsersDo's panel was used to test Burberry's or Maserati's websites, and many actionable insights were found from watching ABC1 users interacting with those sites.

Pre-screener

Some tests require a more specific audience. To find those users, you need a pre-screener or pre-qualifying question. The idea is simple--the system asks a question from the user before the test. If the user gives the answer you are after, they can do the test. Otherwise, the system will look for another user.

For example, if we want to test with people who already have a Samsung smartphone, we could ask: Do you own a Samsung smartphone? This is a bad pre-screener because people could lie to get into the test. A much better one would be as follows:

```
What brand of smartphone do you currently own? (choose all, if you have
more than one phone:
[-] Apple
[-] Huawei
[-] LG
[+] Samsung
[-] Xiaomi
[-] Other / I don't know
[-] None of the above applies to me / I'd rather not say
```

In this example, only the Samsung owners would get into the test. Obviously, we don't want such a narrow audience, so we will not use a pre-screener.

Most of the time, the best thing you can do is to avoid a pre-screener and go with a broad audience. A pre-screener is still a better idea than surveying the panel. That will prolong the test, exclude many users whose test results could have uncovered issues, and probably even cost you extra money--so, *avoid pre-test panel surveys.*

If you really need to create a pre-screener, I have a few tips for you:

- Ask simple, easy-to-answer questions, which can be replied to objectively.
- Avoid polar questions (yes/no questions), transform them into multiple choice questions instead.
- Give objective answer choices. Instead of *I often watch videos on my phone*, it's better to say *I watch videos on my phone at least once a day.*
- Don't start with the qualifying options, and try to hide your intentions as much as possible. Remember, you want people to tell you the truth, not a lie to get into the test.
- Add more non-qualifying answers than qualifying. If most answers are qualifying, then you should consider removing the pre-screener instead. An example for this is if you ask the brand of the smartphone just to find out who don't own a smartphone. It would be better to avoid the question. If someone who doesn't own a smartphone gets into the test, you can treat that test differently and separately, but you can still learn from it.
- Always end with an opt-out answer. The default opt-out is usually something like *None of the above applies to me I'd rather not say.*

Don't overdo the number of answers. Usually, seven is enough. Remember, people need to read all answers. If you need to have more than seven answers, ask the users to "select the first true answer" instead.

Often a test design is better without a pre-qualifying question, but not always. For a test we ran a few years ago, we were looking for people who work in healthcare or related professions and people who were recruiters for healthcare. We created the following pre-screener, and it worked flawlessly:

```
Please select the first true answer.
[-] I am not currently employed
[-] I work in recruitment for energy, oil and gas
[-] I work in recruitment for IT
[+] I work in recruitment for healthcare
[-] I work in recruitment for accounting
[-] I work in energy, oil and gas and related professions
[-] I work in IT and related professions
[+] I work in healthcare and related professions
```

```
[-] I work in accounting and related professions
[-] I prefer not to answer / none of the choices applies to me
```

In the next chapter, we will see another example where a pre-screener can be helpful. Even in situations where the screener might seem needed, you might end up getting too few users, or none at all as a result. In those situations, try running the test without the pre-screener. You might be surprised at how insightful that can be.

Private panel

For some projects, you could be looking for IT decision makers at medium- to large-sized companies. For example, if you wanted to sell rack-mountable switches, even if you craft a screener for this, chances are that it will not find any users. This means you need a private panel. For other projects, you want to run the test with your actual users--for example, testing an employee-only website or the user account section of a public website.

This needs some extra work on your part, but most remote testing platforms will help you. Basically, you need a list of e-mail addresses from people who agreed to participate in the test. Then, the magic is done by the platform, to make sure that they can do it properly.

 Remember, just because some of your users agreed to take the test, by clicking a link in an e-mail, for example, they might not do it. If they try, they might have technical difficulties, low-quality recording with inaudible voice, or other issues. Some will do the test, but will not tell you their thoughts or do it in total silence. As a rule of thumb, *invite at least four times as many people as you actually need*. So if you want to test with 20 people, invite 80, or better 100.

Private panel tests take longer to fill, instead of hours, days, or even a week might pass until all users will do the test.

If your chosen remote testing platform doesn't support the language or country you are targeting, the private panel might seem to be the only option. Even then, it's worth contacting their support, maybe they can offer a solution, which is easier and hassle-free.

Moderated versus unmoderated tests

In a lab, the facilitator sits next to the user, who will read the tasks, and help if the user gets hopelessly stuck, for example, if the Wi-Fi is not working, the lights go out, or the recording software crashes. For remote tests, the user encounters the facilitator as a voice. This voice can also read the tasks and help with fixing technical issues.

The main purpose of the facilitator is to ask questions; to explore why some things are harder to understand. The facilitator observes the test. They should not interfere with the user's natural journey--well, unless the user is stuck, lost, or has technical difficulties. This can be hard, especially if the facilitator is attached to the solution.

 The facilitator should not take notes during the test. This is why the tests are recorded. Moreover, the observers can take notes, and sometimes even transmit their questions to the facilitator. However, if the facilitator takes notes, their attention is split, while they should be focusing on the user.

The most important task of the facilitator is to encourage users to *think aloud*. The think aloud protocol means that the users will describe what they are doing and why. A good facilitator and test design goes beyond that and asks users about their expectations, impressions, and feelings.

The obvious drawback of moderated tests is the increased cost and execution time. It increases your overhead in the logistics. The success of the test can greatly depend on the facilitator. Moderated tests are also hard to scale for the same reason. Unmoderated tests free up a team member for the duration of the test, so they can work on analyzing other tests, improving the map or any other task.

Replicability will always be a challenge for moderated tests. With RITER or other continuous testing and improvement methods, you want to run the same test again on the improved version of your solution. With unmoderated tests, it's easier for one test to be similar to the previous. I'm not saying that RITE can't be run with a facilitator, just that I prefer not to.

The main reason why I almost never run moderated tests is that they are not natural. How often do you use a website while someone is watching you and telling you what to do, then asks questions about why you did it? Most likely never, unless you are married to a product designer.

For the above reasons, we will do remote unmoderated tests for Samsung. This will also make it easier for you to follow along, as an added benefit.

The scenario

After deciding to run unmoderated remote tests, you need to come up with a testing scenario. *How does the adventure of your user starts?* Have you ever played a great role playing or adventure game? Something like *Dungeons & Dragons* with a few friends on a tabletop or *Mass Effect: Andromeda* on your computer or console. *Think of Eye of the Beholder, Grim Fandango, Quest For Glory, or Baldur's Gate*. What's your favorite? You might remember those because of the great story. They created a truly epic adventure, with a great scenario at its core.

> The scenario helps users imagine themselves in the tested situation. It is fundamental to obtain information that's relevant, natural, and in the moment.

Contrary to a book or a game, to set the scenario for a test you have a couple of sentences, ideally one. If you write a short story before the test, most people would not read it. Also, contrary to most games and books, you should anchor the scenario in the user's life. *Imagine, you have died, and now you are in the Land of the Dead*--this would certainly be an unexpected scenario for a user test, yet it is a brilliant scenario for the highly acclaimed game Grim Fandango from 1998. Instead of something shocking, try shockingly simple and natural. My approach would be *Imagine that you lost your phone, and want to buy a new one.* This scenario naturally leads to tasks, such as *Explore Samsung's website to find a smartphone you would consider buying. Gather as much information about it, as you would normally need before buying a smartphone.*

When creating the scenario, avoid any suggestions or hints about your expectations. Try to be neutral. The best case scenario is if the user doesn't know you are in any way interested in the project, beyond the test. Never say our website, our solution, or anything possessive, really. If the testers think you are somehow attached to the solution, they will not be as honest. You want them to be critical, to be brutally honest. They should not care about your feelings, or anyone's feelings when working on the project. You want their own feelings. If it's not working, you want them to be harsh. If it does, you want them to nitpick minor issues--never aim for a polite answer, even if the CEO is in the observation room.

Remember to ask users to visit the website or give instructions on getting to the solution if it's not a website. Also, double-check the URL before launching the test. For example, `http://www.samsung.com/uk/` is the right URL for Samsung's current UK site. Most test designers copy and paste the URL from the address bar. Make sure to test the URL before launching the test. Even if you copied and pasted it, testing the URL might save your test, and it takes only a click.

You can play into the imagination of your users, and have them help with the scenario. Be vague, and let the user imagine most of the situation. This will lead to the most life-like tests.

Writing tasks and questions

The scenario alone might be enough for a moderated lab test with an experienced moderator. However, even there it would result in tests that are hard to analyze, summarize, and repeat. For remote unmoderated testing, good pre-written tasks and questions will unearth many usability issues.

Tasks require an action from the user, while questions require an answer. Both can be used for user testing. Questions are optional and a good task list will help the moderator; it's an absolute necessity for remote unmoderated tests.

As with any form of communication, try to use simple words, and don't overwhelm the user. Design tasks and questions that result in a relatively short, up to 18 minutes test. Yes, the same length as a TED talk, for the same reason. A test should be long enough to uncover the most pressing usability issues and short enough to hold the user's attention.

Try to design a test which you could complete in 6 minutes tops. It will take at least twice if not three times as much for the real user with think aloud protocol. This usually means two to five tasks and zero to three questions. My experience is that there is a negative correlation between the length of a test and how actionable the results are. Users will feel cheated if it's a long test, and rightly so. Most people will not spend 40 minutes on your site unless they open it and then decide to cook dinner instead. Why would you force them to be bored by your site?

Try to be clear, concise, and guide users step by step, without telling them what to do or where to click.

When running the pilot test for the mobile prototype for a fashion brand's website, we wanted the user to use the burger menu to navigate, as the other options were not prototyped. So, we gave them the following task: Now, using the burger menu, find something you would genuinely consider buying on our site. This is an early test version of our site, a prototype. So, most things will not work. We also gave instruction on where to find it [If you can't find the burger menu, it's in the top left, the one with the three horizontal lines icon.] This is a terrible task, written in haste, without much of a consideration. Fortunately, we run a pilot with more than one user. The first user got the idea and used the burger menu as intended. However, the second one was outraged. "Why would I buy a burger from a clothing site? If you want to sell burgers, open a restaurant, and make a new site for it", he exclaimed. The pilot tests (more on them later) saved our research and showed a typical test design error. Even if everyone in the development team knows what a burger menu is, your users might not. This could totally derail a test, even to a point where it needs to be repeated. So, don't use words such as header, div, radio button, input, or AJAX. Also, don't call them thingies or stuff. Just describe the elements with simple words. Best case scenario, don't give tasks which refer to a single object on the site. Instead give the users broader tasks, wherever possible.

When writing the task, remember that users haven't seen your wireflows, they have no idea about how your site works and often don't know the technical language.

Asking for opinions and expectations

Questions enhance the test design, as long as you ask for opinions and expectations. Don't test their knowledge and especially not their patience with many pointless questions.

Avoid leading questions and polar questions (yes or no questions). Closed answer questions restrain the users to what we think will be true; open-ended questions will help us discover things we wouldn't imagine. Instead of starting with *Is this page clear for you?*, you should try, *What are your first impressions when you look at this page?*

NN/g has a great blog post about open-ended versus close-ended questions. I would suggest reading that article at: `https://www.nngroup.com/articles/open-ended-questions/` The table with close-ended questions, and how to replace them with open-ended ones is a good starting point.

You should ask for expectations on a page or interaction before users actually see it. If you ask after they see it, the users will most likely say that what they see is what they have expected to see. As users move through the journey, they shape their ideas accordingly. They adapt their perception to what they see, and their behaviors can and will change. Asking *is this what you expected?* at the end of a test is useless. Users are rarely able to remember whether they were surprised at the beginning of the journey.

In order to have opinions and expectations, the users need to have a clear picture of the scenario. This is why it's important to set a good, easy to remember scenario.

When we test, we are mostly interested in observing behaviors, so don't turn user testing into a video survey.

Privacy concerns

The users should always have the possibility of using fake details, instead of their real names, address, or other details. When needed, provide fake credit card details, test accounts, or any other similar measures. If you can't, add "Stop before entering credit card or other payment details." to any task which might lead to such action. It helps to reassure the users that we're not trying to steal money from them. We should never ask users to record their real credit card or bank details.

If users are required to enter passwords or sensitive personal information, you can ask them to pause the screen recorder while doing so. Remind them to resume recording as soon as they have finished entering that information, and the information is no longer visible on the screen. Ideally, you should provide users with the fake credit card details if such things are required for the test.

When I'm prototyping and there are privacy concerns from the client, I use logo placeholders, instead of real logos. Moreover, I tend to not show any branding elements, unless necessary for the user experience test.

This works the other way around too. Although testers usually sign a non-disclosure agreement, don't share any secrets with them in a remote test. Remember, the users can take photos, screenshots, or even their own video recording.

Exit questions and exit surveys

The exit question is usually not recorded on the video, and the user will only hear or see it after finishing all tasks. I would avoid exit surveys altogether. You should ask questions during the test, in the moment, not after. I would ask a maximum of one question. The only exit questions I'm not completely against are short and easy to reply.

My favorite exit question is, *How likely is it that you would recommend this site/app/solution to a friend or colleague?* Yes, this is the standard **Net Promoter Score** (**NPS**) question. After this, users are presented with a scale of 0 to 10 to select from. This will enable us to categorize them in three categories: promoters (9-10), detractors (0-6), and passives (7-8). Net Promoter Score is a KPI for many organizations to measure customer satisfaction. Ask this after your test. This can help you understand why certain users give you a specific score, and how to increase your overall NPS.

Test script for our smartphone buying journey

You can use this task list as an example, and a starting point for your own tasks. You might need to modify it slightly if you want to run a guerrilla or lab test instead of the remote test.

Start the screen recorder. Ensure that you follow every instruction and speak your thoughts as you do so. Remember, we are testing the site, not you.

Imagine that you lost your phone, and want to buy a new one:

1. Which website would you visit first, if you wanted to buy a new smartphone? You can briefly show us that website. Why do you like it?
2. Now, go to http://www.samsung.com/uk/. What are your first impressions when you look at this page? Please comment on the layout and the design.
3. Explore Samsung's website, and find a smartphone you would consider buying.
4. Gather as much information about the phone, as you would normally need before buying a smartphone.

5. Now proceed to buy the phone, but please stop before entering your name, address, credit card details, or any other personal information.
6. Find a cover, case, or other protection you would normally buy for the smartphone you have chosen.
7. If you had a magic wand, how would you improve Samsung's website?

This concludes our test, thank you for your participation. You can now stop the screen recorder.

The pilot test

Instead of launching a test for all our users, I would recommend a pilot test. This means trying our test with just one or two users.

The pilot test is usually done during the first day of a lab test. You just invite two participants with maybe a third as a backup plan, just in case one or both do not turn up. Two tests will not take the whole working day, so you could use the rest of the day to improve and correct the test, based on how smoothly the pilots run.

With remote testing, it's even simpler as we will see in the next section. Just launch the test with a user, watch the resulting video, and correct the test design if needed. This can be done in two or three hours tops, and then you can launch the improved test. When you launch the pilot for a remote test, chances are, you will have some users who are online and willing to take the test if your user base is broad enough. Of course, if you are only interested in corporate treasurers with five cats, you may need to wait considerably more. Or ideally, reconsider your profiling criteria.

Testing with WhatUsersDo.com

WhatUsersDo.com is an innovative remote user experience testing platform from the UK. In the past few years, I used them for most of my remote testing, and they never fail to deliver high-quality user testing videos within hours. Oh, and I used to be UX director at WhatUsersDo until 2015. It was great fun! Oh, the good old days…

Anyhow, let's use the platform to set up and launch the test we designed in this chapter. After logging in, you simply have to click on the big red **Start a test** button:

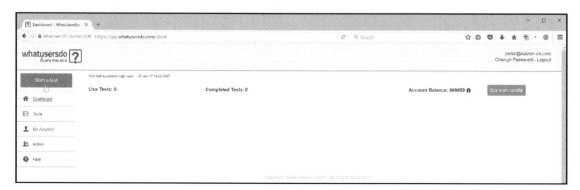

Starting a new test

Giving your test a meaningful, detailed title will help you later. When you have many tests on the platform, the titles can help you to easily identify older tests:

Deciding a title for your test

For a pilot, I usually choose just one or two desktop users, with *any* in all dropdowns, except the country. If your targeted country is not on the list, you can use a private panel, or contact your remote panel. Most of the time, they can help you, even if the country is not listed among the supported countries:

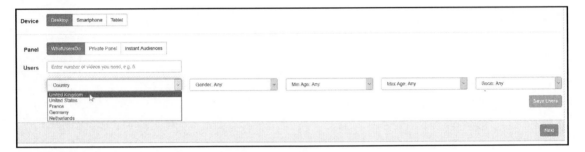

Now, save your first and only user group for the pilot:

You can have as many user groups as you wish. For example, if you want to test with 10 users, 50% women, you would create two user groups, one with 5 females, and another with 5 males:

Finalizing the details for the test

Now that you selected your users, click on **Next**--it will lead to the **Test Script** tab. Here, you can set a pre-screener question to filter the panel even more, but for most tests, you want to avoid doing that. Instead, we start with the scenario, by clicking on the **Set a Scenario** button from the list on the left:

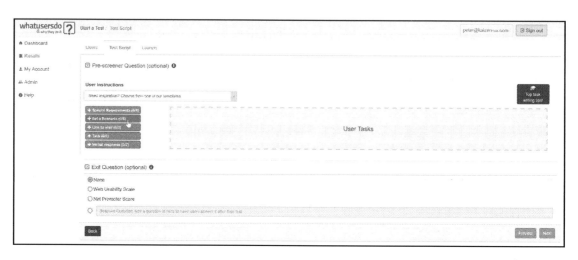

Available instruction types: special requirements, set a scenario, link to visit, task, verbal response

You need to type in the scenario. You don't need to start with *Please make sure you follow every instruction and speak your thoughts as you do so. Remember, we are testing the site, not you.* That is something WhatUsersDo panel members already know. It is part of their induction. If somehow they don't follow the think aloud protocol, you can replace the video. You will get a new user for free:

Setting a scenario

Using the task list elements from the left, you can recreate our written task list from the previous section. Don't forget to test any links you add with the **Open Link** option on the top right of the box (It will open the link in a new tab):

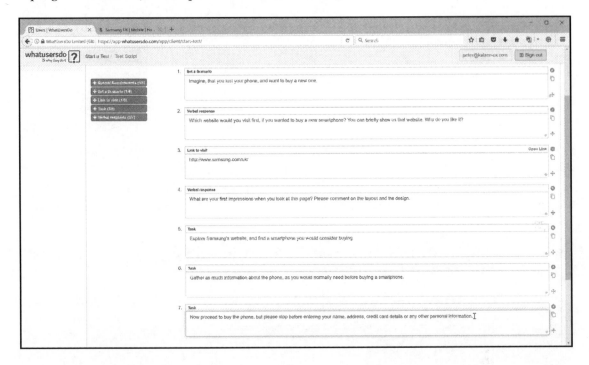

Adding tasks

After adding all tasks, you can add an exit question. This question will not be recorded on the video, and the user will only see it after finishing all tasks. If you choose a bespoke question, the users will need to type in their answer, so I would avoid it. You could simply ask all your questions during the video. Instead, I would suggest **Net Promoter Score**. After setting the exit question, you could go to the **Launch** tab or better, you can see the tasks the way the users will, using the **Preview** button:

I would encourage you to preview your tasks before launching the test by clicking on **Next** > until you arrive at the last task or question:

When you are happy with your tasks and after reviewing them, you can proceed to the final tab, the **Launch**. This tab gives you an overview of the test you are about to launch, with all user groups and the full test script:

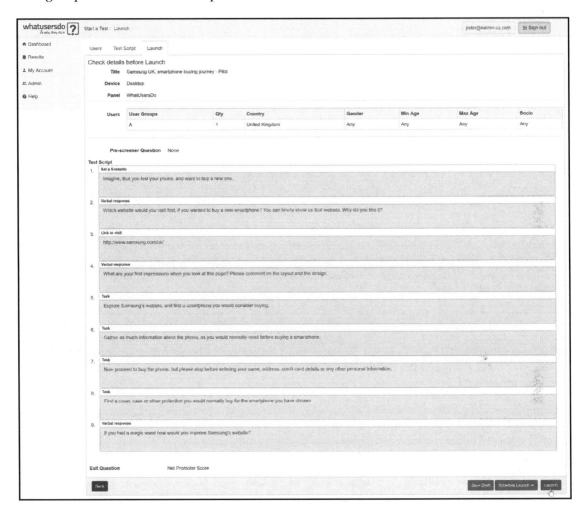

Checking the details of the test before launch

Now, you should be ready to launch the test. After pressing the **Launch** button, you should see a confirmation. Although there is a **Schedule Launch** option, I always want to start my tests as soon as I'm done designing them. I would also avoid automatically repeating the same test, even with RITER. Just launch it again manually for each iteration:

The testers will see your tests and they can start it, right after you have launched it. It will also appear as a live test on your dashboard:

The test we just launched appears on the dashboard

If you launched with just one user, it will complete shortly after, even if you launch tests outside of normal working hours. This chapter's example pilot was launched at 23:17 and it was completed at 23:30. (When I wrote this book, I was working full time as a corporate senior manager, so had to work on the book during the evenings, but I would not suggest launching tests late at night. You and your users might be tired, and this can reduce the quality on both ends.)

When the test is completed, you should click on the **View Results** button:

The results are obviously **Videos**, which you can play. The **Metrics** will not be relevant for the pilot with just a single user:

Now, watch the video. In the next chapter, we will learn how to tag or analyze the video. For now, you should just watch it, the way you would watch a user, peaking over their shoulder:

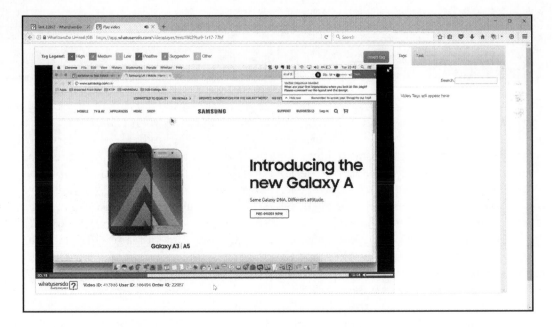

You can watch my video at `https://app.whatusersdo.com/tMks` or better, record yours. When watching a pilot, you should focus on the shortcomings of your test design. Did the user misunderstand any of your questions? Did you forget to ask anything, which might be important?

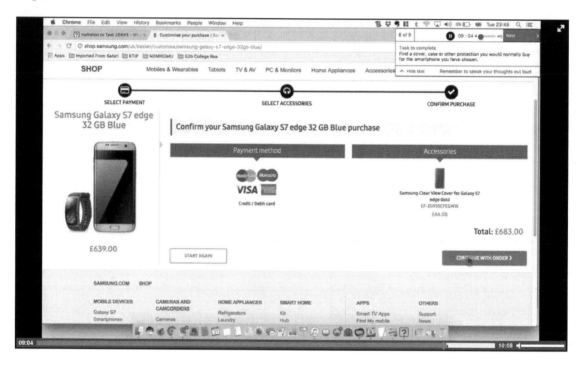

Watching user testing videos is not just for UX or product teams. You can involve everyone in it. A famous example is *AO.com's Pizza Fridays.* You can follow their example too, or even copy the idea as it is. All you need is cartloads of pizzas for all employees, a large room, and big screens showing remote testing videos. This way everyone from senior managers to warehouse staff will be exposed to the users. They will see what the users do on your website, app, or other solution. This will lead to true user-centric products. When things work, and the users have positive or even "wow" moments, all can celebrate and have a sense of achievement. This will also help user experience to become an integral part of the organization. I believe, that in a few decades, UX as an independent team will disappear, instead, like "digital teams" in marketing, user-centricity will be a prerequisite for all teams. Some companies, such as Amazon, already expect all their managers to start with the customer and work backward. Being obsessed with the customer is in Amazon's DNA, and not in small part contributed to the e-commerce giant's success. Everyone working for your organization should work vigorously to earn and keep customer trust. Maybe this will start with a pizza on a Friday. Can you make it happen this Friday?

Summary

To deliver outstanding digital experiences, user-centricity should be part of your corporate culture. Watching users struggle with your solution, and seeing how they behave on competing sites is the first step to understanding and acceptance.

The test-driven user experience process will provide a genuine competitive advantage, as we will see in the last chapter of this book. Recording users will help to understand and communicate user experience issues, even before the implementation of Kaizen-UX or other tailor-made methodologies.

In this chapter, we designed a test. In the next one, we will analyze videos, and do much more than that. Are you ready to turn remote user testing videos into actionable experience maps? Are you ready for the one-and-only silver bullet in product design? Get closer to your users in the next chapter!

6

Solution Mapping Based on User Insights

In the previous chapter, we learned how to design and run tests with real users. In this one, we will continue our epic adventure to understand the users. We will analyze videos and create maps based on the results. We will also design a unique experience tailored to our user's needs.

 A solution map is a tool that will help us find solutions and communicate them. They are visual representations of an actionable project plan. Ideally, solution maps should be based on user testing sessions with real users.

To graphically *solve a real-world business problem*, we will do the following things:

- Start with a new opportunity, showcasing a new test design and an exciting problem to be solved.
- Tag the remote user testing videos. This means watching them and analyzing what we see, highlighting the user insights. To tag, we need to do the following things:
    - Know what to tag
    - Write good tag titles and comments
    - Select the tag type, with the help of the behaviorist issue severity model
- Summarize our tags, finding patterns, and common pain points.
- Create a solution map, following a five-step process.
- Finally, put the solution map to action.

What's your business problem? Can we solve it together?

Contiki adventure

We could have continued with the preceding chapter's opportunity. However, when I started working on this book, I decided to give you 11 opportunities. In all, 11 different projects, to showcase how versatile user experience mapping can be, not just to show you various applications of mapping, but also to ignite your creativity. In this chapter, our opportunity will also have another test design example. I believe that this chapter's example will help you to understand the preceding chapter a bit better. Now, let's start the adventure.

Contiki is a travel company, specializing in vacations for 18-35 year olds. One of our personas is *Adam, the Adventure Seeker*. He needs inspiration. We want to find a new and exciting way to inspire our users.

We could create a big searchable database with all possible adventure travel destinations. Would that be the most exciting way to find an adventure? Would Adam's friends share that link on social media? Would Adam consider that as a boring way? What would work? To find an answer to that question, we need to run some tests with real users. Then, we will analyze the test to create the solution map.

To make our job easier and faster, in the first iteration, we run the test with only five users. Remember that we need many consecutive iterations and a continuous improvement process to create outstanding digital experiences. However, every process starts somewhere. This process begins with the initial five users. They are selected from 18-35 year olds belonging to the ABC1 socioeconomic group because that's our target audience.

Users selected for testing					
Qty Users	Device	Country	Gender	Age	Socio
5	Desktop/laptop	United Kingdom	Any	18 - 35	A, B, C1

We want people who seek adventure when they travel. In the previous chapter, we avoided a pre-screener. In this one, we will use checkboxes for the pre-screener. Checkboxes represent a special screener type, where the user can select all answers that apply to them.

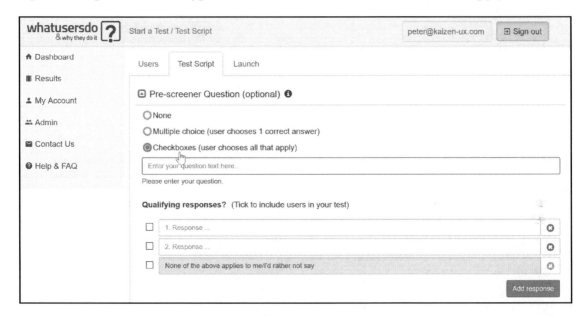

Adventure seekers are hard to define as a group. So, I left the definition to the user. For some people finding a good hotel with strong Wi-Fi is a true adventure. Those people will probably not define themselves as adventure seekers. It's possible that someone is both budget conscious and an adventure seeker, or looking for culinary pleasures as well as adventure. If the user selected, they get into the test, even if they selected other answers as well.

Advanced Profile

Question: How would you describe your holiday planning? What's important for you, when searching for a travel destination?

Show 10 entries   Search: [   ]

Answer	Qualify Answer	No of Answers
I'm budget conscious, I usually look for the best deal when traveling.	No	7
I'm an adventure seekers, looking for the adventure wherever I go.	Yes	7
I'm a foodie, looking for great food and culinary pleasures.	No	2
I just want to take great photos to post on Instagram, Facebook or other social network.	No	0
I'm inexperienced. I haven't travelled outside of UK before.	No	0
None of the above applies to me/I'd rather not say	No	0

This pre-qualifying question is terrible, to be honest. Don't ask questions like this in a survey, or if you want to pose as a respectable qualitative researcher or better, don't ask pre-screeners at all. So why did I do it? To make sure that the test will be fun for my audience. If you want to test a car with real users, ask them whether they want to test a car. Those who don't will probably feel terrible if you force them to do so, not to mention they might not even know how to drive.

I started with a simple scenario **Imagine, that you want to go to an adventure abroad**, which naturally led to the test design. For the test script, I have opted for a lightweight, easy-to-do task list. First, I wanted to see how the users normally search for an adventure holiday. We are interested in what other sites they choose, and what they do on those sites--not to copy the sites, but to create a better, unique experience.

Then, I gave them a task to see how they use Contiki's existing site. Contiki provides awesome adventures, and the site is visually pleasing while not hard to use. We will see how to make the experience even better.

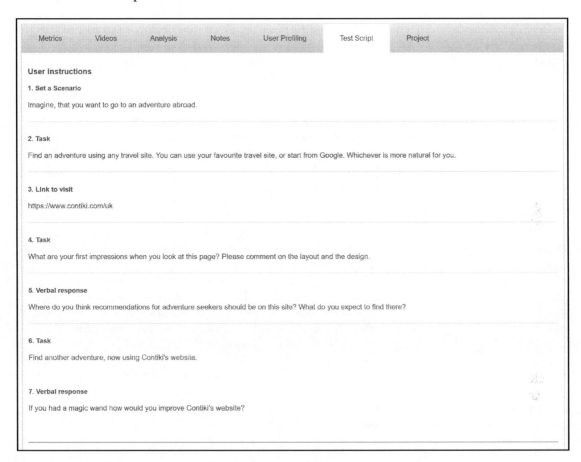

You should be familiar with designing and launching tests from the preceding chapter. I would encourage you to create your own test scripts and run your own test. The most important advice I have is to keep the test script short and simple. My script didn't produce any videos longer than 11 minutes, and the shortest was less than 6 minutes.

Tagging - the science of active watching

We could just watch the videos passively, as we do with a *Game of Thrones* episode. We would surely have fun and learn from it. Chances are, we will not see any dragons or dire wolves in user testing videos. Instead, we might see much scarier things, such as conversion blockers. They are UX issues slaughtering the well-crafted user experience, leading to abandonment; in other words, they are so bad that the users will leave our site.

An even better way to watch user testing videos is called **tagging** in the UX research lingo.

 Tagging is a form of insight identification for user testing videos. As a result, short video snippets are created, with a textual description and a quick scaling, based on the issue severity model. Those tags create an independent multi-voice view on the whole experience. They help us to jump straight to the issues and easily spot trends across a set of tests.

Tagging provides a hidden ace up my sleeve. The video short snippets pack a real punch when you want to convince stakeholders. They will help you to communicate the issues by showing them. They incite quick action. They can help you to get more budget for your team, and thus you can do some more user testing.

The benefits of tags are unmistakable when you need to communicate with your clients. Maybe you work for an agency, or the internal UX team works similarly to the agency-client model. Tags will allow your clients to jump straight to the issues, saving them time and resources. They will not need to watch hours of footage, just a few short clips.

Although tagging is important, tags will not solve your problems. They don't provide recommendations. They don't communicate, and they are not maps. Ultimately, they are just tiny video snippets with some added data. You need to use them to form a map, to communicate and most importantly to solve problems.

How to tag videos

Tagging means stopping a video each time we observe user insights and create snippets from them. Don't worry, a remote research platform will help you with this; you will not need Adobe Premiere or Apple Final Cut Pro. In this chapter, we will use the built-in tagging feature from the WhatUsersDo platform. However, if you are recording your own videos, for example, with Skype or Cisco WebEx, you might need some basic video editing skills. If you need to edit videos, I would recommend Lightworks, a free video editing software, available for all major operating systems from `https://www.lwks.com`. This software is used in Hollywood; for example, *Pulp Fiction* and *The King's Speech* was edited with it. However, you don't need to be a video editing pro to use it. With Lightworks, you can splice out a few seconds from a video and compress the results. Also, you can go even further than that, and add Hollywood-like effects to your tags, or rather, please don't.

What to tag

Some analysts only tag issues that they need to prove their point. This is wrong. You should try your best to gain a good understanding of the user experience, and ultimately improve it. This doesn't mean that you should always tag everything. You need to tag as much as you need for a summary. The goal is to clearly communicate how the users interacted with the solution. The tags are both signals and proofs. The stakeholders will not care about your tags. They should care about the users. The tags, those short video snippets, will get them closer to the users.

When you find something that might be an insight, stop the video. When using the WhatUsersDo platform, you can press the space key or left-click on the video to pause or resume playback. Then, click on the big **Insert tag** button. As a result, the movable **Add new tag** modal will appear.

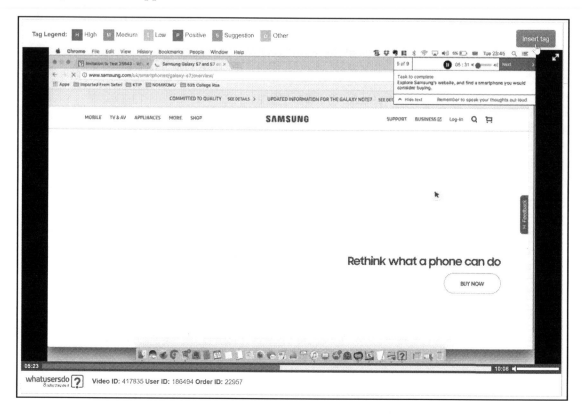

If you are a more experienced tagger, you can press the *Shift* and -> (right arrow) keys to speed up playback. This works on all modern browsers. If it becomes too fast, you can press the *Shift* and <- (left arrow) keys to slow it down. While I would not recommend this for your first few videos, it will save you a considerable amount of time if you need to tag dozens of user testing videos.

At first, setting the start time and end time will prove to be a bit tricky but after some practice, it's really easy. You need to move the playhead a bit. The playhead is where the before (usually blueish) and after (gray) areas of the timeline meet. When the mouse is over the timeline, a playhead icon (←‖→) will appear. When you click on the timeline, the video will jump there. Once you find the correct start time, you need to click on the **Use current time** link in the **Add new tag** modal. After setting the **Start Time** and **End Time**, it makes sense to **Preview** the tag. Remember that we want tags showing the whole issue, while not being too long.

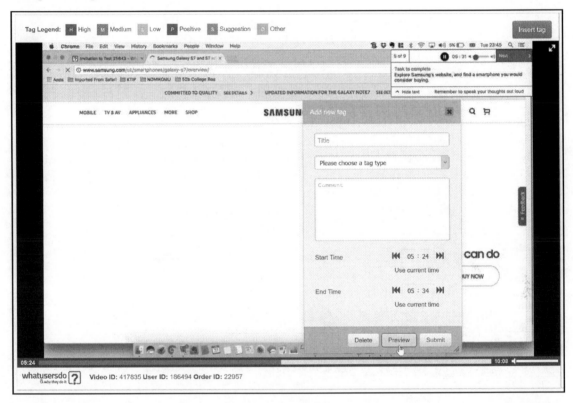

The difficulty in tagging is that tags are not always verbalized by the user. For example, if we see that the user is moving back and forth between pages, not finding what they are after for a few seconds, that is an issue, even if the user is silent.

Tag title and comment

A tag is more than a snippet. It's a form of communication. The tag title, type, and comment should describe the insight. I always suggest treating tags as standalone information pieces. The tag should be understandable without the context. Don't assume that the reader of your comment has watched any part of the video, or read the other tag comments you made.

You don't need to be verbose. Usually, one short sentence will cover the issue and the context needed for standalone understandability.

The language of the comments should be impersonal and formal. The terminology should be consistent throughout all videos you tag. The obvious exceptions are the user's own words. Those can be used in quotation marks to provide more detail of the issue and what they are feeling.

The comment should also uncover the insight's cause. Sometimes, a quote from the user is the best comment, and the only comment needed. However, a tag comment should not always be a partial transcription of the snippet. For example, during one of the Contiki videos, a user said "[…] there is something there, but I don't know what it is, I don't know how to scroll", referring to the top regions menu on the bottom left. This is not a scroll issue, although the user thinks it is. *A tag comment should always reflect the experience the user had.*

Adding a tag to a video

A tag's comment should not investigate the issue in-depth or suggest a solution. It should just point to the issue while being impartial. Later, when we have analyzed all videos, we can suggest solutions, taking into account all tags. This particular issue was encountered only once.

Tag types

Tag types are categories. They group our tags, making them easier to find. For example, we might want to focus on the highest severity issues, the outright conversion killers.

The WhatUsersDo platform uses six categories for tag types, which can be selected from the tag type drop-down.

Selecting the tag type

Let's go through different tag types in the next section.

Positive tags

Positives mean great user experience. Something that's not just working, but the user is happy that it does, or the way it does. If the user commented enthusiastically on a positive aspect of their experience, select **Positive** from the drop-down. I usually don't tag a positive experience if the user is not vocal about it. If something simply works, you don't need to tag it as a positive unless the user is enthusiastic about it.

Positives are actionable. You want to preserve those experiences for the next iterations or the next product. Those features can be used to showcase what's working, and what makes your users happy. They are also mini-achievements for the team.

Suggestions

You can't expect the users to solve your problems, but sometimes they are really helpful. If a user makes a suggestion, tag it as a Suggestion, unless there is a clearly positive or negative tone to it. Use this tag type for genuine, constructive recommendations given by the user.

I usually collate all suggestions in the summary. Later, the team can decide what to do with them. Sometimes true gems can be found, making your life as a product designer or UX expert much easier.

The negatives: High, Medium and Low

Our goal is to solve issues. To make the users' lives easier, we need to find their pain points. The best source for that is watching our users. When we see something that's not working, we tag it with **High**, **Medium**, or **Low**, depending on the severity of the issue.

In most cases, the user will describe the difficulty they are experiencing. Sometimes, the user may not realize there is a problem, but you should tag it if you see it in the video.

If the issue is a conversion blocker, tag it as **High**. These are the issues that are likely to cause the user to leave the website or abandon the task in real life. Include any exit points in the test where the user states they would now give up and go elsewhere. Because the users are paid to complete the test, they are less likely to actually abandon the task, compared to a real-life scenario, so it is up to your judgement to decide whether you have found a conversion blocker or not.

Not all issues are conversion blockers. If the user might be able to work out how to overcome the issue, but it still stops them in their tracks and they get fairly annoyed by it, you should tag it as **Medium**. If you encounter a niggle that may need addressing but is unlikely to hamper the overall user experience, tag it as **Low**. Those minor annoyances should be fixed only if they are easy to fix, or after you fix all high and medium issues.

The behaviorist issue severity model

There is a more scientific way to distinguish the three issue severity types. Dr B.J. Fogg, the director of the Persuasive Technology Lab at Stanford University, came up with The Fogg Behavior Model. Behavior, or the willingness to complete a task, depends on the motivation, the ability to complete it, and the trigger. In other words, the users will complete a task if they have the ability to do it, a trigger exists, and their motivation is strong enough.

For example, I could ask you to send me a hundred quid. This would be the trigger. I would also give you a link to make it even easier, so I have reduced the ability need. You would probably still not send me the money. Unfortunately for me, your motivation, in this case, is very low. What if I said that in exchange, you will get an hour of my time in form of a Skype call? This might still not be enough for you. If that's the case, my proposal is below your activation threshold. That's OK, because each person has a different activation threshold for each event. From this example, you can learn something more important than my current hourly rate--*The same issue might be high for one user, and low or medium for another user.*

When the trigger is present, an issue is tagged as low, if it's easy for the user and their motivation is high. It's high if it's hard and the user is not motivated to do it. If the user would do something normally, even outside of the test, it means that it's above the activation threshold. If it's close to the activation threshold it's a medium, otherwise a low.

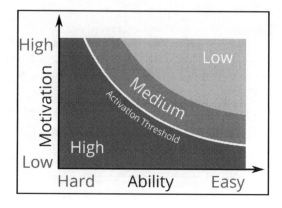

While the activation threshold provides a sharp division between high and medium, there is no well-defined boundary between medium and low. This is normal because that can depend on external factors, such as the mood of the user or the wording of the task. Moreover, most users will perceive a low severity issue as a medium, if they encounter it frequently.

The research summary

The summary is a document we usually create after tagging all user research videos. In this step, we review all tags created. This is more important in large projects, where multiple UX analysts work together, creating hundreds of tags. However, you can benefit from a good summary even for a small five video project.

The WhatUsersDo platform has a button labeled **Watch a playlist of ## video tags**.

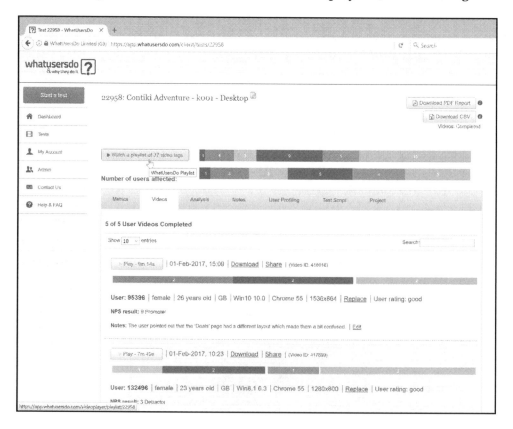

We try to find common patterns and shared pain points across multiple users. This becomes easier with a higher number of videos, but even with five, we managed to find similarities in behavior.

In this desktop test when users were asked to find an adventure using any travel site, all users used Google to find their destination. Almost all users searched for *adventure travel holidays*, and only one user searched for *cheap adventure holidays*.

Three out of five users found the site crowded. They often called it a *"very busy looking site"*. The moving images distracted their attention, and it raised a greater level of frustration. A quote from one of its users is a great example for this: "It's interesting maybe. I don't really like the design because it gave me like videos and pictures."

Don't get me wrong, the 2017 February version of the site was not bad at all. The results of the remote research were positive overall. All users finished the tasks with ease, and nine clearly positive comments were found. The reviews and the clear pricing resonated well with the users. To be fair, after the negative first impressions, the users managed to navigate the site and found what they were after.

The solution map

A solution map is a tool that will help us communicate our solution with stakeholders. It's also a visual summary of the experience we want to create.

 Mapping based on the issues and positive findings of remote user testing will lead to better communication, user experiences, and products. To be able to create solution maps, we need to analyze the tests, categorize the findings, and then collate and summarize the results. We also need to add our creative thinking to come up with a solution.

Our opportunity was not to redesign Contiki. The redesign should never be chosen as the opportunity of a project. Even as an output, or part of a solution, a total redesign is drastic, but sometimes needed.

We need to create a tailor-made experience for adventure seekers. User experience is moving toward custom experiences for smaller and smaller user groups. Eventually, for unique users, based on the data we know about that specific person.

Each solution and each solution map is unique and should never be copied without fully understanding the problem and the users. Even if you are working for a travel brand, please don't copy this solution map. It will be sub-optimal at best, a total waste of time at worst. Try to understand the logic behind solving the problem, then run your own research to create your own solution. The best practice solution is a toxic myth.

Learning from others is great, copying then adapting the processes can be helpful. Copying a ready-made solution without understanding the users results in failure more often than not. Even if it works to a degree, you will be a few steps behind the competition.

Five steps to create the solution map

As always, there are many software products you can use. You can also draw a solution map on paper. For creating the solution map, I have used Adobe Illustrator. This chapter will not have a detailed Adobe Illustrator tutorial because I have already introduced the basic tools needed in `Chapter 3`, *Journey Map - Understand Your Users*. Just use the same tools you used when creating a task model or user journey map. I'll let you in on a secret: you can create a good-looking solution map with just the rectangle (▦) and line segment (◨) tools.

Step 1 - put the issues on the map

The first step to a solution map is to list all medium and high severity issues from user testing. Add all issues coming from other teams and business goals in the form of issues. For example, if the business wants a better conversion rate, then a low conversion rate becomes an issue we need to solve with the aid of the solution map.

Also, add any issues coming from other teams or other tests. Don't add issues if they are only your hunches about user behavior if real user tests don't confirm them.

Put all your issues in boxes, and you are done with the first step. If you do this on a wall, sticky notes are amazing for solution mapping.

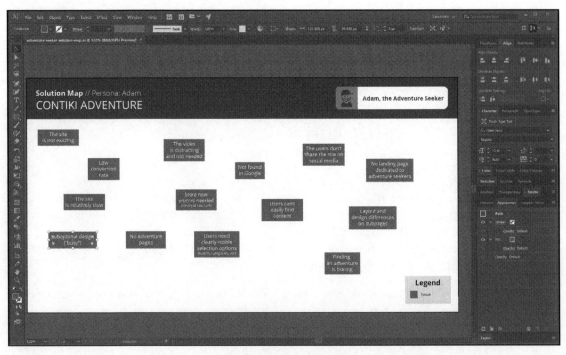

Starting the solution map with the issues

Similar to journey maps, I would recommend that you use personas. Different personas might require different solutions. Jump back to Chapter 3, *Journey Map - Understand Your Users*, to learn about personas. If you are familiar with personas and already created them for your dream project, continue with *step two, arranging the issues*.

Step 2 - form the issue trees

Now that we have listed all issues we know of, we need to arrange the issues into one or more issue trees. We want to build **cause-effect trees** from our issues. If you are familiar with data structures, we want to create a forest of directed rooted trees. We want multiple directed graphs in which any two vertices are connected by exactly one path. Don't worry, if you are not a big fan of graph theory, I will explain how to create the trees in a minute.

You can start with any issue from the previous step. An issue alone is arranged. The rest of the issues are considered unarranged. Then, we ask why? If we find another issue that is the cause of our targeted issue, we add that to the map. We place this newly found issue above our chosen issue, and draw an arrow, pointing to the new one.

Then, we select this new issue and ask why again. We will keep asking why until we find no issues within our context. It's important to note that we only look for issues within the context of our opportunity. We also never add issues that refer to the past. In our example, we could find an issue that caused the suboptimal design. That's not constructive and would probably point to something in the past. It's important to focus on how we can have a design that resonates better with our users.

After we find no cause for our issue tree's top element, we have found our root issue or root cause. This is an upside-down forest, so the roots of the trees are on top, don't worry about it. It's also possible that we picked a root cause first, so this could still be a single issue standing alone.

Now, we select another issue, which is not part of any tree and repeat the process. The difference is that now it's possible that our issue has a cause, which is already part of the tree. In that case, our selected issue will be part of the same tree, below its cause.

After you have arranged all issues into cause-effect trees, you need to test your forest. To do this, ask why for each root issue, and see if any of them would somehow fit in another tree. For solution maps, we want to have as few trees in our forests as possible, ideally one. Don't apply this principle to any real forest with living trees.

If there is more than one root cause, you should prioritize them. To do this, add an importance number to them based on their impact on the users and the business. I tend to use a scale from zero to ten, where nine or ten is the most important issue. The zero is reserved for issues that might become issues in the future, but they are not at the moment. Most of the time, I don't put those zeros on the map.

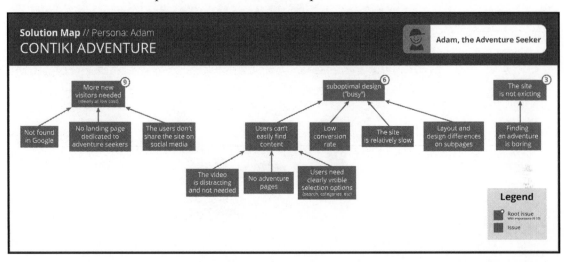

This step will lead to a better understanding and visual representation of the issues we have and their relationships with each other. In an ideal situation, we find one issue that's the root cause of all other issues we have. If not, we will have a bit harder time in the next phase, but it's no reason for despair, even if you find quite a few root issues.

Step 3 - solve the root issues

Now comes the fun part. The main reason for creating the issue trees was to identify the root issues. First, we will focus on the root issue with the highest importance and try to find an actionable solution, within our limits. Then, we try to extend the solutions, so it solves as many, ideally all root issues. When found, add a box, with a different color and point arrows to it, starting from the root issues to the solution fixes.

Add a legend with the different colors/box styles to your solution map. This will help people who are new to solution mapping. Experienced solution mappers will guess what's what without a legend from the placement of the items.

Sometimes, different root issues call for different solutions, and there is no elegant single solution for all issues. That's perfectly normal and not even a rare case in solution design, just draw as many solution boxes as needed.

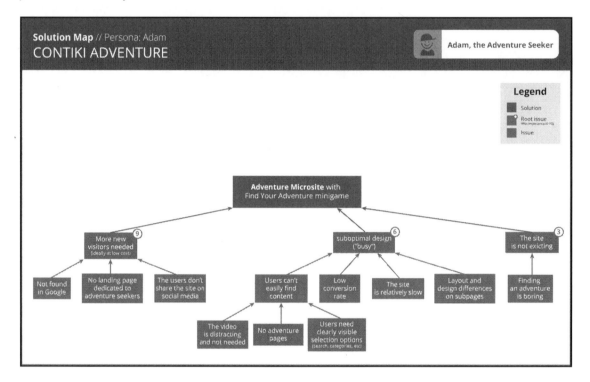

Finding the solution requires creativity and teamwork. Ideally, you want a brainstorming session for this with the wider team, if possible, otherwise just the four amigos. To anchor the issues in reality, you can start with showing one or two snippets from user testing videos showcasing the issue. Those few second-long videos will help everyone understand what's the problem and often lead to solutions.

Thinking small is a self-fulfilling prophecy, so always think big. In our example, we found the solution by creating a microsite on a new domain, with a new design. This elegant solution enabled us to solve the problem much faster and without breezing many feathers. It's not as risky as modifying the main web estate, and usually, it's faster to create a new microsite from scratch than modify a gargantuan project.

When possible, look for reversible solutions. They don't need an extensive study if they are easily undoable. You can learn from them, and change course if the solution doesn't meet the expectations.

Execution time is important for solutions. If a digital solution takes a year to build, it's probably a bad idea. This doesn't mean that you need to lower your standard, and always create quick patchworks, instead of making sure that things you fix stay fixed. Just try to simplify things and split long projects into small, meaningful sprints and aim for quick wins.

Re-think!

There are many solutions to all business problems, many paths to overcome any obstacle. It's always worth considering different angles and rethinking the solution you found. The next iteration of the solution map could have different solutions. That doesn't mean that your first solution was wrong. It means that you reworked it into a better one. This is the path to success.

User Centric Solution Design is a topic that could easily fill a book, a book I might write one day. The essence of that book might be, *balance business goals with real user insights to create actionable solutions*. Reaching those decisions and communicating them needs a solution map. However, that solution map doesn't stop with the solution. Every solution meets resistance.

Step 4 - identify obstacles

After we reach a solution, we need to find out what other teams think about it. Each team might have a set of obstacles, preventing your solution from happening. I add all possible teams here. As each team tends to have a long list of obstacles in a corporate environment, I usually just add the team name.

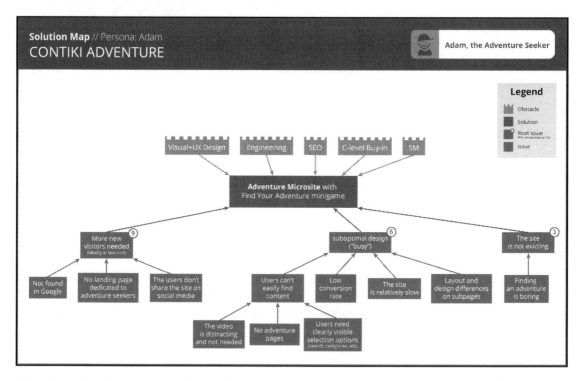

If we have the buy-in from the senior management, those teams will figure out the obstacles real fast.

Step 5 - create actions to remove the obstacles

The final step is the actions phase. We need to find out what we need to do, to remove the obstacles. Some of those obstacles are simple communication exercises, such as getting buy-in from the CEO, for a microsite. Others can be more complicated. For example, the engineering team might need to research the ideal framework for the minigames, or which content delivery network to use.

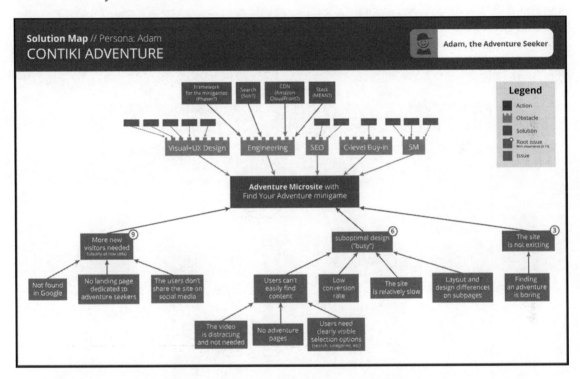

I usually put the actions on the map on a much smaller scale, then the rest of the map, because actions are many and mostly team specific. As long as the team knows them and works on them, I'm happy. Sometimes, some actions are harder or take a considerable amount of time. Those can be scaled up, so we can tick them on the printed map and have pizza after. In a corporate environment, everyone is fighting for engineering resources, so we aim the pizza at the engineers. I mean we aim our attention at them. Throwing pizza at engineers might not be an effective solution design action.

Congratulations! You have just created a solution map. The bad news is that the solution map will not magically solve your problems. You need to put it in to action.

Put the solution map to action

After you get your buy-ins and the other teams start working on their respective action points, you can sit back and enjoy the show--if you want the project to fail, that is. Otherwise, I would recommend putting the map to action. In this book, we create maps to improve communication, solve problems, and to create other maps.

You should be able to create a task model and a journey map based on the solution map, and the skills we discovered in Chapter 3, *Journey Map - Understand Your Users*. We aim to create journeys that have lots of depth, many possible paths, but the paths are quite short and always lead to our main goal. The main goal being to book an adventure. This should make both the adventurers (our users) and the company happy. What does your journey map look like?

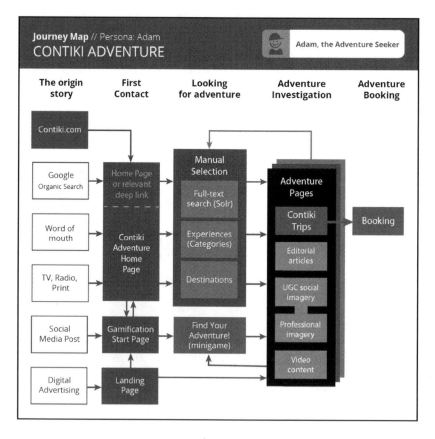

The *Find Your Adventure!* minigame is a good prospect for a wireflow. If you recall, in `Chapter 4`, *Wireflows - Plan Your Product*, we needed to wireframe the relevant views and connect those wireframes with arrows.

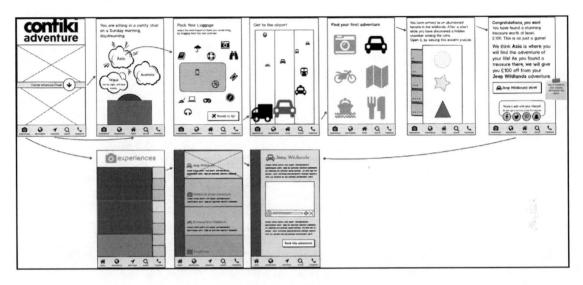

Connecting wireframes using arrows

Now, you need to communicate your solution to realize your dreams. Happy solution mapping!

Five years ago, the solution map failed me. I was consulting for a big client, and my solution map was a total disaster, although it didn't seem like that at the beginning. I was in a meeting with senior managers from the client company. I showed them my carefully crafted presentation. When I played the remote user testing video tags, most managers were nodding, asked questions, and were quite positive. The video snippets worked as they usually do. Then, we reached the solution map, and I lost the audience. I kept talking, but they became uninterested. Sometimes, I talked too much, so I tried to switch to active listening mode, like when I do experience coaching. It didn't help. So, I asked for a 10 minutes break.

During the break, I opened the .ai file and deleted the upper half of the solution map. All that remained was the forest of issue trees with their root issue. A few people left during the break, but the people who remained became engaged. They loved the challenge and brainwork. We found an ideal solution, one that was much better aligned to the business goals. Ultimately, the resulting product was a great success. Mainly because I had the strength to destroy my solution map.

While you can create the first version of most maps alone, for solution maps, that can be a trap. If you are a consultant, it's better to lead the client to the solution than to present a ready-made solution. The solution should be the result of a conversation, not just a starting point. Establish a dialog about the issues. The rapport you create leads them to judge your skills, your trustworthiness, your maps, and ultimately, all the deliverables you create. **I believe that a solution in your head is not a true solution until it is reforged in a dialog.**

Summary

In the preceding chapter, I promised you the one and only silver bullet to product design. By now, I'm sure that it's obvious: *base your solutions on real user insights.*

Solution design relies heavily on solution maps. Solution mapping starts with the pain points coming from our users and the business. With creative thinking, teamwork and communication, we can create amazing solutions. By focusing on the root issue, we change the product or even the whole world. When we meet blockers or obstacles, we overcome them with swift action.

This is a process of innovation and simplification, leading to better new products for the same old users. This concludes the easy part of this book. Changing the world is easy, compared to changing the mind. In the next chapter, we will create a mental model map, and in Chapter 8, *Behavioural Change Map - The Action Plan of Persuasion* we will change behaviors. Are you ready to map the depths of the human mind?

7

Mental Model Map - A Diagram of the Perceived Reality

Mental models are the frames of our reality. They are assumptions and perceptions of how the world works, and beliefs of how it should work. Mental models help us live and survive, by predicting the future. To be able to understand the mental models of our users, we will create mental model maps, then use the maps to provide the best solutions for the users.

In this chapter, we will do the following things:

- Understand what a mental model is
- Explore how mental models work and how people buy a car
- Conduct a longitudinal research, covering a longer time period with the same test users
- Discuss logging types and prompts to be able to conduct a successful longitudinal research
- Then, analyze the research to find units, towers, and mental spaces
- Draw the mental model map
- Add our existing solutions to the mental spaces where they support the users
- Use the map for the benefit of our users

To be able to do all this, first we need to understand what a mental model is.

What's a mental model?

To be able to anticipate and understand events, our mind creates small-scale, greatly simplified models of the **perceived reality**. This helps us to communicate with others, arrange, store information, and ultimately to survive.

Let's take the Earth's highest mountain as an example. My mental model tells me that if I would attempt to climb Mount Everest, I would surely die in the process--probably, early in the process. For me, this is in the category of near impossibilities, such as riding a T-Rex. I would also have no idea how to approach this task. For other people, climbing Everest might be more than a terrible possibility, maybe a dream and passion. They would surely know how to start, or maybe they have already started preparing for it. For a select few, it's something they already did, and they have a first-hand experience about it.

Most mental models are less extreme. For example, Americans visiting the United Kingdom for the first time might try to plug their device into the wall socket. However, the UK uses a different plug and socket type, so they will not fit. This will no doubt cause them to think that this side of the ocean uses a different plug type. Our American friends might even buy an adapter. This will solve their problem while they are in the Queen's England. However, then if they decide to visit France, they will be shocked by yet another plug type. Soon, they will understand that there are about 15 types of electrical outlet plugs in use today around the world, thus expanding their mental model.

As a solution design or user experience researcher, you are most likely interested in more practical mental models. For example, how users search for home insurance, and how they get one or how people buy a car, from the first idea, through visiting numerous websites, then finding a car and considering financing options.

 A mental model map is a visual representation of a user group's or persona's thought process and patterns related to a subset of the world, relevant to our solution. It also contains our solutions supporting the users' thought processes. The mental model shifts focus from designing a solution to understanding the user's state of mind and how we can support those states.

Mental model maps are not intended to change the user's state of mind or influence behaviors. For that, you need to wait until `Chapter 8`, *Behavioral Change Map: the action plan of persuasion*.

Contrary to previous map types in this book, mental model maps are not intended as a wider audience communication tool. This is because they can be overwhelming, and the business usually cares about the solution and improvements to the solution, not what our users think. Mental model maps are tools for people who want to understand the user's mind states and the thought process of why they choose to do what they did. They will also serve as a starting point for the behavioral change map in the next chapter.

Within three years, 92% of start-ups fail. This data is based on Startup Genome Report Extra on Premature Scaling (https://s3.amazonaws.com/startupcompass-public /StartupGenomeReport2_Why_Startups_Fail_v2.pdf). *From the same report, we also know that 74% failed due to premature scaling. The authors analyzed 3,200 high growth web and mobile start-ups to reach this conclusion. Most of the time, scaling up involves hiring more employees, attracting more capital, and spending more on marketing--also, as data suggest, going under shortly after. One of the main reasons for this is that premature scaling leads to many early adopters. They look deceptively the same as a market or stable user base. However, if you analyze their mental model, you can often see something odd. One of their main driving force can be curiosity. Sure, they are quick to adopt your solution and start using it, but they are equally quick to abandon it. How can a mental model help you to avoid premature scaling? First, it can turn the business focus to what happens in the user's mind from the sheer number of users. This is probably the most important paradigm change. The second benefit is showing the direction where you should go. This is not always where you want to go. In 2007, The Point was launched, a social activism platform, trying to get people together to accomplish a common goal or support a cause. It would have probably failed, if not for the founders analyzing what their users do and think. Eric Lefkofsky and his cofounders realized that some people used The Point to save money. This cause meant gathering a large group of people and buying the same product in bulk, to receive a group discount. The founders of The Point pivoted to focus entirely on group buying because this was the most successful aspect of The Point. This is how Groupon was born. Now, in 2017, Groupon has a 2.5 billion dollar market capitalization. Even if you work for a large corporation, you should consider mental models and pivot, if needed. Nintendo was founded in 1889 to produce handmade hanafuda cards. In the 1970s, Nintendo realized that a pivot toward electronic games has a huge potential. First, they were only resellers for the Magnavox Odyssey video game console, but in 1977 they started producing their own consoles. As you probably know, Nintendo quickly became successful at the global console market. The company continuously defined the future of gaming and continues to do so even in 2017 with their new Nintendo Switch console. By pivoting into the right direction, Nintendo became a true Japanese success story.*

If we don't understand the user's mental model, we will have little chance to influence it. Even if you are not interested in persuasion, you should try to understand what happens in the mind of your users.

Buying a car

When creating a mental model, we don't start with an opportunity. We start with the desire to learn more about how our users think and act. However, we need a focus area. For this chapter's focus area, I have chosen car buying. It's a serious, well-considered decision for most of us, and choosing and buying a new car can be a lengthy process. This process involves thoughts, motivations, ability changes, reactions, principles, emotions, behaviors, and triggers. It will surely lead to many different mental spaces.

Our research goal is understanding the user, but we will put that understanding to good use by supporting the user with solutions in different mental spaces. We will focus on people, not tools--minds over software. We could claim that our opportunity is to make the car buying an easy and joyful process. That would be an error. Did we just assume that buying a car is hard or not joyful? When creating a mental model, we want to start with a blank slate. The best starting position is to assume nothing and base the mental model on a valid research. Before we conduct that research, we need to know a few things about how mental models work.

How mental models work?

A mental model is not necessarily founded on facts or complete understanding of reality. Let's be honest, most of our mental models are flawed in many ways, and that's perfectly normal. They work because they are fast and simple and not because they are a complete representation of the reality. This is why when people choose between cars, they will not always choose the same car. Also, this is why UFO cults exist. The most important thing about a person's mental model is that it's simplified and very limited compared to what it models.

We will get back to UFO cults shortly, but we also need to mention the cognitive flexibility present in almost all humans above the age of 12 months: using a mental model doesn't exclude another mental model. We can think about two concepts simultaneously or switch between concepts without effort. This is why we can take many factors into account when buying a car. We can look at the brand, price, fuel type, color, and many other categories. It's possible that we like the performance of one car and the exterior design of another. Although those two characteristics are not comparable, we can still decide between the two cars.

Another important characteristic of mental models is selective perception. This means that people will perceive everything through the filter of their related mental models. If we really like how a car looks, we might ignore its fuel economy, performance, or even price. Some people tend to prefer one and only one make. So, they will ignore all other companies in the industry. You might know someone who drives a BMW and would only buy BMWs, no matter what. That's a selective perception, resulting from a mental model.

Mental models can be activated by exposure to specific things, events, words, ideas, or thoughts. This is what we will call **priming**. For example, your car breaking down could prime the buying of your next car, especially if that happens often. Watching a commercial of a new Jaguar model could also prime that mental model. In fact, the whole scope of advertising is to prime your buying a car mental model. However, it goes even further than that. If a movie has a high-speed car chase, just before the commercial break, it will alter how people perceive the aforementioned Jaguar ad. Chances are that it will be better placed than say after an episode of Game of Thrones, contrary to a life insurance commercial, which would work better after seeing a few characters dying or dead.

By understanding how the mental model works, we can harness its power. In this chapter, we will use it to give the users what they want. In the next chapter, we will change what they want, to what they need. We will call this behavioral change.

The mental model map could serve as the base and driving force of innovation. It can also make innovation less risky, and less likely to fail. Remember that failure is not a rite of passage. Even if a mental model doesn't directly lead to a breakthrough, it will always lead to a better understanding of the users' mental processes. You should put this understanding into practice, by creating a better world for the users, one app, one hardware, or one solution at a time.

Longitudinal research

Most user research types will give us in-the-moment results, or at best, a slice of the complete mental model. To create mental models, we need something that lasts for a longer time period, ideally days, if not weeks or months, to gain a better understanding of many behaviors and attitudes, even beyond the typical use-case scenarios of our solution.

Longitudinal research covers a longer time period with the same test users.

Longitudinal research can take a few days, or even months, depending on the research goal and budget. When creating a mental model map, the researchers focus on target behaviors in their larger context during the logging period, based on the recordings (logs), which can be in writing, audio, video recording, pictures, or a mix of all those.

Users struggle at recalling past events in detail. Accurately recalling past experiences, feelings, and attitudes is almost impossible. To demonstrate this, let me ask you a few questions: *What did you eat for breakfast yesterday? How tasty was it on a scale from zero to ten? How long your breakfast took? How did you feel right after breakfast? (sleepy doesn't count). What if I would have asked about a breakfast exactly six days ago? Finally, how often did you use your smartphone during breakfast in the past two months?* This is why logging is the most important aspect of longitudinal research.

The best research type for creating mental models is a **field study**. A field study means a researcher following and logging everything the user does if it's loosely related to our research target, and conducting frequent interviews to enrich the observed facts with what happens in the user's mind. The problem is that the costs quickly become exorbitant. For a complex mental model, we want to observe the behavior of dozens of users for at least a week or two, if not a month.

My preferred longitudinal research method is the **diary study**. This is much more cost-effective because the users will do the logging themselves. This is also less invasive. The users will keep their privacy, and they stay in full control of what to share with the researchers. In developed countries, most test subjects will have a smartphone available, even if it's not a test requirement to own one. This means that they can easily take photos, screenshots, and even short videos to make a true multimedia logging, and capture things that would be hard to describe. While a diary study will never quite reach the detail level and professional rigor of a field study, it's a good replacement. In fact, a field study is not an efficient way to spend the research budget, so most of the time I suggest a diary study with a longer time frame and more participants, instead of a field study.

The only notable exceptions are when the target audience has a high percentage of functional illiterates or when the test requires the presence of the researchers. An example for the second case is creating a mental model that involves a new hardware prototype, still in early stage.

When you have decided what to research and how long, you need to recruit participants or use an existing panel. Then, you need to brief your test subjects or your researchers on how to log.

Logging types - how to log?

The most crucial element of a diary study is the first briefing. If you botch that, it can ruin the research. Worst case scenario, you can end up with a wrong mental model map, completely misleading you. If you do a great job here, then analyzing the logs and transforming them into a good mental model map will be easy.

First, you need to pick a logging method, and brief participants in it, ideally showing log examples from similar researches. There are three widely used logging practices. You should choose one based on the project's requirements and constraints:

- **Post-situ logging**: This means capturing information after the relevant activities. This method will always work, and this is the least disruptive. You tell people to keep a diary and note things in it after they happen. This is how most people write diaries anyhow. Ideally, the time between the activity and the diary entry should be kept to a minimum, but in some scenarios, even end-of-day logging is acceptable. As you can guess, the accuracy of this logging method is the lowest among the three. This method has the highest chance of missed entries when the user simply forgets to include something relevant in the diary
- **In-situ logging**: This means capturing information during the relevant activities. This method has the highest accuracy. This type of logging works best if the users use audio or video recordings for logging purposes, instead of paper or typing in text. A huge drawback of this method is its innate destructiveness. The act of logging will distort the experience to a degree. In some experiments, this can even be impossible. For example, if you want to create a mental model for people who operate heavy machinery, to improve their work efficiency, it would be disastrous to ask them to do in-situ logging while working with an excavator or bulldozer. For this chapter's example, in-situ logging during test drive would certainly be illegal.

- **Snippet logging:** This technique combines the previous two. A short snippet will be recorded during the relevant activities, usually, just a few words. Those snippets will then be expanded into full logs when time permits. This technique became popular with the widespread use of smartphones, as those devices can be used to create the logs easily. For a more in-depth reporting, a laptop, tablet, or desktop device can be used later. For car buying, I would suggest this logging technique, although the test drive snippets would be created right after the experience.

When briefing the users before the study, make sure to teach them how to log, but *don't lead them.* Talk about the preferred method, not about the preferred outcome, business goals, or your ideas about a solution.

Prompts: what to Log?

After deciding the logging method, you need to choose prompts. While it's tempting to say that you want everything relevant to the project logged, that's not a reasonable request. If you are doing a diary study, you can't expect the users to know about your research objectives, and guess what's relevant and what is not. Even for a field study, the prompts are vital in synchronizing the logging of multiple researchers or analysts. Prompts are what we use to prime the logging mindset. Remember that car buying can coexist with other mindsets, including the participation in a longitudinal research mindset.

Habit prompts are related to when and how often things happen, related to our research target. For example, telling participants to record the hours and minute when they start a workout is a habit prompt. Note that some log entries, like this one, can be timestamps instead of a detailed description. However, you can encourage participants to give more context to habit prompts, by asking them what they did before and after the given habit prompt. An example long entry could be as follows: *[5 Mar 2014 4.10pm] Started workout, after reading 2 hours of 'relax time' (reading).* For almost everyone, buying a car doesn't lead to habit prompts. It's unlikely that you want to buy a car on each Sunday morning. You could say that you buy a car bi-annually, but that's not a habit prompt unless the research takes 10 years.

Usage scenario prompts mean writing down the user's own task list. From those task lists, you can create test designs for remote user experience research (as seen in `Chapter 5`, *Remote and Lab Tests for Map Creation*). For example, you could tell the users to write down what they wanted to achieve and later add notes on how easy it was, or whether they failed the task for some reason. The user's solutions to common problems can even lead to improvements in our products. An example log for a study revolving around an HR software: *[4 Sep 2016 10.07am] I need to find _____'s phone number. [4 Sep 2016 10.09am] _____ didn't add her phone number to the database so that I will send an email to _____ instead.*

Journey prompts require the users to write down a few steps of what they are doing, and ideally add why. Those can reveal the user's perceived cause-effect relationship, relevant to our focus. An example would be as follows: *[2 Dec 2016 9.12pm] we discussed pros and cons of buying a new car with my husband -> we believe that we need a new car -> agreed to search the internet, read and ask around about the pre-owned car market.* This is a good example to journeys happening during a discussion, outside of our solution, yet still relevant for us. Obviously, journey prompts can happen inside our solution or in a competing solution.

Change prompts are probably the hardest prompt types for logging purposes, particularly for a diary study. In theory, they should happen when something changes. This can be a behavior, motivation, perception, ability, or trigger change, even a change in the user's evaluation or information processing style. The most common change prompt is the learning prompt--show how adept they are with a solution. By plotting all learning prompts, we can draw a learning curve for each user. Self-evaluation can be misleading here (as with all change), instead small tests should be used if needed. When you ask the users to rate their ability or skill with a solution, they will most likely rate their processing fluency, the ease and speed with which they process information. This processing fluency is greatly influenced by the previous prompts, and the actual events, and not a good representation of one's abilities or skills. Let's take driving a new car as an example. The log for after an hour on the highway on a Saturday afternoon will be different compared to an hour in the city during rush hour. If the city driving happens after the highway driving, does this mean that the car somehow became harder to drive, or less pleasant to drive? Did the motivation or ability of the user change? It's still valuable to note that the car is used in multiple scenarios, and the experience differs, but that's hardly a surprise. However, change prompts can results in meaningful log entries; consider this for example: *[16 Oct 2016 7.49am] I just realized that the camera system is really useful in traffic, not just for parking. This morning I felt safer while maneuvering. Before today, I usually kept my eyes on the road, practically ignoring the 360° camera.*

The problem with change prompts is behavioral consistency, which makes self-documenting change hard, most of the time unusable. Numerous studies in social psychology confirmed that people want to avoid the discomfort caused by cognitive dissonance. To do this, people change their attitude to match their previous behavior-- probably, the best-documented example is the Seekers cult. They believed that the world would end in a great flood before dawn on December 21, 1954, but members of the cult would be saved by UFOs. I mean literally, they were expecting to be rescued by flying saucers. Unexpectedly, the world didn't end, and the aliens from planet Clarion didn't show up, but this did not shake the cultist's beliefs. Instead, they claimed that the God of Earth had saved the world from destruction, because of their devotion and night-long vigil. In fact, their beliefs and commitment became much stronger. Fortunately for us, this was a field study and researchers infiltrated the group to conduct this longitudinal research. If it had been a diary study, the results might have been entirely different.

Since changes are hard to capture with diary study, I recommend an interview with the participants before the research and one after. You can ask non-leading questions, trying to reveal whether anything has changed. Probing questions can reveal how, when, and why those changed occurred.

Free prompts are the researcher's last hope. I usually tell the users to record anything they wish, even if it's not closely related to any of the other prompts. The best free prompt I have ever read was *Today my bf popped the question and I said YES!* While this was not related to the gaming habits of young females, the whole team was smiling. That lady made our day for sure. More importantly, this explained why the next few day's entries were overly positive. Other than life events, free prompts can also provide great side notes and describe activities, plans, and sometimes even behaviors.

Mental model mapping

Indi Young's famous book from 2008 showed a visual way to represent mental models. In *Mental Models*, she described the full process of mental model mapping. In the nine years that followed, our methods and even the terminology changed. Our understanding of mental models is much broader, but still, that book is the gold standard of the mental model mapping for large scale projects.

A mental model map is the visual summary of all research we did to understand the user's mind. I prefer to base mental model maps on a longitudinal research, with at least two interviews, before and after the logging period. *The mental model map helps us to find new ways to support the users in different mental spaces, thus creating new solutions.* It's a real idea-machine.

Analyzing longitudinal research

A mental model map is a really powerful tool, and as the cliché goes, with great power comes great responsibility. I need to mention the ethics of modeling the mind, especially with the intent of behavioral change. Mapping is, of course, neither ethical nor unethical. Mapping is just the visual representation of knowledge. It's up to you how to use that knowledge. I don't want to take the moral high-ground here, but consider the user's best interest all the time--*never create solutions or experiences with malicious intent; don't deceive the user.* That's a shortsighted approach. Black hat UX never leads to long-term benefits.

Another responsibility of the user experience cartographer is to strive for accurate depiction. Attention to detail when analyzing longitudinal research is even more important. This analysis can be a long and tedious task, and you absolutely shouldn't rush it. Even if you have the best intent, if your maps are not accurate they will fail. In this regard, user experience maps are similar to nautical maps. It doesn't matter whether the mapmaker had bad intentions or it was an honest mistake, if the maps are not correct ships will sink and so will your products.

Even user experience analyst has a slightly different way of analyzing longitudinal research, so it's important to synchronize if more than one analyst works on a research.

I suggest a three-step process for the analysis: finding units, grouping them into patterns, then forming mental spaces.

Find units

Split the log entries into units, then merge duplicates. The units are a common name for atomic thoughts, motivations, ability changes, reactions, principles, emotions, behaviors, triggers, and knowledge the user has. They are small but self-contained. Try to find the smallest unit that's still meaningful, and the user would think of it as something separate, not a part of something else.

Units have many names in the literature. For example, Young calls them tasks, while Kalbach named them boxes. I started calling them units because usage scenario prompts lead to tasks, but we are interested in many other prompts for a complex mental model, not just usage scenario prompts. It doesn't really how you name them, as long as they represent a single idea.

Merging duplicates makes the mental model manageable. Each user will have slightly different variants of the same unit. The challenge is to find similar units encountered by other participants and merge them into one unit. If you find one user having a log entry for *establishing the price range for the car*, and another for *decide the car budget*, those can safely be merged into *establishing the price range*. On the other hand, a user could have a log entry, *I just imagined how I would feel if I would spend more than [a certain amount] on a used car*. Now although it's related to the previous two, they are not mergeable into a unit. However, both units belong to the same group, or as we call them, the same tower.

When merging units, I usually add notes of how many units were combined into one, then represent this visually. To keep the map simple, I often exclude narrow and specific user groups. For example, people working for a car manufacturer have a unique mental model for buying a car. Similarly, a billionaire or someone living in absolute poverty would approach this differently compared to the majority of the population in the UK, but then again we would not recruit those people, to begin with. If we exclude extremes and edge cases, the mental model becomes simpler. It will be easier to use and communicate. Always try to achieve simplicity; if a mental model is too complicated, people will simply avoid using it.

Group units into towers

Group the units into towers. It's important to base your towers on unit groups, and don't try to force the units into premade towers. You should start with a unit, and if you see similar units you group those together. It's possible that a unit fits into multiple towers. That can mean two things. Either it's a complex pseudo-unit, which means you should refine it some more, to reach an atomic, true unit or it's possible that you went too far, and created a subatomic unit, a trivial subunit, which is actually so small or insignificant that our mind doesn't treat it as a separate entity. For example, when the users were asked to test-drive a vehicle for a week with a new user interface, pressing the brake pedal happened often, and it could have been part of almost all patterns. However, in reality, it's not something the users treat as a separate action unless it's their first day behind the wheel.

For this grouping, you need to find natural links, patterns, and similarities among your units. Following the previous example, *I just imagined how I would feel if I would spend more than [a certain amount] on a used car* and *establishing the price range* (the result of merging quite a few similar units) would be part of the same tower. Another unit of this tower will be *discuss budget decision* (also a result of many units merged together).

When you have your towers, you should name them for easier referencing. Continuing the example, there could be a *decide the purpose* tower or a *test drive* tower, or simply a *pay* tower to collect all units of the mental processes happening at the time when the user buys the car and pays for it.

Mental models lack the time dimension. This can be a bit misleading, as people assume that a tower right from another happens after the tower to the left of it. In reality, they can occur at any time when the user is in a given mental space. Quite often, they happen at the same time. For example, the *decide the purpose* will be our left-most column; that's more or less arbitrary. Most people start their diary with something resembling a purpose, such as *We decided to buy a new car. Our current one is too small for our family. (We got two small children.)* For some other users, the purpose gets defined after the *discuss the possibility* column, for example, their partner suggests a PHEV (plug-in hybrid car). For some other users, the *decide if/when to buy* column is the only column in this mental model, because they choose not to buy a car this year.

Form mental spaces

The easiest step is to group the towers into larger sets called mental spaces. Since the number of towers should be quite small, this will be really quick compared to the previous two steps. Just move the towers close together if they represent the same mindset. If you are using Adobe Illustrator, just create a group for each tower; select its content, then press *Ctrl + G* or *Command + G*. For example, in the *budget* mindset, you would have towers related to the car-buying budget: *savings, financing,* and *decide the budget* towers. Now, in this example, the *decide the budget* tower might look like something that belongs to the *decision* mental space. In this research, the users treated this particular decision quite differently to all other decisions. Note that this is most likely caused by the relatively high value of the purchase. If you are doing the mental model map for buying jeans, you would probably find different behaviors related to the budget, which is quite reasonable. You would probably not impulsively buy a nice looking car with your credit card. Instead, you might think about how much you want to spend on a car, which cars can you afford, different financing plans, and so on.

I have used Adobe Illustrator to create the mental model map for this chapter. The units are white, the towers are a lighter gray, and the mental space is a darker shade. I usually differentiate the rarity of the units, resulting from merging units. In this example, I have drawn a bigger stack (three layers) for common mental units, encountered by four or more people. For uncommon units, I have used a smaller stack (just two layers). Two or three people encountered those. Finally, for rare mental models, I just used a single rectangle, without a stack. Those are shortened versions of a log entry by a single participant.

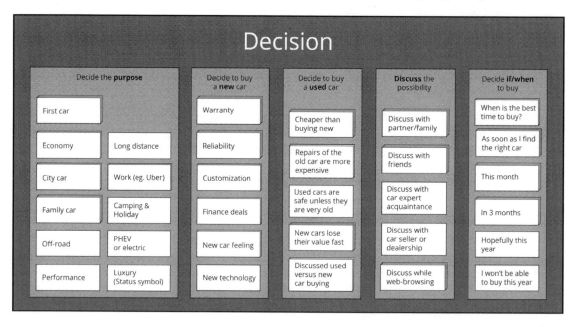

Most authors, such as Young or Kalbach, use thick vertical lines between towers to mark mental spaces. My problem with this is that the resulting mental model map will not be easy to print unless you have a plotter. It's night impossible to include it in a PDF or presentation at a readable font size. Also, between you and me, it's quite ugly. So, I use another rectangle, usually shaded differently, which will hold all towers in a given mental space.

Supporting solutions

Real-world solutions can and should support people in different mental spaces. If we already have solutions, we can match them with towers and mental spaces. For example, the *Finance helper* view of our web application should help with getting some financing for your next car. On the other hand, *History check* aims to reduce your risks and the resulting nervousness when buying used cars. Don't worry about terms such as V5C or MOT. This mental model is relevant for the purchase of a car in the United Kingdom, but in different countries, the process or specific terms can be different. It's critical to create new mental model maps for each country or region, which you want to support with solutions.

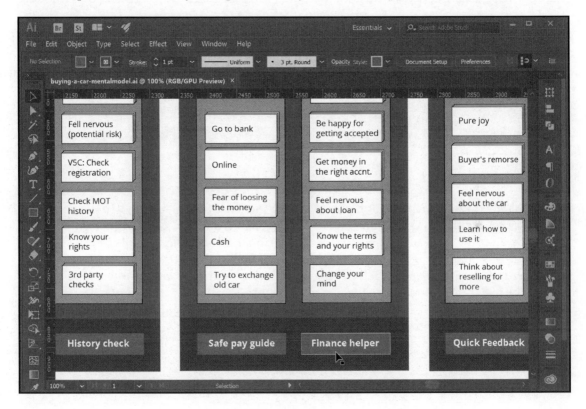

Finishing touches

For more complicated maps, it's important to include a legend. This simple guide to the symbols found on the map will make your map easier to read and use. Also, keep the number of symbols to a minimum, more than eight symbols will result in a hard to read map, even with a legend.

After adding a title, we should have a map.

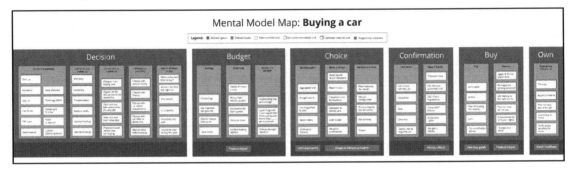

A wide mental model map

The problem with this map is that it's too wide for most purposes, such as being a book illustration. A mental model doesn't have a temporal axis, and no other axis is needed. So, we can arrange the map any way we want. The **Artboard Tool** (*Shift + O*) in Adobe Illustrator was made for this purpose. We define the size and shape of the artboard, and then move every mental space inside those boundaries, resizing them if needed. We can have more than one artboard, even an artboard within an artboard if needed.

Illustrator's artboard tool is more flexible and powerful than setting page/canvas dimensions in other applications.

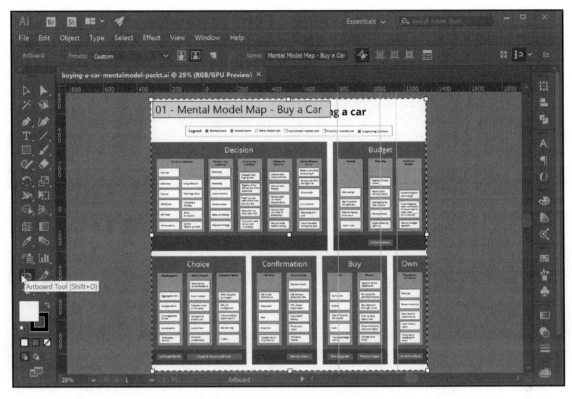

Use the Artboard Tool to arrange the map elements

The other benefit of using an artboard is that we can export our map with just a click. Go to the **File** > **Export** > **Export for Screens…**, as follows:

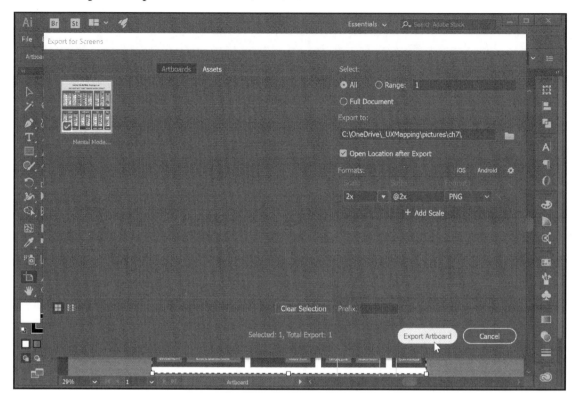

The resulting map will be the right size to be included in this book, although the text will be still small.

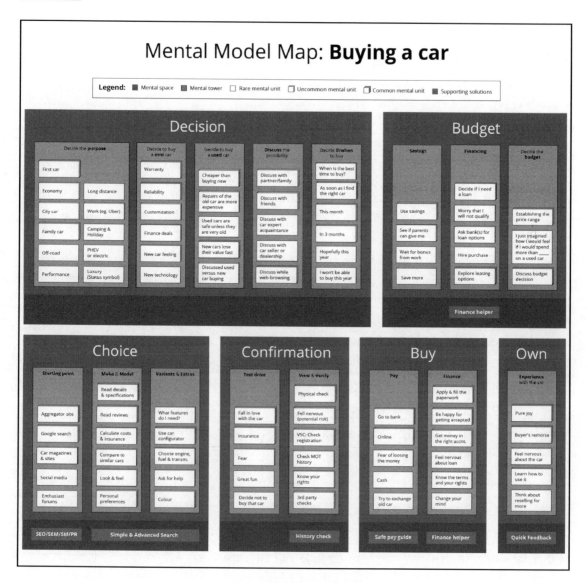

The finished Mental Model Map

However, we don't create maps because they are pretty. Well, sometimes I do, but most people don't. So, let's put our map to good use.

Using the mental model map

The mental model map helps us to find new ways to support our users. To be able to do this, we need to place the existing solutions on the mental model map, and ask the question *can we create something that would make the user's life better, happier or easier in this mental space?*

Another use of the mental model map is to improve existing solutions. For example, based on this mental model map, the search should include aggregated reviews of the cars at the results page, while detailed specifications, cost breakdown, and insurance on the car details page. It should enable easy side-by-side comparison. The personal preferences might suggest an add to favorites feature, while the look and feel might be enhanced with high-quality pictures and videos.

If people don't really need some of our existing features, we can hide them or even remove them. Instead of designing many features, we should always design use-cases, supported by the mental model of our users.

Current business goals can be updated or reconsidered based on a detailed and accurate mental model map. Mental model maps are inspiration sources and can lead to innovation.

Earlier in this chapter, I mentioned selective perception. If we understand what is filtered by the user's mental model, we can focus on what reaches the user. By understanding how the mental model message changes our message, we can provide the information in a way to minimize distortion. Alternatively, we can take a step further, and instead of providing what the user wants, we shape their mental model toward what they need. This is a powerful tool, and it was often misused in the past. So, don't start a UFO cult, just because you can.

Summary

A mental model map is a visual representation of a user group's or persona's thought process and patterns related to a subset of the world, relevant to our solution. It also contains how our solution supports the user's thought processes. The mental model shifts focus from designing a solution to understanding the user's state of mind, and how we can support those states.

To be able to create a mental model map, we can do longitudinal research. This research type covers a longer period with the same test users. When creating a mental model map, we focus on target behaviors in their larger context during the logging period, which can take days or even a few weeks. Then, we analyze the results, creating mental units, group them into mental towers, and then group the towers into mental spaces.

The mental model map helps us to find new ways to support the users in different mental spaces, thus creating new solutions or improving existing ones. We can use the mental model map as a starting point to change the users' behavior.

In the next chapter, we will discover a framework to change people's behaviors. We will create a behavioral change map to make the process transparent and easy to communicate. Continue if you are ready to make people's lives better, by changing what they think and do.

8

Behavioral Change Map - The Action Plan of Persuasion

In this chapter, we'll improve people's lives by shifting their behavior to what is more beneficial for them. You will learn about a framework that will increase your sales while making your customers happier. To do this, we will do the following things:

- Introduce behavioral change
- Study the Amazon miracle to provide us with examples for this chapter
- See whether a behavioral change is possible, and if yes, how?
- Understand credibility and its impact on behavioral change
- Explore the cue-routine-reward framework
- Talk about automating repetition
- Investigate the two different modes our mind uses to process information
- Use, my method, the LEVER framework to change user behaviors
- Draw a behavioral change map, based on the LEVER framework
- Use the map for the benefit of our users

 A behavioral change map is a visual representation of a path to change a user group's behavior. It should be simple and impactful. Behavior change maps should be based on a good understanding of our user's mindset and thought processes, ideally on a detailed mental model, backed with longitudinal research.

A single chapter in a book is hardly enough to explain behavior change. I will try my best to scrape the surface of the psychology and behavioral economics behind this new science. However, my goal here is not to teach you how to change behaviors. Instead, I will show you how to plan and map those changes. If you want to delve deeper into the subject, BJ Fogg's book, *Persuasive Technology*, is probably the best start.

> *In* Chapter 2, *User Story Map - Requirements by Collaboration and Sticky Notes, we have seen the INVEST principles working to create user stories. The "v" in INVEST stands for valuable and by valuable, we mean value to the user and to the business. However, for most user stories, value is forced at best. Sometimes, the users will not perceive something particularly valuable. For example, cloud storage was initially not perceived as valuable neither for the users nor for the businesses. Why would the users install an application, set it up, and give access to their data to a third party? Why would they allow the app to use their Internet connection for this? From the company's perspective, why would they sacrifice resources (storage on their servers, bandwidth, developer time, and so on) to provide this service? Today, I have 1.12 TB total storage on OneDrive, which I got for free (most of it as a gift with my Office license, but you can get OneDrive storage without spending a dime on Microsoft software). I use it to store many gigabytes of data. You might use Dropbox, Google Drive, or one of the other similar services; however, chances are, you have access to at least one, if not many, cloud storage services. Cloud storage-based file hosting services, such as Google Drive, were initially not perceived as valuable. What happened? How could the behavior of both the users and big corporations change so fast? Is behavior change even possible?*

Most of you might think that behavioral change is not possible. The free will is one of our most treasured abilities. We would want to choose between different possible courses of action and between different paths and different goals. Actually, those free choices and behavioral change are not mutually exclusive. Amazon is a great example of how those can coexist on a great e-commerce platform.

The Amazon miracle

In this chapter, we will map how Amazon changes users' behaviors. Please don't get me wrong, I'm not blaming Amazon for their behavior change solutions. In fact, I'm thankful for their great service. I never leave home without my Kindle, and I buy 80% of my books there. I believe that we can learn from Amazon. They successfully disrupted the e-commerce industry, starting with books, expanding to cover many different areas. Nowadays, you can get home delivery from restaurants through Prime Now, or store petabytes of data storage on AWS.

Amazon moved far from selling books in the early 90s. They have surpassed Walmart as the retailer with the largest market capitalization in the States.

No matter what you do, you can learn from the simple and more advanced techniques used by Amazon to make the customers happier, their lives easier, while balancing that with their business goals. Even if you don't want to be the next Jeff Bezos, you should aim to create a solution that has an impact on people, changing them for the better.

For example, you can support a charitable organization without spending your money or time, just by shopping on Amazon:

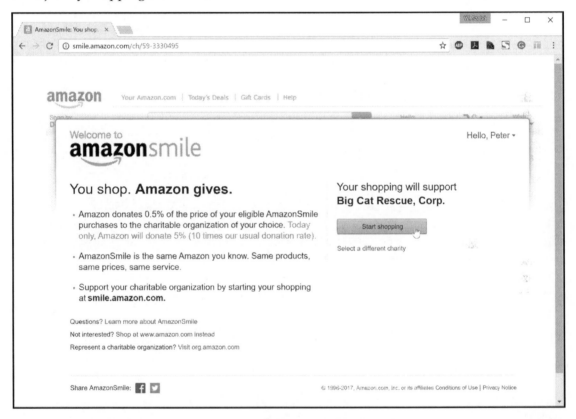

As a positive side effect of using AmazonSmile, you will likely donate more money to *big cat rescue*, or as a worst case scenario, a charity not interested in saving cats. You might also share your favorite charity's smile link. How's that possible? How could Amazon achieve that? This chapter holds the answers to some elements of the Amazon miracle and some of the less altruistic elements of the Amazon miracle, too.

Is it possible to change behaviors?

We hate being manipulated or told what to do and how to do it, even if it's for a good cause. Although people love a degree of guidance, this is dwarfed by the loss of choice. Luckily, unnoticed change works brilliantly. Although some people would say it's a deadly sin to even try such techniques, I will show you that it's possible.

Soon, I will tell you a story about a lucky dwarf, but first a quick trick. Think of a number between one and ten! Don't think much about it, just make a mental note of the first number that came to your mind; my bet is that it's the number seven. Did it work?

I learned this trick from the mind reader and author Nick Kolenda. This is probably the best example of priming I have ever encountered. There is no mind reading or magic involved. Nick's trick works, because of the exposure to certain words in that paragraph, notably dwarf, lucky, and deadly sin. Even a subtle exposure to those concepts will activate a schema or a thought pattern. Priming is the reason why you were thinking of the number seven. This is what I call Nick Kolenda's story of the lucky dwarf. If you are interested in persuasion and practical applications of it, I would recommend his book, *Methods of Persuasion*.

If the lucky dwarf trick didn't work, that is because you expected to be manipulated and picked eight instead. Yes, you could have picked any number between one to ten, but chances are, you picked eight. This happened, because of a previous priming, chiefly that this is chapter eight. Moreover, seven acted as an anchor, so you were likely to choose a number next to it. Since I asked you to pick something between one to ten, you will have a tendency to pick a bigger number, close to the high anchor ten. Up or higher is associated with the schema for good, better, and positive that might have led to the number eight. You wanted to pick a better number, more than the one I wanted to implant in your mind.

It's also possible that you picked a number lower than seven. You might have even failed to comply with my request, and didn't pick a number at all, or picked your favorite number, and that's perfectly fine because behavior change intends to change the behavior of the masses. It works for groups of people, but not for all individuals in that group. If you are not performing in a mind-reading show, you don't want 100% accuracy. Instead, you want to influence or persuade just some of the people getting in contact with your solution. If you are selling yachts, you don't need to persuade that many people, but if you are running an e-commerce site, you need to think about thousands. You need to create a behavior change map, which might work for the majority of the target audience, then continuously improve to increase its efficiency.

Real-world persuasion is hard. Most of us lack the needed persistence, and even if we are persistent, this is not scalable. No matter how good you are in sales, you can't do more than a handful of sales pitches per day, but chances are that you do much less. We can also lack flexibility and discreetness needed for persuasion. Fortunately, our computers, websites, and apps can be much better at this, but they are not perfect. One of the critical areas where they need help from you is improving their credibility.

Credibility

Imagine that you have reached a website that claims that you just won £10,000. You just need to give your name and home address. Chances are you would close the site right away. Now, imagine that you go to a brick-and-mortar grocery store; when you enter the building, you are greeted by loud music and a man in a suit who gives you an oversized check while a camera is pointed at you; he tells you that you won £10,000, requesting your name and home address. The message is exactly the same, yet you would react to it quite differently. Why? This is because your trust for the website is quite low, especially compared to men in suits.

Let's take another example. Let's say you feel pain when you place weight on your leg. You search the Internet. Most likely you will find that you have three different kinds of terminal disease, but for the sake of argument let's assume that you find out that it's a sprained ankle from a close friend on Facebook; she suggests elastic bandages and taking ibuprofen. Would you do that? What if you went to your doctor, and they had the exact same suggestion. Even if your trust for your close friend on Facebook was quite high, you might have had questions about her expertise.

Credibility = trust × expertise
To maximize your credibility, you need to maximize both trust and expertise. The credibility score toward your solution will be unique to each user, but it can be aggregated. (When I talk about credibility, I mean perceived, aggregated credibility for the given user group.)

As we can see from the above examples, credibility is important, because low credibility means low influence potential. While influencing will most likely fail with low credibility, a high credibility will not guarantee success alone.

In the past, before the Internet era, computers had an innate credibility, according to BJ Fogg. So, what went wrong? People trusted computers much more than most humans. Since the late 90s, this has been eroded. With the advent of phishing, scams, and fake news websites, credibility became contested and disputed. People no longer believe everything they find on the Internet. This is a beneficial behavioral change, as the Internet had many sites with malicious intent even in the early years.

Amazon has a good trustability, but Smile might increase this even further. One of the proven benefits of corporate social responsibility is increasing trust. If we believe in a charity, and someone supports that charity, we will start to trust that person or company through association.

The cue-routine-reward framework

The classic behavior change model is based on the cue-routine-reward framework. This works by the simple principle that a trigger makes you act (cue), with a consistent behavior (routine), possibly resulting in a positive event (reward). For example, you may feel sleepy in the morning. This is the cue, which triggers the drinking coffee routine, possibly resulting in being more alert, increased concentration, and increased dopamine levels. Overall, you might feel good, as a reward. This, in turn, strengthens the association between cue and routine, so it's more likely that tomorrow morning you will also have coffee.

For the routine, conscious thought is not required. If you are a coffee lover, you will most likely not think whether to drink a cup or not, you just drink it. The cue-routine-reward framework is so strong that sometimes it can go against your conscious decisions. This is what people usually call an addiction.

> *The most direct way is using a highly addictive substance, opium, for example. In 2004, over 200 restaurants were closed in China because the officials found out that they were seasoning their meals with opium poppies. To avoid detection, the restaurants mixed opium with chilli oil. The opium addiction created this way served as a cue for customers to return to the restaurant. Those people had no idea that they were addicted to opium. Their reward was the euphoric feelings opium induces. Getting another dose reinforced the addiction, and the circle continued. Tragically, the story was not over in 2004. From time-to-time, restaurants try this trick. In January 2016, the China Food and Drug Administration closed 35 restaurants with similar charges.*

Addictions are not always related to a substance. For example, problem gamblers can experience cue, feeling that they don't have enough money, or even that they are in financial ruin. This could have been caused by gambling, to begin with. However, their routine is to try to win a large sum, even by risking what little they have left or using illegal means to get money to fuel their habit. Gambling can be fun, a form of entertainment. Some people spend money on going to the opera or a fancy dinner, while others spend that much at the casino tables. That's perfectly fine, as long as it stays in the fun zone, but what if you became a problem gambler? Although far from being easy, the solution is to remove the cue, which triggers the routine. This is why socially responsible online casinos have self-exclusion options. You can set up a period during which you can't play. This can be as short as half a day, but it can be a couple of months if you need that much time. This will obviously not stop at-risk gamblers from joining another casino. Probably, the best solution for them would be to hand over control of their money to a close family member. This essentially removes the cue, and hopefully, in time the behavior will fade. If you are interested in the mechanisms involved in addiction, for a more in-depth view, I would suggest *Addiction and Self-Control*, edited by Neil Levy. I hope that your interest in addictions is in helping addicts, not inducing an addiction.

Behavior change is applicable outside of addictions, too. Conscious thought should not be required for many simple behaviors. For example, when the phone rings most people will answer it, without much of a decision-making process. They simply repeat their habit by pressing the green button on their phone. This is certainly not an addiction, but still, it fits into the cue-routine-reward framework. Also, you can use the cue-routine-reward framework to create a recurring desire for your solution, a drive to use it again and again. This is what Nir Eyal calls *manufacturing desire* in his 2012 TechCrunch article available at `ht tps://techcrunch.com/2012/03/04/how-to-manufacture-desire/`.

To be able to manufacture desire, you need to understand how cues work. There are two types of cues. External cues come from the environment of the user; this is what you can change directly.

From external to internal cues

External cues come in many shapes or forms. A search result in Google, a social media share, or a huge billboard can be an external cue. However, a friend can casually mention a new book, or we can see someone reading it on the train. Sometimes, they are huge billboards, or sometimes just a hint in an interview with a famous author.

Targeted e-mails are one of the best examples of external cues. If I get an e-mail from Amazon with a list of books to read on my Kindle, based on my previous shopping behaviors, chances are this will trigger my book buying behavior yet again. Based on the sheer number of books I buy, I will start to feel like a book addict.

Through the repetition of the cue-routine-reward process, the external cues become internal cues. This means that from time-to-time I will go to Amazon and browse for some books I haven't read. This happens even if I have more than 10 books in the waiting-to-be-read list, sitting idly on my Kindle. It's fairly obvious that I have an Amazon addiction. I simply can't imagine my life without reading. Amazon sent me many cues (including free books with Prime), made the routine easy (Kindle, one click order, Prime), and the reward obvious and powerful (I just love reading).

The reward reinforces the external cues when we encounter them next. Moreover, repeated action can create internal cues. They are more powerful and more cost efficient. Those are the things we genuinely want to do, just like reading new books on Kindle is an internal cue for me. Even if Amazon would stop all its advertising activities, all newsletters, and even public relations, I would still buy books from them.

The reward also has a randomness element here. Sometimes, I just buy terrible books-- poorly written, low-value junk. However, the brain just loves random rewards. The monetary reward for gambling is random by nature, yet it still works as a powerful reward.

Probably, the best online cue I have seen so far is Amazon's Kindle First. It has three powerful elements, which would work alone, but together they multiply in effect:

1. Editors select (usually) six books, from different categories, which will appear next month.
2. You will get one of them for free, instead of the usual pre-order price (around £4 in March 2017).
3. You get to read the book before their release date next month, even today if you are a Prime member.

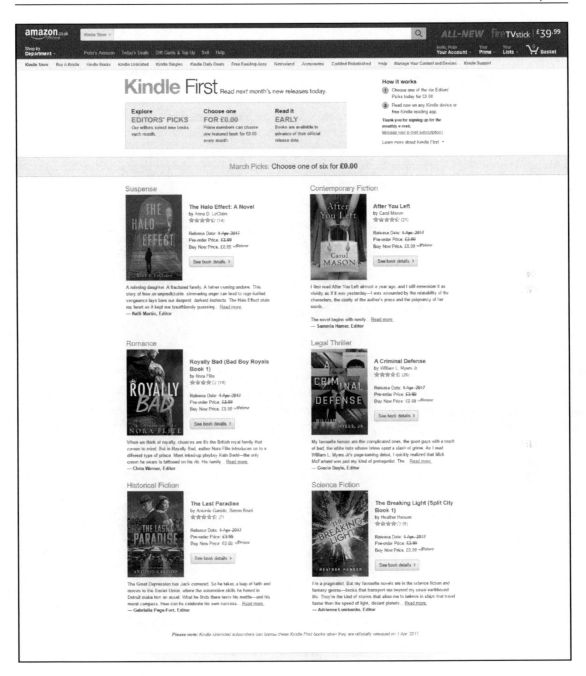

Amazon Kindle First

What's not so obvious is that the process of choosing activates intrinsic motivation, as in a motivation that emerges from a genuine personal desire, another source of internal cues. I'm always motivated to choose one of the books, and then read it. I love the freedom of choice Amazon gave me there. By limiting people's choices to six books, all from different genres, Amazon overcame the decision paralysis. Decision paralysis, in a nutshell, means that a huge amount of variants can trigger a delay in the decision-making process, sometimes even the avoidance of a decision. For example, Audible (Amazon's audiobook production and retail company) give me one credit each month, which can be used to get any audiobook title from their catalog. So, I get to choose between more than 200,000 titles. This can be overwhelming. Sometimes, I end up not using the credit in a given month. (Luckily, they carry over to the next month if unused.)

A third source of internal (thus more powerful) cues appears when there is no obvious reward at all. Our mind will try to enforce congruent attitudes with our behaviors. Without the psychological lingo, this means that if we do something, we will then develop a favorable attitude toward it. It works to a degree for Amazon book-buying habits. If someone would buy and read a book and realize that they don't really like reading, they might buy another book because they now consider themselves a reader. Those are the book snobs. However, they are an elusive, hard to define, and hard-to-research user group.

> *Please, don't get me wrong. I have drawn a forced parallel between buying books and using drugs. I respect the battle recovering drug addicts fight each day to overcome their harmful habits. The only reason I'm comparing buying books and reading them to drug addiction is to emphasize similarities. Most of the relevant literature is about serious and harmful addictions and how to help people suffering from those addictions. I'm sure that you don't want to induce addictions, but you might be interested in creating the next Amazon or Google. As I mentioned before, I love Amazon. Amazon doesn't pay me to advertise them. Yet, I still do it, for free. There is a psychological reason for that:*

Uri Gneezy and Aldo Rustichini published a fascinating research in *The Quarterly Journal of Economics*, back in 2000. The test subjects were students collecting donations. The researchers created three groups. Members of one group received 10% of the total money they collected, members of the second group received 1% of the money, whereas the third group received no incentive at all. What shocked the scientific world is that the students who got no monetary incentive managed to collect the most money. Those who got 10% collected the second most, and those who received a small incentive collected, by far, the lowest amount. How that's possible? The answer is that the students who worked for free developed a congruent attitude. The authors titled the article *Pay Enough or Don't Pay at All*. This is also the reason why people work more enthusiastically, and perform better at charities, working for free, than at low-paying jobs. Low salaries can decrease the performance of even high-performing team members, who somehow ended up in that job.

The cue-routine-reward framework is the most important element of behavior change. To summarize this section, I have created the following simple diagram, the starting point for most behavior change maps:

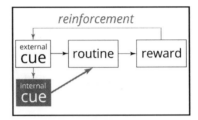

AmazonSmile will constantly remind us of the donations made as a result of our shopping habits. This is a good example of reinforcement. Through this reinforcement process, we are likely to develop congruent attitudes.

This might increase the likelihood of donations to our chosen charity. We will also associate Amazon with the charity we love and trust, so this is a true win-win situation.

Automate repetition

One of the most well-known behavioral change techniques, which also improves user experience, is automating repetition. Basically, the solution makes the users' lives easier by removing repetitive tasks--automatic save with cloud synchronization, and automatic updates for software. Automatic transmission, automatic parking, or even rain-sensing wipers for cars are more and more accepted and expected. Essentially, they remove the need for the cue or any trigger and replace the routine with an automatic solution.

Of course, Amazon capitalizes on this with the subscription buying model. For items that users buy frequently, Amazon replaces the classic buy button with a subscription button. Although you can switch back to one-time purchase, it will be more expensive. Moreover, the delivery frequency also defaults to the most common value, so you can still use the easy checkout process for the first purchase, but the repetition will be automated. In two months (or whatever is the delivery frequency for your item), you will get the same item again.

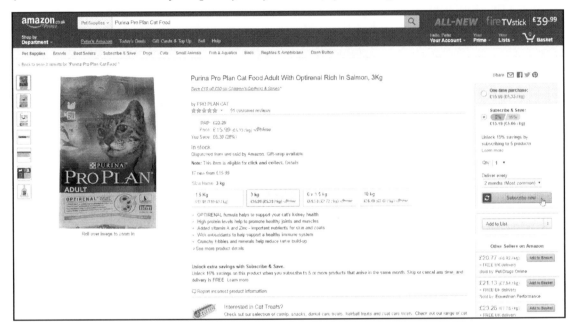

Subscription buying model for Amazon

Amazon Prime is also a subscription, quite a popular one. There were over 60 million Prime members at the time of writing this book. It is a complex benefits package, but the automation part is that it's a fixed fee you pay each year, recurring. Just like a magazine subscription, which replaces buying a magazine each month. The difference is that you don't get anything tangible, just a few nice benefits bundled together. Amazon didn't publish the cancellation rate for Prime, but I assume it's fairly low. What's interesting is that this benefit package benefits Amazon more than the buyer. The average monthly expenditure of non-Prime members was $138 a month, whereas for Prime members it was $193, according to `Recode.net`. This is mainly because Prime members order more frequently.

The free next day delivery--one of the main benefits of the Prime membership--successfully changed people's online shopping habits. Yes, Amazon has a brilliant behavioral change solution: the users will pay $99/year to change their own behavior into something more aligned with Amazon's business goals. Do you remember *Pay Enough or Don't Pay at All* from the previous section? Amazon went a step further. Uri Gneezy and Aldo Rustichini didn't include a fourth group, where the students had to pay a small amount just to be able to collect the donations. However, if they had, I'm almost certain that group would have collected the largest sum.

If you run a charity, or are just about to start one, you can still benefit from automating repetition. Not just with AmazonSmile, but directly on your site. Instead of asking for one big donation, suggest a monthly recurring donation to your supporters. You don't even need to worry about developing such a solution. You can use PayPal's ready-made one, such as *big cat rescue* does.

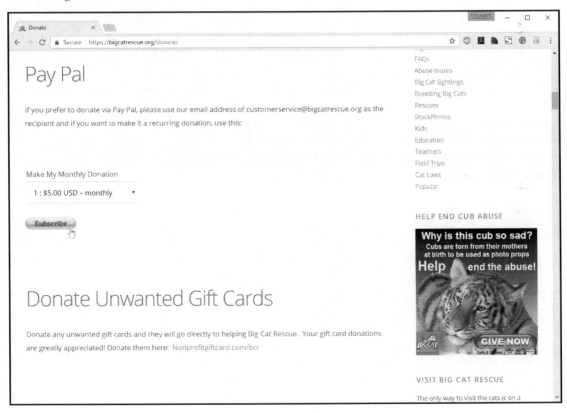

Heuristic and systematic processing

Behavior change is not mind control. You are not exerting some sort of evil super-power to enslave the users' minds. Instead, your solution should provide guidance and support. To be able to do that, we need to understand how our brain processes information from the outside world.

We have two modes to process information. Most of the time, we use **heuristic processing**, or at least we are closer to the heuristic processing end of the processing spectrum, which means we pretty much effortlessly and mindlessly choose. When we are in a good mood, this is more likely to happen. When the price is relatively low, or the action is easily undoable, we use heuristic processing. When the message is seemingly too complex, we also tend to use this processing mode. For example, when buying a PC laptop, if you are not tech savvy, you might be easily overwhelmed by different specifications.

In the heuristic processing mode, the user is easily influenced by attractiveness or esthetics. This is probably one of the reasons why Apple products are so popular. The volume of presented information is also a positive influence here even if the content of it is not. If you list 12 features for a laptop, then 6 for another, people will be more inclined to buy the one with 12, even if they don't know what those features mean. For example, one element listed among the specifications of the current gen MacBook Pro 15 is *Turbo Boost up to 3.6GHz*. Most customers will not know what that is, but it sure sounds cool. It's hardly new, introduced in 2008, and hardly unique to MacBook Pros. Some PC laptops offer Turbo Boost up to higher GHz numbers, for example, those with Intel i7-7700HQ or better processors.

Most users might not even encounter a scenario where Turbo Boost is important. So, why bother listing it in the first place?

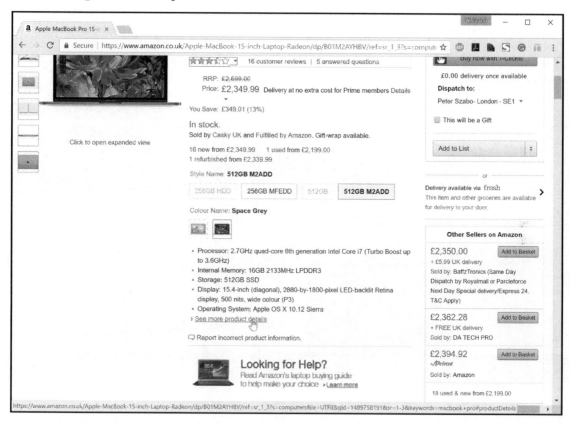

Another way to convince users in heuristic processing mode is by instilling authority. Listing many features at a source which we trust. From the preceding screenshot, I would emphasize the laptop buying guide. It promises to help you choose, so you can rely on an expert to guide you to the best laptop. Going even further, with Amazon's choice, you only need to select the purpose, and Amazon will give you the best laptop, fully capitalizing on your heuristic processing mode. Chances are that you will end up with a great laptop, at a good price, so everyone wins.

Amazon's laptop buying guide

On the opposite end of the spectrum, there is systematic processing. Sometimes, we make a conscious effort to evaluate the information we received. This happens when we are highly motivated, something grabs our attention, and it's relevant and important for us. High-value purchases, such as buying a car or a property, are usually closer to the systematic processing end of the processing spectrum.

If you want to convince people in this processing mode, you need to show as much information as possible, with both positive and negative aspects. This is where reviews are helpful. People in systematic processing mode want to see the downsides of a choice. There is no perfect choice. If you have just 10 positive reviews on your site, people will simply not believe them, and you will lose their trust. On the other hand, if you have a negative, two neutral, and seven positive reviews, people will find that more convincing.

Reasons and arguments are important here. People will put some effort into understanding the message, so try to emphasize a few important elements with justification and possibilities to go even more in-depth.

The LEVER framework

Early in my career, I used the cue-routine-reward framework to change the users' behaviors for their benefit. The operant conditioning resulting from the perceived possibility of reward always worked with the majority of users who arrived at the reward stage. Amazing marketing teams provided the cues, and the rewards were many, varied, and choosable, often with a bit of randomness mixed in. However, for a significant number of users, the behavior change failed.

To remedy this, I came up with the LEVER framework. It is an extended version of the cue-routine-reward framework. I have used it to provide behavioral change solutions to my clients. This book is the first time I have published it. I hope it will help you to make your users happier.

LEVER is a five-step framework, starting with external cues, which then lead to the namesake LEVER element, which then leads to perceived possible rewards. They reinforce the effect of the external cues. After one or more cycles, the previous routines get replaced by the LEVER-enabled routine, which leads to internal cues, eliminating the need for external cues to trigger the desired behavior. In this aspect, it's similar to the cue-routine-reward framework. However, I have added the LEVER element.

LEVER has five areas, where we support the users, automate repetition, and help them based on their processing mode. The five areas of LEVER are as follows:

- **Limitation**: We show the item as something rare, hard to get, and valuable. So, this is the best moment to get it. For example, we show that only two items are left, or they need to order in the next x minutes to get it tomorrow. With this, we often trigger loss aversion.
- **Elevation**: Instead of removing options, we show many products, but elevate some to increase their visibility. For example, we can elevate a product by saying it's a best seller or a popular item in the category.
- **Validation**: We help the conscious decision of the user by validating their preferred choice. This choice can be what we think is the best for them. There are many validation techniques, a good example is *Frequently bought together* on Amazon. Instead of buying a PS4 console alone, we should suggest a few great games, maybe an extra controller or a longer HDMI cable. This will be genuinely helpful for both the user and Amazon, but some validation techniques are not so straightforward. Most things we do to motivate our users to exert a certain conscious behavior will fall into this group.
- **Ease**: If something is easy, it's more likely that the user will do it. The easiest thing is not doing something. This is where automating repetition and smart defaults really shine. Amazon's 1-Click checkout is probably the best example of something that's not fully automated and still easy.
- **Reversibility**: Even if we did everything and the users were receptive to our behavior change attempts, they might have a second thought. People hate commitments, destructive change, or the potential of a wrong decision. This is where reversibility helps. For example, you can request a cancellation or edit the order after it has been submitted, just to name two examples from Amazon.

We will draw a behavioral change map based on the LEVER framework for the Amazon e-commerce site, but first, let's understand the five areas of LEVER. The user can encounter them in any order. Most of the time, the user will be exposed to more than one element of LEVER. *I will let you in on a secret: the only reason they are in this order is because this way they made a meaningful word. So, I can say that I offer you a lever, which sits on the pivot of the mental model. This lever can be used to lift the user into a better behavior.*

Limitation

People prefer avoiding losses to acquiring equivalent gains. This is what we call loss aversion. If there is only one or just a few items left, we will be more likely to buy the given item. If the item can only be purchased for a limited time, or at least at a discounted price, it adds a sense of urgency and will also increase your chances of selling the item. For example, Parker and Lehman (2011) published some research on wine purchase in brick-and-mortar shops. Unsurprisingly, they found that people were likely to pick the wine with fewer bottles available.

Limitations will also increase the user's satisfaction with the reward. You will enjoy your coke much better if it was the last on the shelf. Even if it's the same old coke, you have been drinking for ages.

Some limitations come from the users themselves. Those are a bit harder to influence or capitalize upon, but if you succeed, they are the most powerful. This is what I call **well-timed triggers**. For example, you just lost your headphones. Then, you see an ad for new headphones or you go to Amazon and see headphones on the first page. This seems like magic. Does Amazon have supernatural powers? Probably what happened is that you became much more responsive to headphone-related content, due to your internal limitations. Losing the headphones already primed the mental model of getting new headphones, and you created your limitation.

Elevation

Elevation might seem like picking the product, the one for which we have the largest margin, and try to make all users buy that product. This is far from the truth. Authenticity is important. Aim to deliver on your promise. For the best selling product, choose the real best sellers, and for the editor's choice products pick the best, based on an objective evaluation. This will increase trust, and your e-commerce site might even become a respected and often referenced source of information in one or more product categories.

Elevation can also come from the information you know about the user. If a user buys PS4 games often, it makes sense to offer them those games. If a user bought cat food two months ago, you might want to suggest buying it again, even if they didn't turn on the automation

If you want to just sell more of a certain item, be honest about it, and create a promotion. Users will also like a price reduction as a form of elevation. Some businesses, including Amazon, have products that they can ship sooner. Marking those is another good form of elevation.

The benefit of elevation is increasing the visibility. This is also the first step we do to help users with their choice, but more important is to make sure that they believe they can choose. We indicate many items but feature some. Even if the user will not immediately choose the elevated object, we have primed that, and the next time the user might be more receptive to buying it.

Validation

A large number of choices leads to decision paralysis. In that situation, the user might postpone the purchase. As we have seen in the previous section, the user can use either heuristic or synthetic processing. To succeed, we need to support both.

Great product images are essential in heuristic processing mode, but so is a nice clean design for our website. Aesthetically pleasing visual design leads to brain responses similar to the biological sense of pleasure. You don't need to study neuroesthetics to know that people will not trust, and most likely leave bad looking, poorly designed websites.

Most of what we do as validation is supporting people's conscious decisions. A good information architecture is probably the most important step, alongside a powerful search.

Social validation is undeniably helpful. As social creatures, we are influenced by what other people do or say. This is why we are interested in customer reviews or frequently bought together items. *What do customers buy after viewing this item?* is another powerful example from Amazon for social validation.

Ease

Ease is closely related to easily actionable on the web. Notifications should be easy to understand and should tell the user what to do next. Instead of hard-to-understand technical notifications, warnings, and error messages, Amazon has messages that tell the user how to solve the issue and what went wrong.

What we discussed in the automate repetition section will come in handy in making things easier for the user. The easiest action is an automatic action, which does not require human input. With automation, we want to make sure that the user is notified of all that's happening automagically. We want them to feel in control and that includes the ability to change or turn off the automation.

A big, visible button for our favored outcome will always help. For our palaeolithic ancestors, the ability to quickly detect contrast in the environment was key to avoid being eaten by a saber-toothed tiger or any other predators. The color can also make a difference here. Yellow, orange, and red colors have a long wavelength and small frequency, compared to other colors. We react much faster to those colors, compared to blue or green. This is probably why Amazon's **Add to basket** button is yellow, and the **Buy now with 1-Click** button is orange.

There are many factors to why it's easy to find the **Add to basket** and the **Buy now with 1-Click** buttons, like placement, the darker border, amount of white space around them, or the icons:

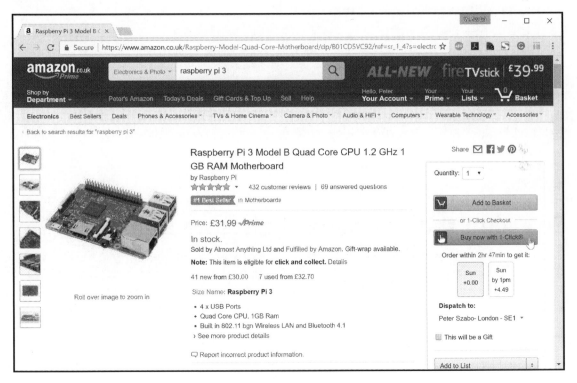

There are many subtle changes Amazon did in the past few years to make their site easier to use. Just remember that, don't copy Amazon, learn from them. The most important thing you should learn is customer obsession, which leads to easy-to-use websites and happy customers.

Reversibility

While commitments are beneficial for the business, people will feel imprisoned by them. Should you ask, *are you sure you want to buy this?*, please don't. That would make things even worse. What people need instead is the option to change their mind.

People absolutely hate long-term contracts, so companies need to offer valuable rewards to get people into them. That's why mobile network operators offer expensive smartphones, just to lure customers into those long-term contracts.

On Amazon, you have the option to request cancellation of a recently placed order or edit it. If it has already arrived, you can return it.

Even before you get to confirm your order, you can review your basket. If you wanted to buy something with a promo code, you will immediately see whether it was successfully applied to your order.

There are many techniques used by Amazon to either give you the ability to change your mind or reassure you that you will not have to. Shipping options with guaranteed delivery dates will reassure you that you will get your items when you want them, so you will not have to buy something else at the last minute, for example, when a birthday gift doesn't arrive in time.

Drawing the behavioral change map

A behavioral change map is a visual representation of what we do to improve the users' behaviors. If you want to base your behavioral change projects on my LEVER framework, I would suggest a map similar to this one, showing the Amazon miracle:

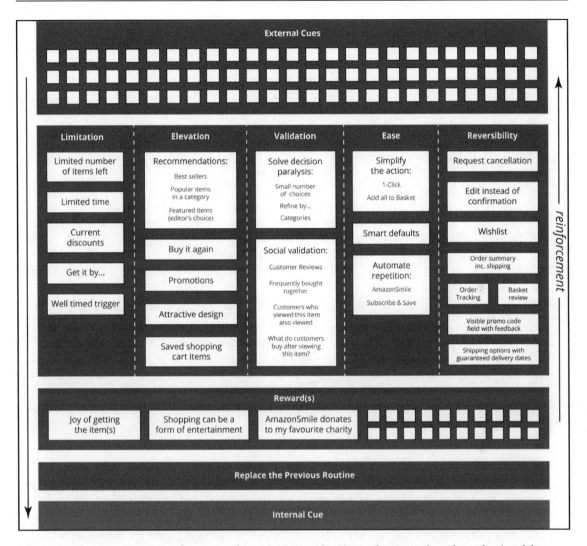

There can be many external cues and many rewards. To make sure that they don't add clutter to the map, I just added empty squares. I have used a dashed line to separate the elements of LEVER, to show that they can often overlap. *Frequently bought together* is also a form of elevation, not just validation. All reversibility options benefit from being easy to use. In fact, an easy cancellation method like Amazon's will make the reversibility aspect even better. We don't just want to undo our mistakes, we want that to be easy.

Drawing this map should be easy based on the mapping techniques we discussed in the preceding chapter. What's more important is to understand how LEVER works and how to use the map.

How to use the behavioral change map

This chapter was a short glimpse into behavioral change. In the future, I might write a book on this subject alone, expanding the LEVER framework, and giving you more tools to improve the users' lives by changing their behaviors. With that said, I hope that you use this chapter's learning even today.

If you work for Amazon, you can add new elements, which might be missing from the LEVER, and then test them with real users. This leads to continuous improvement, better solutions, and happier users. We do behavior change for the benefit of the users, never against their best interest.

If you don't work for Amazon, you can still benefit from creating Amazon's or a competitor's behavioral change map. You can find testable ideas there. Remember never to copy an idea without testing and tweaking it for your users.

Summary

A behavioral change map is a visual representation of a path to change a user group's behavior. It's possible to change behaviors, but for that, your solution needs to have a high level of credibility.

The classic behavior change model is based on the cue-routine-reward framework: a trigger makes you act (first an external cue), with a consistent behavior (routine), possibly resulting in a positive event (reward), which will reinforce the process. By repeating this enough, internal cues emerge, which are much more powerful.

My behavior change model is an extended version of the cue-routine-reward framework. LEVER is a five-step framework. The second, namesake element of the framework is composed of five areas: **L**imitation, **E**levation, **V**alidation, **E**ase, and **R**eversibility. After one or more cycles, the previous routines get replaced by the LEVER-enabled routine, which leads to internal cues, eliminating the need for external cues to trigger the desired behavior. I hope you will only use behavioral change for the benefit of the users.

Now, we are ready to merge all map types together and create the ultimate user experience map. Follow me to the next chapter to harness the power of the 4D UX Map.

9

The 4D UX Map - Putting It All Together

I have always considered communicating user experience as the hardest part of my job. User research is fascinating, and its result can improve a solution or even create a new one if there is a drive for change. For that, you need to convince stakeholders--this is what the industry usually calls getting buy-in.

In the previous chapters, we have seen many different map types, but all of those are just aspects of the user experience as a whole. To get buy-in for innovation, I needed a map type that shows user experience in one big picture.

I wanted to create something I can show to any stakeholder, looks great, and can be printed on paper, a map that can be taped to the wall of an office or included in a presentation. This is how the 4D UX Map was born. In June 2014, I published the 4D UX Map for the first time in my blog, the Kaizen-UX available at `http://kaizen-ux.com/4d-user-experience-map/`.

This chapter is an extended, enriched, and updated version of that blog post. In the past three years, I have created quite a few 4D UX Maps, and thus I have improved this deliverable.

 The 4D UX Map summarizes the user experience in one detailed map. It's a tool to communicate the results to one or more user test, without wasting the stakeholder's time. I have created a high-impact deliverable to visualize how the users' needs are met. The 4D UX Map is my ultimate user experience communication tool. It's a compact, yet highly visual, summary of an UX consulting project.

In this chapter, I will show you how you can summarize your UX projects with a 4D map. To be able to do that, we will learn the following:

- Introduce the opportunity, the restaurant without tables
- Summarize what we have discovered about UX mapping in the previous chapters, and how we can merge them into one map
- Explore how the merged map can be the most advanced yet acceptable (MAYA) map
- Define the four dimensions of the 4D UX Map: milestones, events, importance, and severity of the problem
- Introduce mental model snippets
- Discuss and add ratings to the map
- Create the 4D UX Map for our opportunity
- Use it for the benefit of our users
- See how this map type can evolve in the future, with your help

The restaurant without tables

In this chapter, we will create the 4D UX Map for a fictitious restaurant. Understandably, no company would share the 4D UX Map I have created for them as a summary of a large consulting contract. Moreover, I wanted to choose a vertical we haven't touched in the previous chapters. This restaurant will only offer online takeaway orders. Imagine a talented cook in a well-equipped and staffed kitchen. It's not a three Michelin star extravaganza, but no fast-food either. You can't walk-in, but you certainly can order awesome meals, which arrive in 30 minutes tops. This might not be The Fat Duck in Berkshire, but the chef pours their soul into every dish. Imagine your favorite restaurant, just maybe this is a bit better and, of course, online only.

Our imaginary chef has already provided the tasty food and handpicked beverages to match them, but she needs your help to create the best user experience for the visitors for their website. We will create a 4D UX Map as a visual summary of our project. We aim to have one map to rule all aspects of the user experience, one map to rule them all. Unlike the one ring, this will not bind people into the darkness, but I certainly hope that the 4D UX Map has superpowers.

Sum of all maps

The 4D user experience map is a visualization of the whole user experience. Similar to the first map we created in the Chapter 1, *How will UX Mapping Change Your (Users') Life?*, it is a communication tool. We will improve the users' lives by filling the web with easy-to-use and beautiful websites. We will start with the website of a restaurant.

The 4D UX Map has a narrative flow, composed of events and milestones, similar to the user story map, from Chapter 2, *User Story Map - Requirements by Collaboration and Sticky Notes*. Events grouped into milestones form the backbone of the 4D UX Map. We map every achievement the user has on the road to reach the opportunity, and this will form the horizontal axis of the map. You might recognize those achievements as the milestones from the user story map. The unique events will also be featured under each milestone. I usually display them vertically to make sure that the map doesn't become too wide for complex solutions. This is also a good format for chained events. Sometimes, one event can lead to another, for example, viewing the pictures of different dishes on the menu can lead to ordering one of them when you are in the restaurant, which can lead to picking a matching wine. Those are all in the same milestone, yet they are linked together as a chain of events.

All maps and business decisions can benefit from the four amigo meetings we introduced in Chapter 2, *User Story Map - Requirements by Collaboration and Sticky Notes*. So, when the first version of the 4D UX Map is finished, invite the business representative, the developer, the tester, and of course the UX expert.

When creating the 4D UX Map, you should always keep your solution's primary personas in mind, and if possible mention the other personas where needed. Besides the persona-driven approach, this map still shares many aspects with task models and user journey maps from Chapter 3, *Journey Map - Understand Your Users*. Important tasks, especially evaluations, will become events of the 4D UX Map. The easiest starting point when creating a 4D UX Map is a journey map for the primary persona, with the arrows layer hidden.

In a 4D UX Map, key interactions are represented with wireframes of the relevant views, similar to a wireflow. Contrary to the wireflows in Chapter 4, *Wireflows - Plan Your Product*, in 4D maps we will not link wireframes together with arrows, but sometimes events can be linked with arrows. The 4D UX Map will be complex as it is, and adding arrows to it would add clutter, so it would go against our principle of simplicity. You can still use the wireflows refined after multiple **Wireflow Improvement Workshops**, but keep the low fidelity. High-fidelity wireflows are best created after you have a clear understanding and plan for your solution, usually created after the 4D UX Map has been presented and discussed with stakeholders.

Even if you happen to have hi-fi wireflows, they would add too much detail to the map, attracting attention to themselves, essentially transforming the 4D UX Map into a wireflow with some noise. Sometimes, I even simplify lo-fi wireframes before adding them to the 4D UX Map. The reason why we add wireframes to this map is to gain communication benefits from viewing and discussing wireframes in the bigger context of the user experience. We will use lo-fi wireframes to keep our options open and the solution flexible. *When creating a 4D UX Map, remember to focus on what's really important from day-zero: the user and creating outstanding user experiences.*

To understand real users, we need to watch them while they interact with our solution. From the lab and remote user experience tests we run, we will gain an understanding of people's behavior. Behind every great user experience map, there is a well-executed research. You might want to revisit Chapter 5, *Remote and Lab Tests for Map Creation* before conducting remote or lab UX research.

After analyzing the research, you can create a solution map, similar to the one in Chapter 6, *Solution Mapping Based on User Insights*. From that map, you can add the root issues and solutions to the 4D UX Map with line thickness and colors. We will get back to this in the following sections of this chapter, but essentially you would want to give visual cues to what needs attention, and if a problem was solved, you would want to highlight new solutions.

I would avoid adding the obstacles and the actions directly to the 4D UX Map. However, after the obstacles and actions have been discussed and accepted, you can add markers to the map events with issues, signaling that an action plan was set in motion. I usually use a green dot in one of the corners of the event. The maps in this chapter will not feature this because they were created for fictitious opportunities.

One of the distinctive features of the 4D User Experience map is what it inherits from a mental model map drawn in Chapter 7, *Mental Model Map - A Diagram of the Perceived Reality*. I always include a visual representation of the primary persona's thought process and patterns related to the mapped solution. When possible, I base that part of the 4D UX Map on a valid longitudinal research.

The goal of solution design and 4D UX mapping is not only to support the users' thought processes, but as we have seen in `Chapter 8`, *Behavioral Change Map - The Action Plan of Persuasion* to change their behaviors for their benefit. You can achieve that by creating solutions based on my LEVER framework. Instead of using the visual representation of LEVER from the previous chapter, you can mark its elements on the map. Below the map, I list ratings for each milestone. Those ratings show how successful we currently are in achieving the desired behavior from our users. I list ratings for motivation, ease of use, credibility, and any other relevant factors for the behavior to occur. In a sense, the 4D UX Map is another visualization of LEVER-enabled behavior change design.

Greater than the sum of all maps

When creating the 4D UX Map, I just wanted to create a high impact UX deliverable that visualizes how the user needs are being met. I wasn't sure whether the result would be a map or not, but the map metaphor was convenient because it shows how the users go about reaching a goal. I was influenced by experience maps created by Chris Risdon, Gene Smith, Jesmond Allen, and James Chudley among others. Those maps feature two dimensions, and are often restricted to map a website or an app, instead of a broader approach.

The end result surpassed my expectations. The 4D UX Map is a great tool to facilitate communication with stakeholders, help UX designers understand the project, and ultimately enable us to create award-winning experiences for the benefit of the users. A hidden benefit was presenting behavioral change strategies, without putting behavioral change in the spotlight. Some stakeholders either don't believe in or are afraid of behavioral change. It's a new area, and is still considered uncharted territory in 2017 for commercial use by some senior stakeholders. Fortunately, it leads to a greatly improved user experience, which is measurable with KPIs, such as the number of new accounts created, the percentage of returning visitors, average basket value, average number of visits, and many others. In other words, it means more income for the business while also making the users happy. The 4D UX Map is my favorite way to get buy-in for the elements of the LEVER framework. It helped me in many instances to improve the users' lives, one map at a time.

The MAYA map

Raymond Loewy, the father of industrial design, believed that consumers are torn between a curiosity about new things and a fear of anything too new. Loewy called his grand theory **Most Advanced Yet Acceptable--MAYA**. *To sell something surprising, make it familiar; and to sell something familiar, make it surprising.* You should apply this principle when selling user experience research and design as a service, internally or to a client. When creating the 4D UX Map, or any deliverable, always try to follow the MAYA principle.

In 2012, I had experimented with a more advanced version of the 4D UX Map, called the MAYA Map. It featured seven information layers (dimensions), and there was a software behind it. It was more information rich, and you could switch between the information layers with a click. Each layer represented a view on the user experience, from complex wireflows to a simplified user story map. All elements were connected and rearrangeable in runtime, with connection highlights and easy editability.

The mapping software I was working on had a commercial 3D engine behind it. I thought that I had created a map for a new era--an era when people use head mounted displays, such as Microsoft HoloLens, or virtual reality goggles, such as Oculus Rift. The project started just days after the Oculus Rift Kickstarter campaign ended; it was way too soon. At that time, the MAYA map was clearly too advanced. It didn't run on most of the laptops my clients had, and it was impossible to print or include in a PowerPoint presentation. I decided to put the MAYA map project on hold, as it clearly failed its namesake principle. It was too advanced. Five years later, it's still too advanced. It is possible that MAYA map's time will come in in a few years, or it might never come in the form I have envisioned it. At the moment, I still believe that the 4D UX Map is the most advanced user experience map, which is still acceptable as a communications tool. If you can't use a UX Map to understand and discuss the user experience easily, it's pointless to create one.

Now, let's see the dimensions of today's most advanced UX Map.

The first dimension - milestones

We will tell the users' story through the milestones. As we have seen in the previous chapters, milestones group all events that lead to a common goal. Each achievement the user has on the road to reach the opportunity is a milestone. Milestones give a structure to our map and allow easier organization and communication. The 4D UX Map doesn't necessarily have the same milestones as the user story map, task model, or journey map for the same project, but if you have created any of those, that's a great starting point.

We will focus on the action, and start where the action starts. For high-value purchases or life-changing decisions, this might be the decision or planning milestone. Ordering food doesn't fit into that category, so we will start with the acquisition milestone. Usually, the left-most milestone, the starting point, is the hardest to influence. Moreover, this can be outside of the UX expert's domain. In our case, SEO, SEM, PPC, and other experts should be involved in improving the acquisition journey, which reaches beyond the acquisition milestone, into the understanding milestone. Understanding is what we hope our users will achieve shortly after arriving at our website. They need to get the idea of the tableless restaurant in seconds.

For our tableless restaurant, the user goes through a few stages until they taste our delicious food. First, they need to understand what we offer, then they need to choose what they want to eat and drink, then do the usual checkout with address and credit card details. Then, they need to wait for the food to arrive. We can use this stage to improve their experience, for example, by showing a live feed from the kitchen with sharing and commenting abilities. Finally, the user can reach the last stage of the journey, the **after delivery** phase.

milestones	acquisition	understanding	choice	checkout	waiting	after delivery

Ideally, the user's journey restarts sometime after the last phase, by returning to the site. Frequent revisits should be part of our behavioral change plans for a restaurant.

When creating a remote user test, you can create tasks designed around each milestone, or better you can have a really open test design, which can lead to milestones defined by the users. For example, you could give the users test/fake payment details and ask them to use the site as they normally would. To design great remote UX tests, refer to `Chapter 5, Remote and Lab Tests for Map Creation`.

The second dimension - events

Each milestone contains one or more events. Each user might do one or more events in a milestone, but it's possible that they will do none. For example, they might not do anything **after delivery**, or even abandon the whole journey at the understanding part, if they fail to understand what this site is about.

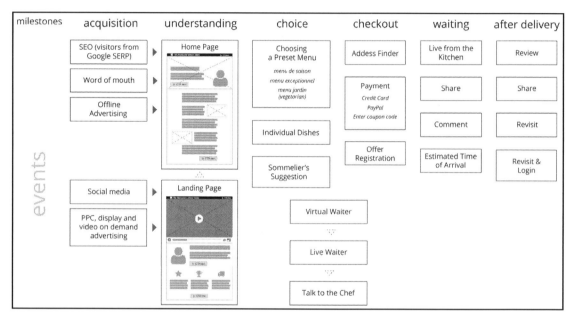

Events can contain wireframes, such as the **Home Page** or **Landing Page** event of this section's example. They can also contain a list of options, such as the **Choosing a Preset Menu** or the **Payment** events.

You want to include as few arrows as possible, but sometimes arrows help with understanding. For example, visitors resulting from our **SEO (visitors from Google SERP)** and **Offline Advertising** arrive at the homepage, while visitors from **Social media**, **PPC, display and video on demand advertising** arrive at a **Landing Page**. Some visitors from the **Landing Page** might go to the **Home Page**, before doing the intended action or choosing something at the **choice** milestone.

Some events are present at more than one milestone, for example, the **Virtual Waiter**, an AI driven chatbot. I usually align those events to touch both milestones, sort of sitting in the middle. Another option is to make it as wide as the two columns together--that's a design decision.

 Remember that the design of a map should make it easier to understand and communicate. If a design decision doesn't lead to those goals, it should not be made. You can always restart.

The third dimension - importance

Each event has a relative importance from business perspectives. This is something that should be decided in a meeting, where the important discussion is led by one of the business representatives. For determining the importance, the order of items in the user story map can be a good starting point. If something is part of the minimum viable solution, it could be of the highest importance, at least in the beginning. In the next iteration, the business might shift focus and other items could gain higher relative importance.

I have experimented with 4D user experience maps created with 3D modeling applications, such as Cinema 4D, Rhinoceros by Robert McNeel & Associates and Google SketchUp. Creating a great 3D rendering of the map certainly adds to the shock value, but unfortunately, 3D rendering makes the map harder to understand and it distracts the viewer. Those maps were also harder to create and modify, not really fitting for our needs.

It's possible to use tint, shadow, or other visual cues for this dimension, or even a number in a corner suggesting importance. I would encourage you to experiment with other visual representations and share your results (adding @wszp on Twitter if you are interested in sharing them with me).

I have found that increasing the line thickness of the boxes based on their relative importance is easy to understand and doesn't add much of a visual clutter. Remember, if something is not important at all, it should not be on the map in accordance with our simplicity principle. If it's important enough to be on the map, but just barely, you should give the events a thin, but visible, border. For the most important things, go with a thick border.

This leaves room for a medium thickness border for the middle importance cases. Obviously, if your project needs more than three levels of importance, you can go with four or five thickness values as long as they are easy to distinguish.

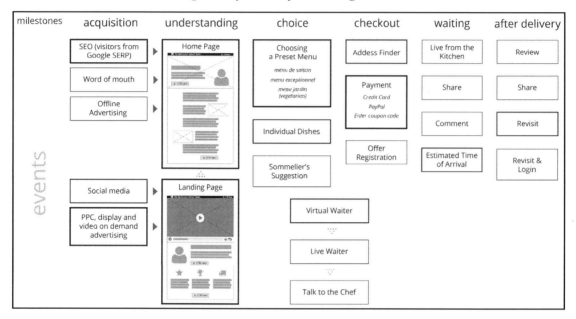

For this chapter's examples, I have used 3-pt stroke weight for the most important events, 1-pt for the least important ones and 2-pt for the middle importance values. In Adobe Illustrator, you can set that from the **Stroke** panel (**Window** > **Stroke**, alternatively use the keyboard shortcut of *Ctrl + F10* or *Command + F10*).

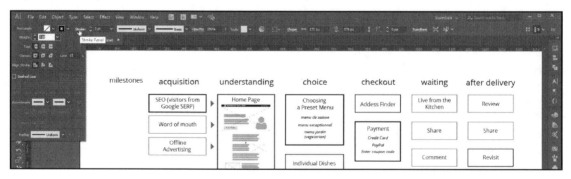

Use of Stroke Panel for setting stroke weight

The fourth dimension - severity of the problems

The analysis of the user experience tests will provide us with medium and high severity issues, as we have seen in the `Chapter 6`, *Solution Mapping Based on User Insights*. The medium and high issues can lead to abandonment. I usually don't add low severity issues and positives, but always mark events where conversion killers were found. To mark them, I use color.

Most of the time, two border colors are enough to mark the medium and high severity. Red is generally understood as an error, whereas orange as a serious warning. This also collides with the color coding we use when analyzing remote UX tests.

The aim is to draw attention to user experience issues that need fixing. This makes the map much more actionable and easier to communicate.

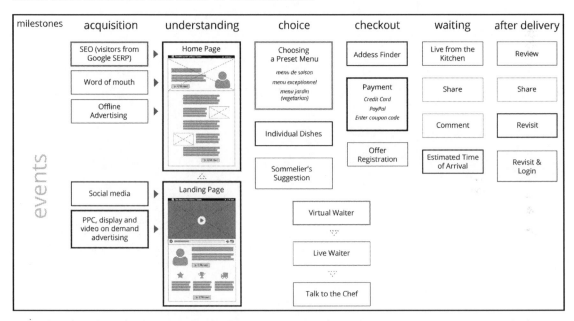

After adding all four dimensions to the 4D UX Map, we have completed the upper half of the map. Most of the time, I would call a four amigo meeting at this stage, to make sure that all amigos are aligned on the four primary dimensions, before continuing with the mental model snippets.

Mental model snippets

Mental model snippets are relevant and frequent thoughts from the users, present at each milestone. I usually emphasize the most common thoughts in comic-book style thought-bubbles to create a clear division between the upper part of the map and the mental model snippets. If you are creating a digital-only map, you can even link video snippets to quotes. *The aim of the mental model snippets is not to create or replace a mental model map.* Instead, they provide a glimpse into the contents of a mental model map. They attract the viewers' attention to behaviors and can link the mental model map to the 4D UX Map.

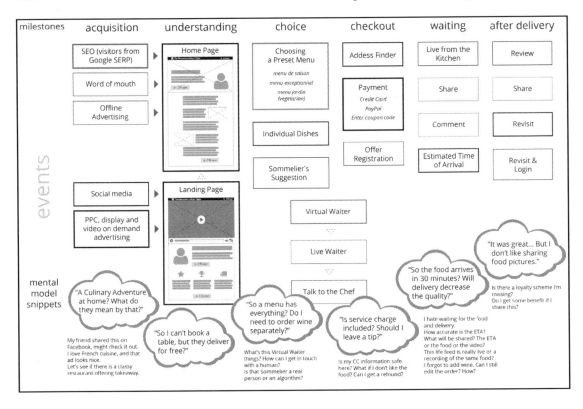

Even if you don't have a mental model map, you can use quotes from any user experience test.

Ratings

The optional bottom part of my 4D UX Maps is dedicated to *ratings*. As we have seen in the previous chapter, there are many enablers for a behavior. In `Chapter 6`, *Solution mapping based on user insights*, we introduced the two basic elements that need to converge at the same time for a behavior to occur: motivation and ability. If the trigger is present, those two can describe all behavior changes, according to Dr. BJ Fogg. However, motivation and ability are broad categories, which are hard to target directly. I almost always include those two in my 4D UX Maps, but often add a few more ratings to paint a more detailed picture of the behavioral change.

Arguably, **trust** is one of the most important factors for a website requiring any monetary transaction. We will offer credit card and PayPal payment options to the customers of the tableless restaurant, but if they don't trust us, they will not pay, simple as that. One of the somewhat hidden tasks of the user experience is to help build trust. To measure trust, I often use a simple question at each milestone of a test: *Based on what you have seen so far, would you give your credit card details to this site, if asked? Please choose one of the following answers: definitely no; probably no; probably yes; definitely yes.*

I always use a rating system, which has no neutral choice. The users need to pick a side. The experience is either good or bad. However, the world is not black and white, so I have added two more steps between the two extremes. I have experimented with a six, eight, and even ten division rating system, but the users were unable to quickly and easily pick the answers.

Another solution is a grading similar to the **net promoter score** (**NPS**), where 0-6 is the negative area, 7-8 is the neutral area and 9-10 is the positive area. By eliminating the neutral area, 0-6 means no, 9-10 means yes, and we simply ignore the 7-8. You can use many methods to determine the ratings, and any scale, as long as the viewer can clearly tell from the map how it works, and what each rating means for the user.

Obviously, if a rating type doesn't make sense for a milestone, you should omit it. For example, the trust rating will be misleading and probably near-impossible to measure accurately in the waiting milestones, when the users paid for the food, but haven't received it yet. The users' trust peaks at the point they submitted their payment details, and then many psychological effects could have been activated. For example, *buyer's remorse*, which is a commonly encountered sense of regret after making a purchase. Since we can't teleport the food to the user, some, especially first-time visitors, might have second thoughts and feel anxiety.

To add visual cues to the ratings, I often use vector icons for each rating type. This makes the map easier to read. You could use stars, plusses, or even design your own icons. I usually do a search on the Noun Project, `ht tps://thenounproject.com`, for the rating's name. This site pairs most English nouns with icons. The icons are downloadable in pixel-based (PNG) or vectoral (SVG) formats, and you can choose between Royalty Free or Creative Commons license.

The icons used in this chapter were created by Charlene Chen (light bulb), Joris Hoogendoorn (feather), and Harsha Rai (handshake). The fun factor is based on Barracuda's smile icon.

Drawing the 4D UX Map

If you put together all elements from the previous sections, you should end up with a 4D User Experience map, maybe a bit similar to mine:

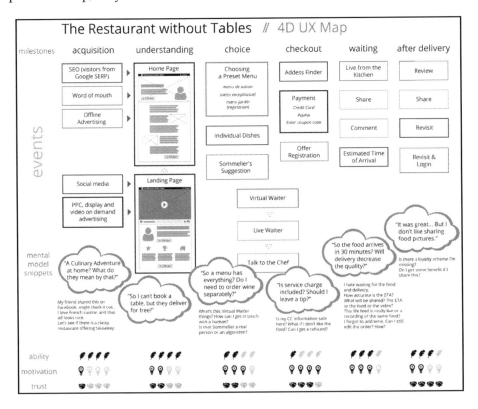

The first 4D User Experience Map, which I published on my blog had quite a few cats, obviously. So, it's only fair if I include that as well, as a reference. The source of that map, my original article on 4D UX Maps from 2014, can be found at `http://kaizen-ux.com/4d-user-experience-map`.

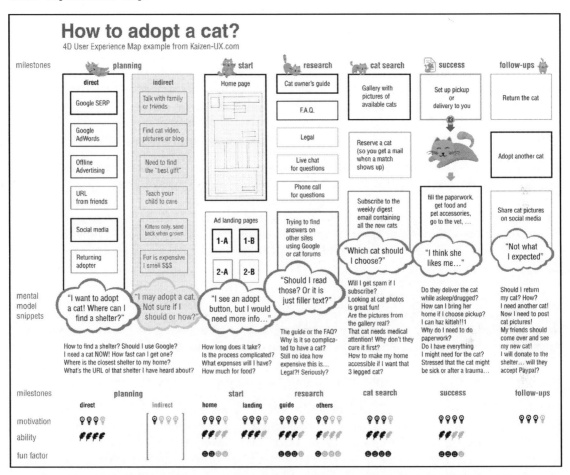

Note that back in 2014 I opted for a more refined rating system, not just milestone level ratings like nowadays. After quite a few successful commercial projects, I have found out that behavioral change, based on LEVER framework is easier to understand and communicate if associated with milestone based ratings, instead of separating different views in a milestone. While this simplification could hide some differences between views or events in a milestone, ultimately we want to make sure that the user progresses to the next milestone. Moreover in complex, non-linear scenarios, often encountered in gaming UX, it would be impossible to create view-based ratings.

Using the 4D UX Map

The main reason for creating a 4D UX Map is to gain an outside view of the users' experience, summarized in a single map. This visualization will enable us to improve our solution for the users' benefit. The 4D UX Map leads to a meaningful and valuable future for our solution.

The 4D UX Map is a high-impact communication tool, which can and should be shared in e-mail, print, or as part of a presentation. However, due to the high information density of the map, I would suggest having a meeting where you can introduce the map, answer questions, and share the map only after the meeting. This can be larger than the usual four amigo meetings. Inviting a larger group can be beneficial for immediate feedback, and you will not need to explain the map to dozens of small groups or individuals interested in it.

If you have access to a large size printer, printing the map is a good start. Stick it to a wall, or place it flat on a table so that the attendees can examine the map in its physical beauty and immerse themselves in the details. If you can't print it in a large size, print a copy for each attendee with a regular office printer in A3 or even A4 if that's the best you can get. Once people are a bit familiar with the map, they will start talking. I never had to artificially generate a meaningful discourse when I had a 4D UX Map. The map itself acts as a natural catalyst for conversations.

For most projects, many elements of the map are debatable or at least a bit questionable. That's actually a great thing because from those debates new opportunities can surface. As long as attendees keep the users' best interests in mind, the meeting will be successful. The 4D UX Map meeting can create an environment where people feel more comfortable than during usual serious business meetings. This can easily lead to new ideas and radical thoughts, even crazy ideas. Embrace a bit of craze and miracles can happen.

Many 4D UX Maps challenge industry-wide best practices, assumptions, and quite often the highest paid person's opinion. However, evaluation and restraint are always needed. No map can be more accurate than the data used for its creation. If you see a great map for a solution, which challenges one of the cornerstone principles of your industry, you should evaluate and discuss it. Fun ideas can easily find champions, and mapping findings can easily be confused with validating findings, especially if you want to believe in those fun ideas. For most ideas found in 4D maps, rapid prototyping followed by a quick and simple remote user testing will be enough as the first idea-validation.

For example, if people have difficulty choosing between the three different menus, we can create a simple quiz or a wizard, which can be integrated with a more pro-active virtual waiter. Would that be a good solution, worth exploring? Should we invest resources into such a project? That's impossible to decide until we run at least a few remote user tests. Afterward, we can improve the 4D UX Map, incorporating this update, or decide to search for other alternatives.

Evolving the 4D UX Map

There are other possible enhancements to the 4D UX Map. For example, you could add a visual storyboard, such as a comic-strip to the top of the map, where each panel would be aligned with a milestone. You could also find a way to add a fifth dimension. You could create two or more states of the map and present them side-by-side in print and one slide after another in a presentation. Those states could represent temporal changes, like the experience now versus our short-term and mid-term plans.

The possibilities are limitless; there are just three rules to follow:

- Keep the users in focus. This is a user experience map. It should be about the users, and only about them. Don't include the internal system, engineering problems, or financial solutions. If it's not closely related to the user experience, it should not be on the map.
- Don't create a map that is too complex, or too hard to understand. Simplicity is the key for all map types, especially for 4D UX Maps, summarizing many other map types.
- Always create maps with the intent of sharing and discussing them with others. This might be bad advice if you are a pirate, trying to hide your booty, but it's the best advice I can give for user experience maps.

I hope that you, yes you, my esteemed reader, will improve this map type. If you do, please share it with as many people as you can, including me.

Summary

Creating the 4D User Experience Map can be a lengthy process, especially if we base it on detailed user research, involving both lab and remote tests, but it's worth the effort. No other visualization can summarize the user experience of a solution as a whole in one detailed map.

This map is based on all map types we have discussed so far in this book, but it's much more than the sum of all UX Maps. The top section of the map contains the actual four dimensions: milestones, events, importance, and severity of the problem. The middle section of the map contains the mental model snippets, and the bottom part is reserved for ratings.

The 4D UX Map is a great tool to facilitate communication with stakeholders, and it helps UX designers understand the project. I hope that after reading this chapter, you will not only create 4D UX Maps, but improve this map type and come up with even better map types.

There is one more user experience map type I need to share with you to make the book complete. So far, we have created maps of our solution and its users. Follow me to the next chapter, where we will gain a holistic understanding of the ecosystem in which our solution will need to survive. Let's map our solution's relationship with other solutions and entities.

10

Ecosystem Maps - A Holistic Overview

Ecosystem maps are powerful tools to facilitate communication and help with the decision-making process. Unlike all other maps we have seen in this book, the ecosystem maps will show our solution's relationship with other solutions and entities in the world, instead of exploring the inner workings of our solution; this is why I'm fascinated by ecosystem maps.

 The ecosystem map places our solution in the greater context of the holistic user experience. This map aids the identification and integration of complex, interdisciplinary information of the user experience ecosystem. The primary benefit of the ecosystem map is finding and communicating threats, enablers, synergies, incompatibilities, motivators, and trade-offs between different entities. Those entities are often solutions our users use or consider using.

In this chapter, we will do the following things:

- Introduce our opportunity
- Define the ecosystem
- Explore how we can map an ecosystem
- Create hexagon maps with Inkscape or Adobe Illustrator
- Build an ecosystem map from hexagon map foundation
- Use the ecosystem map
- Draw a stakeholder map using a similar technique

Shutter Swipe – where photographers and models meet

The opportunity for this chapter is Shutter Swipe. Actually, it's more than an app where photographers and models get to meet, it's a photography social network. Taking the idea from the dating app Tinder, you can easily find models or like-minded photographers. You can even organize shooting trips together and form lasting friendships and professional relationships. Long story short, this is the app the community wanted. It's an early seed start-up idea, which might disappear by the end of 2017, or become the next success story.

More importantly, it sits in a rich and interesting ecosystem, which is simple enough to be easily mapped, an ideal candidate for an ecosystem map. I'm sure that you are already eager to jump into mapping this ecosystem, but first, we need to understand what I mean by an UX ecosystem.

The ecosystem

Our solution exists in a user experience ecosystem. This ecosystem is the sum of all discrete but interdependent components that function together from the perspective of the user interacting with our solution. Those components can be software, hardware, services, information, channels, or even people.

When I talk about ecosystem, I mean the part that we made visible by mapping it. It would be impossible to map the full complexity of an entire ecosystem. Our map will always be a simplification of the reality.

How to map an ecosystem

The **centerpiece** of the ecosystem map will be our solution. Each element of the map will be an **entity**. To map the ecosystem, we will start with six questions related to our solution to find the entities. Those six questions will create the **slices** or categories of the map:

- How?
- Who?
- When?
- Where?
- What?
- Why?

The distance from the centerpiece will indicate the scale. If an entity is closer to the centerpiece, it represents a smaller scale, while entities on the edges of the map represent the broadest scale. For example, the *when slice* will scale as follows: now, today, soon, plan, and strategy. Those are the scales of our app's usage scenarios from the temporal perspective.

On the smallest scale, every action we do in the app happens in the moment. This is also why surveys are less accurate than remote or lab user testing. The users expect the direct results of their actions to happen on the same day. For example, when a photographer searches for a model, they want to find a match as soon as possible, ideally today. This can't be immediate but can happen minutes after, if the model is active at the same time. People expect other users of the app to be active daily. When the match is made, they would want to arrange a meeting soon. This *soon* can mean vastly different things for different users. For some, soon means a Skype call five minutes after, for others it can be a face-to-face meeting during the weekend, or next month, when they are in the same city. After the users gain proficiency with the solution, they start to plan the usage, for example, saying that tomorrow morning they will spend some time to find a model. They will have expectations and a rough time-frame in mind. At this scale, longitudinal research can be used to understand the mental model of the user, as we have seen in Chapter 7, *Mental Model Map - A Diagram of the Perceived Reality*. The strategy scale is when the app is part of a user's long-term strategy. This usually means that the usage is now an essential part of the user's professional activities. The usage can be considered part of the user's life.

It's also possible that there are multiple entities at the same scale level, in the same slice. For example, at the second level of the *how slice*, we can find both the App Store and the Play Store, as people might get the app from either of those. The broadest scale of the *who slice* contains four entities, namely, international media, events, community, and social media. Usually, the smallest scale is an exception, containing a total of six entities, one for each slice. Those microscopic entities are the roots of the slice, and they attach our solution to the broader context of the reality.

For our example, they will be the following six entities, namely, app, user, now, here, search, and need. Putting those together will form the basic context of our solution. The *basic context* can be formulated as a sentence: The *app* is used to find other *users*, *here* and *now*, through a *search*, because those users *need* each other for a collaboration.

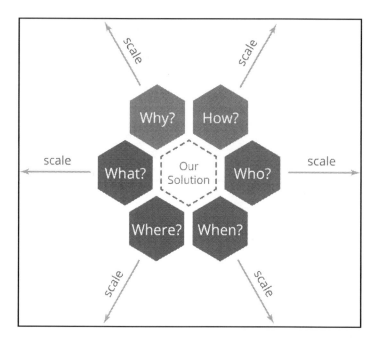

Creating hexagon maps

Probably the best example of an ecosystem map can be found in *Service Design: From Insight to Implementation* (Polaine, A. et al., 2013). That map is composed of hexagons, arranged on concentric circles. I also prefer to use hexagon-based maps for my ecosystem maps. They also remind me of board games and classic turn-based strategy games, most notably *Sid Meier's Civilization* and *Heroes of Might and Magic* series.

In this chapter, we will create hexagon-based maps, but not all ecosystem maps are hexagon based. The circle is the second most common shape, but you could use pretty much any shape to represent entities on an ecosystem map.

Hexagon mapping with Inkscape

The easiest way to create hexagon maps is using the free and open source vector graphics editor, Inkscape (available from `https://inkscape.org`). There is a hexagon mapping extension for Inkscape, created by Pelle Nilsson, which you can download from GitHub, at `https://github.com/lifelike/hexmapextension`.

Pelle Nilsson's *Hex Map Extension* for Inkscape is relatively easy to use, anyhow. You need to download and install the extension. Installing means copying the `hexmap.inx` and `hexmap.py` you have downloaded from GitHub to the extensions folder, then restarting Inkscape.

To use the extension, select **Extensions** > **Boardgames** > **Create Hexmap...** from the top menu and specify your settings in the **Create Hexmap** dialog box, which will appear. If you tick the **Live preview** checkbox at the bottom of the dialog box, you can immediately see the effects of your settings.

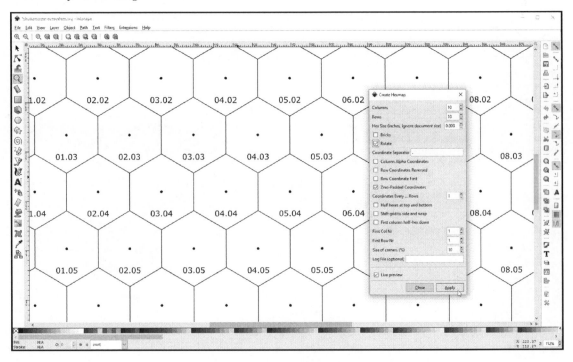

The live preview checkbox will show the effects of your changes in real time

If you use Inkscape with Hex Map, you can skip the next section and jump to *From hexagons to ecosystem maps*, where we turn hexagons into entities. If, however, you prefer Adobe Illustrator, then the next section is written for you.

Creating hexagon maps with Adobe Illustrator

Now, I will show you how to create a hexagon map using Adobe Illustrator in greater detail. After the process of creating the hexagons, the process is similar in Inkscape and Adobe Illustrator. The tricky bit in is creating an editable hexagon pattern. This was handled by the Hex Map Extension in Inkscape, but in Illustrator we will do it manually.

We will start with a single hexagon, which can be drawn using the **Polygon tool**, by clicking on the canvas. To make spacing calculations simpler, I usually draw a polygon with 100 px radius. Later, we can resize the finished map, but in this stage, 100 px is a good starting point.

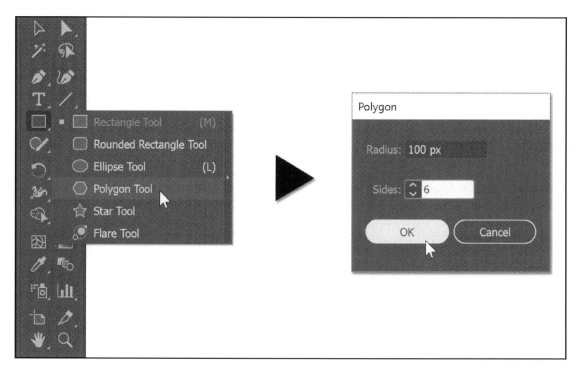

Even if you want border lines for your hexagons, or as Illustrator calls them, *strokes*, you should remove those for now. The easiest way to do that is pressing the / key with your hexagon selected. You can also use the color selector panel, available from the **Window** > **Color** menu, or by pressing *F6*; after that, click on the None icon.

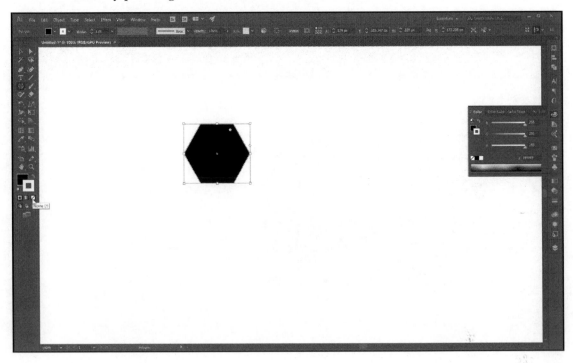

Illustrator's color selector panel

You can also rotate your hexagons, the way they look the best for you. I usually rotate them by 30 degrees. You can do this from the **Object** > **Transform** > **Rotate...** menu, or using the **Rotate tool** (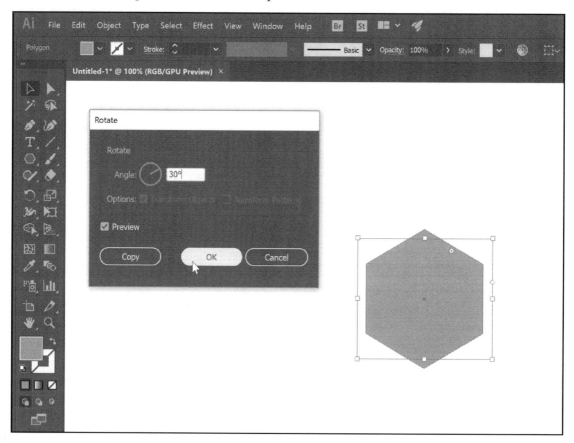). The 30 degree rotation is so common for hexagon maps that it has a checkbox in Hex Map Extension for Inkscape.

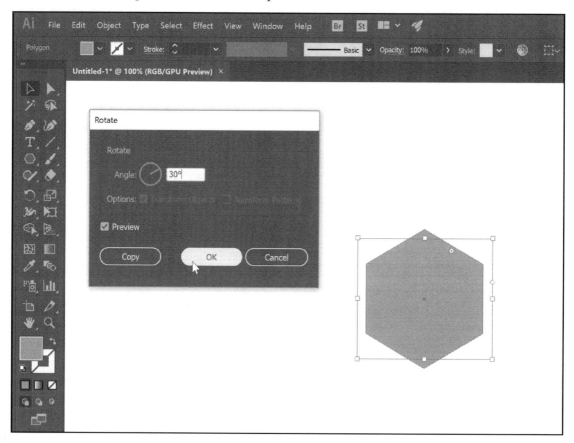

Now, we need to create a pattern. We could manually duplicate the hexagon as many times as we need to, but that's quite cumbersome, and chances are that the resulting hexagons would not align perfectly if done by free-hand. However, the biggest benefit of the method I will show here is that we can see how the hexagon pattern will look before we create it. Thus, we can easily change many aspects of it. As you might have guessed, we will use Illustrator's powerful pattern maker from the **Object** > **Pattern** > **Make** menu.

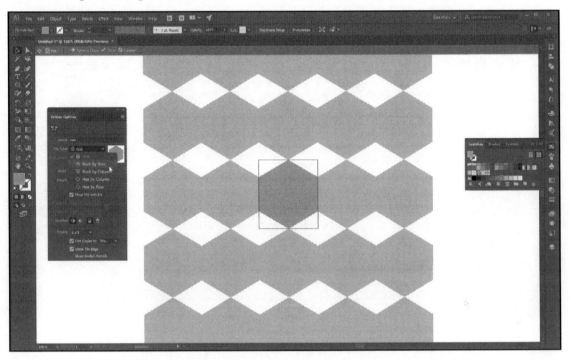

Selecting Tile Type > Brick by Row

The default settings will make our hexagon pattern quite odd. That's why we need to tweak our pattern in the **Pattern Options** dialog, which should have appeared. Naming the pattern is optional, but can be helpful later, when we need to find our pattern among the Swatches. Setting the **Tile Type** to **Brick by Row** will fix some of the issues. The default 1/2 **Brick Offset** is good, but the **Width** and **Height** values are probably not. I have used 200 px width and 170 px height for this chapter's example.

If you would prefer just a small gap between hexagons, use 175 px and 151.55 px, respectively. If you don't want any gap, 173.2051 px and 150 px should be the measurements. Feel free to experiment with different width and height values. You want the angled and vertical gaps to optically look the same width, so don't worry about the math behind it. However, if you are interested in the mathematical formula, the *width = sqrt(3)/2 × height*, roughly width = 0.866 × height. This is a good measurement for small gaps. However, to my eyes, 200 px and 170 px looked a bit better, than 200 px and 173.2 px. Experiment with the numbers to achieve the best result.

Setting the dimensions for the pattern

Now, click on **Done** to add your new pattern to the swatches. Then, create a rectangle as big as your art board, and then click on your new hex swatch from the **Swatches** panel. If swatches are not visible, try **Window** > **Swatches** from the top menu.

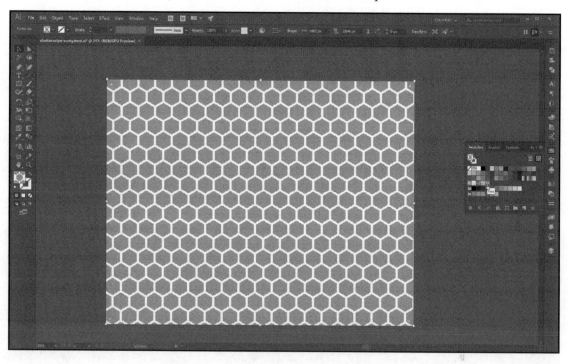

Selecting your new hex swatch

Now, you should have a rectangle with a hexagon pattern, but the hexagons are not editable. First, we need to expand this. To do this, go to **Object** > **Expand…** menu and click on **OK**. Ensure that the **Fill** checkbox is checked. If **Expand…** is grayed out, it means, you need to do **Object** > **Expand Appearance**, then you will have a path as a result, on which **Object** > **Expand…** will work.

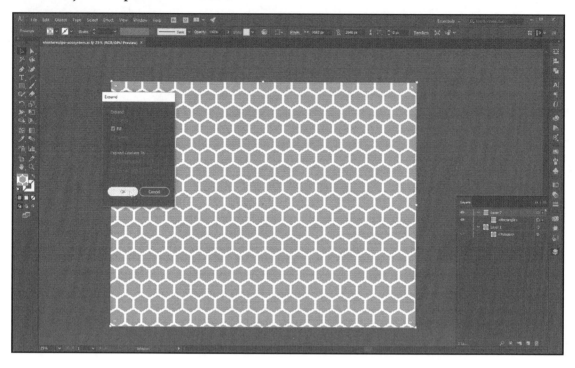

Selecting the Expand option

Now, if you look at the **Layers** panel, you will see that our pattern expanded into rectangular **Clip Groups**, most of them containing five hexagons and a rectangular **Clipping Path**.

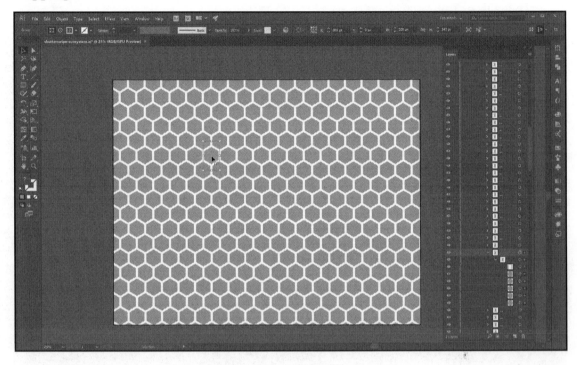

The unexpected rectangular Clipping Path and five hexagons

To reach our goal, we need to merge all **Clip Groups**. We will do this by selecting the new group, created by the **Expand** command, which contains our pattern. Then, we will use the **Merge** command on this group. You can find it at the bottom row of the **Pathfinder**. If you can't see the **Pathfinder** panel, it's available from **Window** > **Pathfinder** as expected.

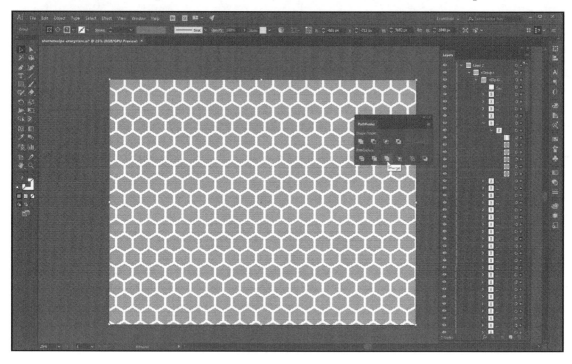

Merging all Clip Groups

Now, you should have separate, editable hexagon shaped paths, serving as the base of our map. It's safe to delete the edge rows, with incomplete hexagons.

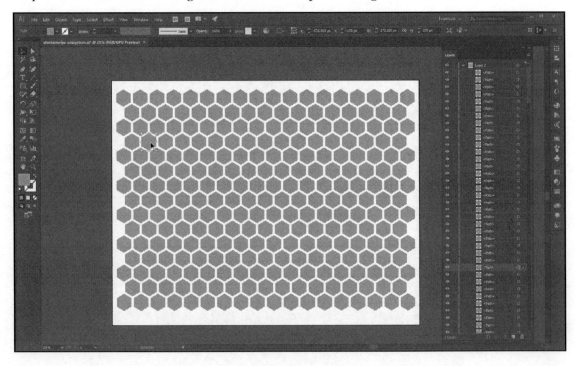

The hexagon grid will serve as a base for our map

Now, we are ready to turn those hexagons into meaningful entities.

From hexagons to ecosystem maps

When we have a hexagon layout, we can color it, according to our slices. Starting from our solution, which could also get a unique design, we can add a different color to each group. I prefer to use different shades or tints of the same color to represent scale. Other authors add concentric circles with labels for the same purpose. Then, you can add the entity names for all six entity slices.

When you are done with coloring, you can add the name or description for all entities of your map.

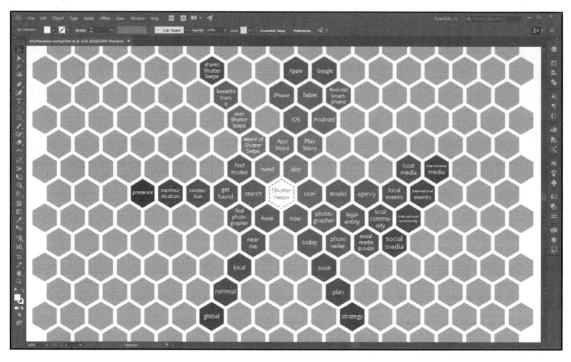

Basic layout for our ecosystem map

Our ecosystem map is now done. I would suggest hiding the gray hexagons, instead of deleting them, because you might need them later, when creating the next version of the map. You can do this from the Layers panel (**Window** > **Layers** or *F7*). Click on the eye icon ( ) before the object's name. You can hold the mouse button and swipe across many objects, to quickly hide or show many objects.

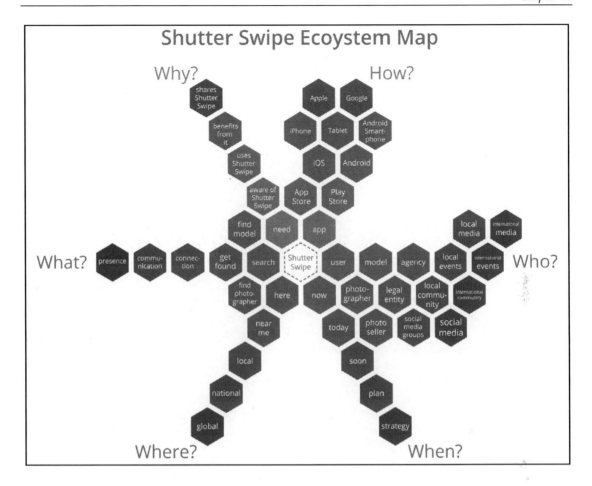

Using ecosystem maps

The most obvious benefit of the ecosystem map is understanding and communicating a holistic overview of the user experience, and how interconnecting parts relate to each other. This can help creating a holistic strategy, and it can drive innovation, as we discussed before.

We can use the map to identify enablers to our solution, and flag threats. For example, if we want to create a gambling app, the Google Play Store would be flagged, because it will not allow such an app. Gambling apps are allowed in Apple's App Store, so that would be an enabler. For Shutter Swipe, the biggest threat is awareness, found on the second scale level of the *why direction*.

Some authors (for example, Polaine, A. et al., 2013) also mark motivators on their ecosystem maps, by adding a red border around certain hexagons. Those motivators are almost always found in in the why direction, and I think it's not really necessary to mark them. Most of the time they are trivial. In our example, the motivators would be the benefits of our app.

For this book's example, I have chosen not to mark anything on the map, because that should happen during or after a meeting. The best approach is to start the meeting with an unmarked ecosystem map and an open mind.

Stakeholder maps

Stakeholders are people, or a group of people, with the power to change our solution. They are essential for the success of the solution. To be able to efficiently manage them, you need to know who they are and what level of reporting they expect. If you neglect to manage them and their expectations, it can doom your solution, because some stakeholders will start to work against you and your solution. This is true, even if you work at the agency side.

I often use a hexagon-based map for stakeholder mapping, and the stakeholders can be defined as parts of the solution ecosystem. Unlike the ecosystem map we created previously, the stakeholder map doesn't have directions, only scale levels. Those scale levels represent the detail level and frequency of reporting they need, for example, the project owner can require frequent, detailed reports, while regulators or the users are on the opposite end of the spectrum. The four amigos represent the inner circle of stakeholders, right next to our solution.

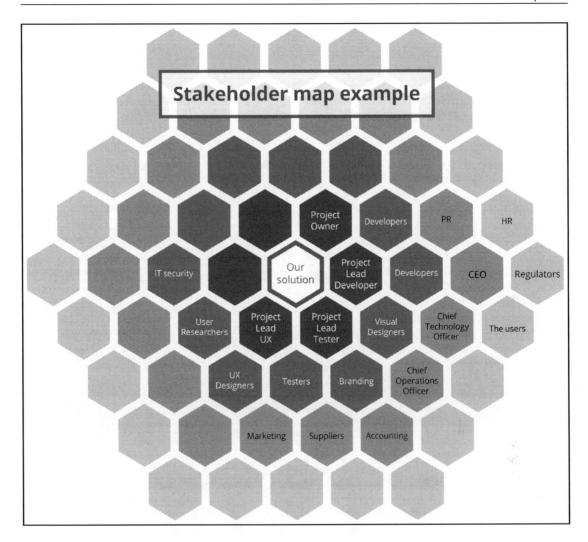

Summary

The ecosystem map places our solution in the greater context of the holistic user experience. Our solution will be the centerpiece of the map. To map the rest of the ecosystem, we will start with six questions related to our solution to find the entities. The distance from the centerpiece will indicate the scale of those entities. We will use the ecosystem map to understand and communicate a holistic overview of the user experience. A stakeholder map is a special ecosystem map, lacking the six directions, containing only the stakeholders for our solution.

I hope that you have enjoyed creating the user experience maps of this book. For me, writing the first 10 chapters was an amazing journey. In those 10 chapters, I have covered all map types I use through my day-to-day work as a user experience consultant. In fact, this chapter could have been the last. There are no more maps that I can show you. I have shared all my mapping knowledge with you.

However, this is not the end of the journey. In the last chapter, we will discuss the role of user experience maps in agile product management. We will see where maps fit in a project's lifecycle. The last chapter will also serve as a sneak peak into Kaizen-UX, the management framework I developed for agile UX teams. So, get ready for the final thrill of this book!

11

Kaizen Mapping - UX Maps in Agile Product Management

In this chapter, we will celebrate. I hereby declare today as our special day. You have reached the last chapter of this book. It was an awesome journey, full of challenges, and we were victorious, together. Now, we celebrate the discovery of user experience mapping and we celebrate you, dearest reader.

Do you feel a sense of achievement? I hope so because this is the most important rule of the Kaizen-UX management framework. Celebrate! Not just big wins, and breakthroughs, but all achievements. You and your team members or co-workers should have a mini-celebration for small victories. Did you finish a map, or analyze all videos in a remote research? That's awesome.

I'll let you in on a secret, sometimes I even celebrate failures with my team. Imagine that the client was not happy with a redesign project because it failed to generate the expected uplift in sales. We have invested countless hours in it, and now we need to find out why it didn't work as expected, then redesign. Maybe even from scratch to avoid replicating the mistakes resulting from reused wireframes.

Before redoing the research and redrawing the maps, we would have a celebration. No, I don't treat failure as a rite of passage. I always try my best to avoid it. With that said, we should reward ourselves for the effort, for the hard work and struggle, for pouring our enthusiasm into a solution, even an unsuccessful solution.

Above all else, we always celebrate teamwork. To have something to celebrate, we will have to do the following:

- Find an opportunity
- Manage ourselves and possibly a team
- Proclaim the Kaizen-UX manifesto
- Understand agile, beyond the buzzword
- Explore the three UX roles
- Discover the Kaizen-UX framework
- Create a UX strategy, and put it on paper in the form of a UX strategy document
- Change the world

Your opportunity

This chapter is all about you and your opportunity. Each of the previous chapters contained a unique opportunity, chosen by me. This chapter gives you tools beyond mapping. It gives you a framework to change the users' lives.

We can solve any real-life product design problems with an agile approach and an open mind. Most of the time, picking your fight is the hardest decision. Most problems found in product design or UX design are daunting. If you have just started working on a project, or you are about to build your start-up, you can pick from dozens of opportunities. After watching a few videos of users struggling with your solution or similar solutions, the number of issues can skyrocket. Before the end of the day, you are faced with more issues than you can hope to solve in a year. So, how do you pick a fight?

Your first opportunity should always be a quick win--a fruit hanging so low that it ripens on ground level. At first, most organizations will be skeptical at best. You need to prove your worth, and the *raison d'être* (reason for existence) of experience maps. If there is no tradition of using maps, they might be seen as a waste of time. It certainly takes a bit of time until maps become part of the corporate culture, and from oddity or curiosity, they become expected and needed elements of decision-making and communication. You can speed this up by finding projects, which are easy to do and will make a noticeable difference to the users' lives.

After you have found your quick win opportunity, you can start creating a map for it.

The manager and the map

You absolutely need a manager to create a UX map. The good news is, you are one. Even if you only need to manage yourself, that still counts as management. This is the reason why Richard Templar split *The Rules of Management* into two sections: *Managing your team* and *Managing yourself*.

The even better news is that experience mapping is not about following a set of rules and constraints. I hope that you don't take my book as a collection of rigid rules and UX dogmas. Yes, I had to give you a few rules, for the same reason as master painter gives rules to their apprentices. However, now it's time for the most important rule of mapping.

 When creating user experience maps, you need to keep an open mind and innovate. You create maps to understand and communicate experiences. For this, you need to continuously rewrite the rules of mapping.

This means being passionate about your maps--create outrageously bold maps. Being obsessed with experience maps is great, but it's also acceptable to put maps aside when you can communicate better without them.

There are countless books and articles about saying no. Saying no starts to become the gold standard of management. Managers are expected to say no. To respectfully challenge everything is the second nature of all good managers. Does this sound familiar to you? When it comes to mapping, say *yes*, instead. If a team member or your manager comes up with a new idea to map, or a new mapping idea, try it. Creating a new map takes a couple of hours tops, maybe two working days if you spend 80% of them on Facebook. However, when you say yes to a new map, magic happens. This magic is often called innovation. Even if the result is a totally, utterly useless heap of failure, you gain from saying yes. You have recognized the possibility of a new way. If you don't, the next idea might not reach you. It might reach someone else, or die in someone's mind, without reaching another soul. This is how you can start building a culture of continuous innovation. This culture of innovation is where Kaizen-UX thrives.

Kaizen-UX manifesto

Kaizen-UX is an agile management framework, which uses maps to communicate and understand the users. The core of Kaizen-UX is the continuous innovation in an agile way. We value the following things:

- Maps and communication over comprehensive UX documentations
- People and interactions over processes and tools
- Customer collaboration over contract negotiation
- Responding to change over rigorously following a plan
- The users' needs over business goals

If you think that this is the agile manifesto tailored for UX teams, you are spot-on. I was inspired by `agilemanifesto.org` and SCRUM when creating the Kaizen-UX framework.

If you are familiar with the Agile Manifesto, you might have noticed that our manifesto has five elements, instead of four. If not, here are the four elements of the original Agile Manifesto:

- Individuals and interactions over processes and tools
- Working software over comprehensive documentation
- Customer collaboration over contract negotiation
- Responding to change over following a plan

The middle three elements of our manifesto are analogous to the Agile Manifesto, and the first element emphasizes maps and communication, for the obvious reason that UX doesn't directly produce software. However, the fifth element is unique--I mean the sci-fi movie. I'm pretty sure that putting users first is hardly unique for Kaizen-UX. I hope that all user experience professionals champion the users' needs over business goals. All organizations have people in charge of defending business goals, starting with the chief executives. Sadly, the user needs rarely get enough support. A visionary business leader balances business goals with users' needs in all projects. We, the UXers, represent the counterweight. We are the users' voice in all meeting rooms. We use maps to make sure that voice is understood, not just heard.

Agile beyond the buzzword

The problem with agile is that it has turned into one of the most overused and probably most often misunderstood buzzwords of the IT development industry.

A few years ago, I was doing user experience consultancy for a big retailer. They told me that their development team recently "turned agile". I had to work closely with the dev team, mostly because one of the first issues I identified was the site speed. In other words, the site was awfully slow, and senior management looked puzzled when I tried to explain why 200+ HTTP requests are bad. So, here I was asking why we have 50+ CSS and 30+ JavaScript files. The head of the team said: "Well this is all because we are agile. You see, we stopped writing documentation to become agile. As soon as something needs to be done, we just do it. No more wasting time with requirements. As a side effect, the developers need to do so in a different CSS and JS file, as a best practice." Now, it was my turn to look puzzled. "Why don't you just merge them into a single minified file before deployment?" The guy was expecting this, so he had an answer ready: "There was no such task before, but we can certainly add it to the next sprint. You just need to fill this briefing template and get it approved. This influences the whole site, so I'm afraid you need director level approval." That was the point when I realized that the challenge was not site-speed, but their understanding of agile.

For me, the essence of agile is the bias for action. I always prefer jumping in to the middle of the problem. This doesn't mean jumping in front of the train. It means sitting in the driver's seat and hitting the emergency stop button at the first sight of trouble. Then, we remove the obstacle as a team effort, so we can hit full-steam minutes after the debris has been cleared. It goes without saying that we need a map to see where that debris could be, and how to remove it efficiently.

We have already discovered Rapid Iterative Testing and Evaluation or RITE in `Chapter 5`, *Remote and lab tests for map creation*. For most of my projects, both time and money is a scarce resource. This is why I prefer RITER, as in RITE done remotely.

The three UX roles

If I didn't see an UX versus UI post on social media for a week, I would start to suspect zombie apocalypse. What people rarely mention is the separation of UX roles within a UX team. Ten years ago, if a company had a single UX/UI person for one hundred engineers, that was a sign of forward thinking and user-centricity. Nowadays, both the public and the private sector is swarming with UX designers. Usually, a handful of UX designers are led by a head of UX or UX manager. This is miles better than what we had ten years ago, but far from ideal.

In my experience, high-performing UX teams have three distinct roles: design (**UXD**), research (**UXR**), and management (**UXM**). Every person in each role should understand the other roles. Maps and communication bind the team together.

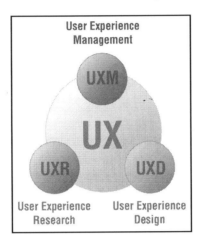

The Kaizen-UX framework

Those three roles are responsible for different processes and deliverables. UXM doesn't just mean someone acting as a people manager. In fact, most of the UXM doesn't revolve around managing the UX team itself. The most important UXM function is to act as a buffer zone between the world outside of the UX team and the team members. This means ownership over the UX strategy and UX delivery. It also involves communicating with stakeholders and championing user-centricity in the whole organization, and sometimes even outside of it. Three of the map types we have explored in this book are mostly UX management deliverables. The user story map, the 4D UX Map, and the ecosystem map should be owned by UXM roles. They require input from outside of the team, and multiple team members inside of it. They should be owned by someone who can set standards and find the right people for the right tasks. At agencies, UXM roles are often called UX strategists, UX directors, UX managers, principals, and sometimes account managers. (To be honest, I would never call anyone an account manager because clients don't prefer talking to account managers over "real" UX people, and most account managers also hate being called that.)

It's much easier to define the boundaries between researchers and designers. At most companies, researchers don't create maps, and designers don't design tests. In my team, solution maps and mental model maps are created by researchers, maybe with some graphical enrichment or post-work by a designer.

Who creates maps? When and why are they created? To solve this puzzle, naturally, I have created a map. It shows one iteration, one Kaizen-UX cycle, with many deliverables, including all maps of this book.

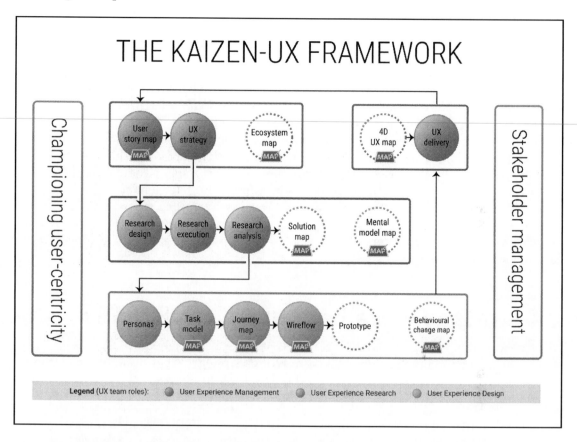

Some maps are updated during each iteration, whereas others are rarely created or updated. The later category is shown as a circle with dashed outline on my map.

The three roles are not cast in stone. I often move people from one UX role to another, and I expect every team member beyond the junior level to have a good understanding of all three roles. A role in a Kaizen-UX team is a never-ending learning experience. Any role beyond junior level is also a mentoring and coaching experience. When you stop learning and teaching, you stop being part of a Kaizen-UX team.

There are two ongoing UX team functions, which are outside of the iterative circle. Those are essential parts of the Kaizen-UX framework. They represent ongoing communication between the UX team and the outside world.

Championing user-centricity is our continuous effort to put the users' needs in focus. No organization is completely user-focused, not even charities; this is a good thing. An entirely user-focused shop would sell all goods for free, while a charity which focuses only on its beneficiaries would not raise any money. Similarly, no organization could completely ignore the users. All organizations sit somewhere between the two extremes. The UX team's job is to pull it toward the users, essentially creating a force, which counters other directions.

Stakeholder management is the other ongoing function. To suggest that managing stakeholders is like herding cats is to give cats a bad name. With a stakeholder map (see `Chapter 10`, *Ecosystem Map - A Holistic Overview*) and excellent communication skills, it becomes less daunting. One of the cornerstones of stakeholder management is to set optimal targets--this means, not overly pessimistic, but also not easy-to-achieve ones. You need to know your limitations and your team's limitations if you are leading one. It's easy to confuse stakeholder management with corporate politics. Hidden agendas and backstabbing can become parts of corporate life. This is why I prefer to lead a small but action-focused team, a team that gets things done, without getting entangled in the web of politics. Even if you are an independent consultant, you might get stuck in it. Honesty and hard work are the only ways to escape.

UX strategy – the beginning of all maps

UX strategy is the cause of our mapping efforts. You create a map because there is strategical thinking behind it, even if it's an unwritten strategy. When you put the learnings of this book into practice, you will create and follow a UX strategy--even if you work alone for your own start-up, and even if you don't do it consciously.

Jaime Levy's (2015) *four tenets* is the most commonly accepted UX strategy framework. His formula is *UX Strategy = business strategy + value innovation + validated user research + killer UX design*.

By business strategy, we mean how a company tries to achieve competitive advantage. This usually means cost leadership and differentiation. In other words, being the cheapest and doing things better. For example, you can create the best smartphone, or the cheapest one to have a chance at gaining market share, ideally both.

I prefer to use the word vision instead of business strategy, an idea of how the solution will make the users' lives better. Yes, this can mean selling cheap or creating an improved version of something, but what's more important is a clear direction or a goal.

Value innovation is more than coming up with a new idea. It's how you align newness, utility, and price. You need to create something new, original, and important enough to shake up the market--think of the Tinder dating app or the Nintendo Switch console.

Validated user research goes beyond simply conducting user research. You need to make sure that it's measurable. It's a reality-check. Instead of hunches and assumptions, you test your solutions with real users. This also means that you might need to call a solution a partial or total failure.

Finally, a killer UX design involves collaboration and communication. It means drawing maps to aid communication. It also means learning about the solution and its market. A bad UX designer creates maps and prototypes based on hunches. A good one creates them based on valid research. A killer UX designer guides the value innovation of a solution, identifying critical features, removing any friction. A killer UX designer creates seamless experiences across all touch-points.

In Kaizen-UX, a strategy has four pillars, namely **Vision**, **Innovation**, **Research**, and **Design**.

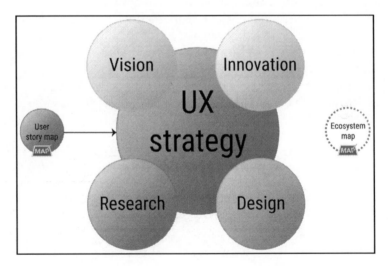

The UX strategy document

UX strategy is like sex in the seventh grade. Everyone talks about it, almost no one is doing it, and the learning material is all about its consequences. We have seen what a UX strategy is; now let's put it on paper.

A good UX strategy document is short. It should fit on a single page. At its core, it's a document aimed at senior management. It's a form of communication, and a successful strategy one-pager starts a discussion, with the unmasked goal of getting the organization more focused on users. Its shortness and simplicity will increase the chances that senior management will read it. To further increase this chance, start with how the strategy will help the organization succeed, how it will change the life of the users, and how it will serve the company to meet its business goals.

A good UX strategy doesn't pounce on UX design solutions. I almost always omit any reference to actual UX design issues in my strategy documents. UX design consists of tactical solutions to the problems, while the strategy should be concerned about the business and user goals, obviously within the limitations of the available resources. This is why the second part of the strategy document should be dedicated to goals, cost, and schedule of research, design, and management.

The UX strategy should be a short and simple answer to four fundamental questions *why*, *what*, *how much*, and *how long*, usually, in that order.

Although we create strategy documents for senior management, it should also be circulated inside the team. There is an anecdote of three workers doing exactly the same work. They split heavy rocks in the scorching summer heat. One of them is troubled, drudges slowly while cursing every now and then. When asked, he complains about the heat and the low quality of his equipment. The second one is indifferent. He says that he is well paid and needs the job to support his family, so he toils. The third one works with passion, harder than the previous two combined. He is seemingly euphoric with the same job. When asked, he proudly replies, I'm building a temple.

The first part of the strategy document gives reason to the team members' efforts. They will work to make people's lives better in a joint effort. This increases morale and helps you to retain your best employees. This is one of the reasons why it's awesome to be part of a Kaizen-UX team.

Summary

You can use the Kaizen-UX framework to structure your product design and user experience efforts. The agile framework is more than just a process resulting in experience maps. It defines the three basic roles within the UX team, namely research, design, and management. It has a UX strategy at its core, and it leads to better products and better communication within the team and with stakeholders.

Kaizen-UX also served as the skeleton of this book. Every map we created and every research we discussed was a result of the Kaizen-UX framework. I have introduced the basic concept in the first chapter, without directly calling it Kaizen-UX. I started the book with a bold and overused promised, to change your life. I did this to influence how you perceive the information presented in the rest of the book. The reason for starting the book with the seeds of the Kaizen-UX framework is the primacy effect. Now, at the end of the last chapter, we will summarize the Kaizen-UX framework. I have orchestrated this to benefit from another effect, called **recency**. Studies have shown that you will most likely recall the first (primacy) and the last, most recent (recency) idea I share with you (Murdock, 1962).

Now, you know how, why, and when to create experience maps. You can use the Kaizen-UX framework to manage the process. You are ready; *go and change the world!*

References

Adzic, Gojko. *Impact Mapping: Making a Big Impact with Software Products and Projects.* London, UK: Provoking Thoughts, 2012.

Adzic, Gojko and Evans, David. *Fifty Quick Ideas to Improve Your User Stories.* London, UK: Neuri Consulting, 2014.

Allen, Jesmond and Chudley, James. *Smashing UX Design: Foundations for Designing Online User Experiences.* NJ: John Wiley & Sons, 2012.

Barrington, Barber. *The Complete Book of Drawing: Essential skills for every artist.* London, UK: Arcturus, 2004.

Bowles, Cennydd and Box, James. *Undercover User Experience Design.* San Francisco, CA: New Riders, 2010.

Card, Stuart K. et al. *The Psychology of Human-Computer Interaction.* NJ: Lawrence Erlbaum Associates, 1983.

Caddick, Richard and Cable, Steve. *Communicating the User Experience: A practical guide for creating useful UX documentation.* NJ: John Wiley & Sons, 2011.

Charan, Ram. *What the Customer Wants You to Know.* London, UK: Portfolio Hardcover, 2007.

Cockburn, Alistair. *Crystal Clear: A Human-Powered Methodology for Small Teams.* Boston, MA: Addison-Wesley Professional, 2004.

Cooper, Alan. *The Inmates Are Running the Asylum: Why High-Tech Products Drive Us Crazy and How to Restore the Sanity.* Carmel, IN: Sams - Pearson Education, 2004.

Evans, Vaughan. *25 need-to-know strategy tools.* Harlow, UK: Pearson, 2014.

Fogg, B. J. *Persuasive Technology: Using Computers to Change What We Think and Do.* Burlington, MA: Morgan Kaufmann, 2003.

Fried, Jason et al. *Getting Real: The Smarter, Faster, Easier Way to Build a Successful Web Application.* Chicago, IL: 37signals, 2009.

Fried, Jason and Heinemeier Hansson, David. *ReWork: Change the Way You Work Forever.* Chicago, IL: 37signals, 2010.

Festinger, Leon et al. *When Prophecy Fails: A Social and Psychological Study of a Modern Group That Predicted the Destruction of the World.* NY: Harper-Torchbooks, 1964.

Gneezy, Uri and Rustichini, Aldo. Pay enough or don't pay at all. The Quarterly Journal of Economics, 115, no. 3 (2000): 791-810.

Hunt, Andrew and Thomas, David. *The Pragmatic Programmer.* Boston, MA: Addison-Wesley, 1999.

Johnson-Laird, Philip N. *Mental Models.* MA: Harvard University Press, 1983.

Jeffries, Ron et al. *Extreme Programming Installed.* Boston, MA: Addison-Wesley, 2000.

Kalbach, Jim. *Mapping Experiences.* Sebastopol, CA: O'Reilly Media, 2016.

Klein, Laura. *UX for Lean Startups: Faster, Smarter User Experience Research and Design.* Sebastopol, CA: O'Reilly Media, 2013.

Kolenda, Nick. *Methods of Persuasion: How to use psychology to influence human behavior.* London, UK: Kolenda Entertainment, 2013.

Krug, Steve. *Don't Make Me Think: A Common Sense Approach to Web Usability.* San Francisco, CA: New Riders, 2013.

Krug, Steve. *Rocket Surgery Made Easy: The Do-it-yourself Guide to Finding and Fixing Usability Problems.* San Francisco, CA: New Riders, 2009.

Levy, Jaime. *UX Strategy.* Sebastopol, CA: O'Reilly Media, 2015.

Levy, Neil. (ed.). *Addiction and Self-Control: Perspectives from Philosophy, Psychology, and Neuroscience.* NY: Oxford University Press USA, 2014.

Lichaw, Donna. *The User's Journey.* Brooklyn, NY: Rosenfeld Media, 2016.

Martin, Judy. *Drawing with Colour.* London, UK: Quarto Publishing, 1989.

Mckeown, Max. *The Strategy Book.* Harlow: UK: Pearson, 2012

Murdock Jr., B. B. "The serial position effect of free recall." *Journal of Experimental Psychology,* 64, no. 5 (1962): 482

Nickelsen, Alyona. *Colored pencil painting bible: techniques for achieving luminous color and ultrarealistic effects.* NY: Watson-Guptill Publications, 2009.

Patton, Jess. *User Story Mapping.* Sebastopol, CA: O'Reilly Media, 2014.

Polaine, Andy et al. *Service Design: From Insight to Implementation.* Brooklyn, NY: Rosenfeld Media, 2013

Parker, Jeffrey R. and Lehmann, Donald R. "When shelf-based scarcity impacts consumer preferences." *Journal of Retailing* 87, no. 2 (2011): 142-155

Ries, Eric. *The Lean Startup: How Constant Innovation Creates Radically Successful Businesses.* London, UK: Portfolio Penguin, 2011.

Schwaber, Ken. *Agile Project Management with Scrum.* Redmond, WA: Microsoft Press, 2004.

Templar, Richard. *The rules of management.* NJ: Pearson Education, 2005.

Unger, Russ and Chandler, Carolyn. *A Project Guide to UX Design.* San Francisco, CA: New Riders, 2012.

Vii, Paul. *User Stories: How to capture, and manage requirements for Agile Product Management and Business Analysis with Scrum.* North Charleston, SC: CreateSpace, 2016.

Wendel, Stephen. *Designing for Behavior Change: Applying Psychology and Behavioral Economics.* Sebastopol, CA: O'Reilly Media, 2013.

Young, Indi. *Mental Models: Aligning Design Strategy with Human Behavior.* Brooklyn, NY: Rosenfeld Media, 2008.

Index